Praise for
A Well-Regulated Militia:
The Founding Fathers and the Origins
of Gun Control in America

"This intelligent, carefully rendered history of gun policy in the United States . . . is challenging but essential reading for scholars, specialized undergraduates, and readers interested in law, criminal justice, and public affairs."

—*Library Journal*

"If proof were still needed that the study of the Second Amendment remains a fruitful source of inquiry, Saul Cornell's new book provides it. Crisply written and vigorously argued, *A Well-Regulated Militia* advances an often hackneyed debate by looking beyond the original concerns of the Revolutionary era. Cornell concisely demonstrates why so many of the contemporary fictions swirling around the meaning of this vexed clause depart from its real history."

—Jack Rakove,
author of the Pulitzer Prize–winning *Original Meanings*

"Saul Cornell provides a wonderful, original treatment of a much discussed subject. Based on a meticulous review of American history, Cornell shows that both sides of the debate over the Second Amendment are mistaken. This is a must-read."

—Erwin Chemerinsky,
Duke University School of Law

"Jettisoning the rancorous partisanship and historical distortions of both advocates and opponents of gun control, Cornell recovers the lost civic dimension of the constitutional right to bear arms. The point of departure for any future, historically informed discussion of this most controversial amendment, *A Well-Regulated Militia* clears the way for fresh and constructive thinking about the rights and responsibilities of gun ownership in America today."

—Peter S. Onuf,
author of *Jefferson's Empire: The Language of American Nationhood*

"A provocative alternative in the debate over the historical meaning of the Second Amendment. Anyone interested in how the right to bear arms was thought about in the early republic will need to take this book into account."

—Keith E. Whittington,
author of *Constitutional Interpretation*

A WELL-REGULATED MILITIA

THE FOUNDING FATHERS AND THE ORIGINS
OF GUN CONTROL IN AMERICA

SAUL CORNELL

OXFORD
UNIVERSITY PRESS

OXFORD
UNIVERSITY PRESS

Oxford University Press, Inc., publishes works that
further Oxford University's objective of excellence
in research, scholarship, and education.

Oxford New York
Auckland   Cape Town   Dar es Salaam   Hong Kong   Karachi
Kuala Lumpur   Madrid   Melbourne   Mexico City   Nairobi
New Delhi   Shanghai   Taipei   Toronto

With offices in
Argentina   Austria   Brazil   Chile   Czech Republic   France   Greece
Guatemala   Hungary   Italy   Japan   Poland   Portugal   Singapore
South Korea   Switzerland   Thailand   Turkey   Ukraine   Vietnam

Copyright © 2006 by Oxford University Press, Inc.,

First published by Oxford University Press, Inc., 2006
198 Madison Avenue, New York, NY 10016

www.oup.com

First issued as an Oxford University Press paperback, 2008

Oxford is a registered trademark of Oxford University Press

Library of Congress Cataloging-in-Publication Data
Cornell, Saul.
A well-regulated militia : the founding fathers and the origins of gun control in
America / Saul Cornell.
p.   cm.
ISBN 978-0-19-534103-4 (pbk.)
1. United States. Constitution. 2nd Amendment.   2. Firearms—Law and legislation
—United States.   3. United States—Militia.   I. Title.
KF45582nd .C67 2006
344.7305′33—dc22   2005036605

Printed in the United States of America
on acid-free paper

For Emma and Julia

CONTENTS

PREFACE

Writing the history of a topic as divisive and emotionally charged as the Second Amendment and gun control has posed a number of unique challenges. If I had set out to write a historical justification of gun control or a defense of gun rights, I would have certainly written a different book and done so in far less time. In contrast to advocates engaged in promoting a particular agenda, historians have an obligation to place such agendas temporarily aside while they pursue their research. In the course of researching this project and writing this book, I had to jettison many of the assumptions I had originally brought to this study. The history of the Second Amendment and the struggle over gun regulation proved to be far more complicated and contentious than I had imagined. Rather than fit into either a simple gun control or gun rights framework, the story of the struggle over this issue was filled with innumerable ironies and unexpected historical twists and turns. Partisans on both sides of this controversial issue are likely to find a number of surprises in these pages. Readers who come to this book with an open mind will be gratified to learn that the current impasse over guns in America was not inevitable.

I stumbled into this topic quite by accident. While completing a book on the Anti-Federalists, I noticed that a handful of writings by the opponents of the Constitution were frequently cited by scholars and partisans in the contemporary gun rights movement. Having spent more than a decade working on Anti-Federalism, I found it hard to reconcile the claims being made about Anti-Federalist ideas with what I knew about the opponents of the Constitution. It seemed particularly odd to me that scholars who claimed to be seeking the original understanding of the Second Amendment would lavish so much attention on the losing side's thoughts in the original struggle over the Constitution. Even if one acknowledges that the Anti-Federalists were the other founders of the American constitutional tradition, it seems curious that their thinking should be accorded as much, if not more, authority than the Federalist Founders. I decided that I needed to write a short article on this subject and expected to quickly move on to another project on Thomas Jefferson and the Enlightenment. As I dug deeper into sources, however, I realized that not only was the individual rights model of the Second Amendment trumpeted by gun rights advocates deeply flawed, but that the rival collective rights model also seemed difficult to reconcile with many of the sources I encountered. As I struggled to make sense of the evidence, I began to think that a new paradigm was needed to explain the understanding of the right to bear arms dominant in the eighteenth century. What emerged from these efforts was a pluralist model that acknowledged that there were a number of different views of the right to bear arms in the Founding era. The dominant model fit neither the modern individual nor collective rights models, but seemed more civic in character. It is important to recall that the Second Amendment was drafted and ratified by a generation of Americans who feared standing armies and had witnessed a systematic policy to disarm their militias. With these concerns in mind, America's first constitutions explicitly protected the right of citizens to keep and bear those arms necessary to meet their militia obligation. Having discovered that the individual and collective rights models were minority views in the Founding era, I set out to discover when these two interpretations rose to prominence in American law. Although I found some scattered evidence for both of these theories during the Founding era, it became clear to me that both of these models gained a strong hold on American legal thinking only in the decades after the adoption of the Second Amendment.

Tracing the evolution of American thinking about the meaning of the right to bear arms in all its complexity required looking in places that previous scholars had ignored. I realized that I would need to unite the top-down perspective of traditional constitutional history with the bottom-up perspective of social and cultural history. In my story, the perspective of the backcountry farmers who took up arms during Shays's Rebellion would have to be accorded the same respect as the learned disquisitions of Supreme Court justices. Having resolved to look beyond the traditional types of sources used by legal and constitutional historians, I discovered hundreds of new sources never before consulted by scholars interested in this topic.

It is impossible to write or talk about this topic without being asked where you stand on the gun issue today. I am always amazed when people ask me if I am pro-Second Amendment or anti-Second Amendment. It is hard to imagine anyone asking a scholar with a particular view of freedom of the press or federalism if he or she is pro-First Amendment or pro-Tenth Amendment. Although I am strongly in favor of gun regulation, I do not consider myself anti-gun. Growing up in Brooklyn I did not have that much experience with firearms. Most of the shooting I did was at arcades in Coney Island. Like so many young boys in America, I was fascinated by guns and played with every conceivable type of toy gun, including a collapsible AR-7 rifle with infrared scope that fit snugly in my James Bond attaché case. As a teenager I even acquired my own BB gun (illegally purchased), during a vacation in the Catskills. Although I had great fun with the gun in upstate New York, once I got back to Brooklyn I realized that there was not much one could do safely with a gun in a crowded Brooklyn apartment building. Guns are deeply embedded in American culture and history, and one must respect that fact if one wishes to understand the complex history of gun regulation and gun rights. Since beginning my research on this topic I have tried to learn more about firearms and their hold on the American imagination. I owe a great debt to Captain Scott Dawson, USMC, for taking me down to the Ohio State firing range and teaching me something of the power and allure of guns. Sadly, learning that I was a left-eye dominant and right-handed shooter probably dashed the last remaining James Bond fantasies left over from my childhood. I think I now understand why most colonial militia statutes exempted college faculty from reporting to muster. My brother-in-law Bill Hill also took me out shooting on his farm and helped me understand the important role that firearms continue to play for those who live in rural areas of the country.

The research for this book fills an entire six-drawer lateral file cabinet, and it would have been impossible to undertake a project of this scope and complexity without generous financial support. Funding for this project was provided by the National Endowment for the Humanities, the American Council of Learned Societies, and the Gilder Lehrman Institute. Much of the research for this book was done in conjunction with my work as director of the Second Amendment Research Center at the John Glenn Institute of Public Service and Public Policy. Generous funding for the center was provided by grants from the Joyce Foundation. Roseanna Ander, program officer at Joyce, has been an enthusiastic supporter of the center's work and of my scholarship. I would also like to thank Ellen S. Alberding, the president of the Joyce Foundation, for recognizing the need for high-quality historical research on the role of guns in American law and society. The staff of the John Glenn Institute provided a congenial home to work on this project. Particular thanks are due Larry Libby, Deborah Jones Merritt, Don Stenta, Deanna Stewart, Senator John Glenn, and Annie Glenn. Invaluable research assistance was provided by a number of graduate students at Ohio State University and elsewhere: David

Bernstein, Nathan Dedino, David Dzurec, Amber Esplin, Steve Gara-
bedian, Nathan Kozuskanich, John Maass, and Joe Stewart-Pirone.

Several colleagues in the history department at Ohio State read
the manuscript and provided thoughtful suggestions, including
Michael Les Benedict, John Brooke, and Geoffrey Parker. Randy Roth
shared with me evidence drawn from his own forthcoming study on
the history of violence in America. My thinking about the historical
issues relevant to this project has benefited from the comments and
insights of a number of scholars: Robert Churchill, Jan Dizard, Carole
Emberton, Paul Finkelman, Robert M Goldman, Leslie Goldstein, James
Henretta, Don Higginbotham, David Konig, Peter Onuf, Jack Rakove,
Lois Schwoerer, Robert Shalhope, and Lou Falkner Williams.

In the age in which the Second Amendment was drafted most
lawyers obtained their legal education by pouring over classic texts
such as Blackstone's *Commentaries* and serving long apprenticeships.
Although I have never attended law school formally, I have spent hours
reading Blackstone and other eighteenth-century legal texts. I have also
sought counsel from a number of legal scholars on the fine points of
constitutional law and interpretation, and particular thanks are due to
them: Akhil Amar, Erwin Chemerinsky, Michael Kent Curtis, Michael
Dorf, Bernard Harcourt, Kurt Lash, Sandy Levinson, James Lindgren,
Frank Michelman, Bryan Wildenthal, David Williams, and Adam
Winkler. I owe a particular debt to Dean Larry Kramer of Stanford
Law School for his support and guidance on many issues of constitutional law and interpretation.

A number of the ideas developed in chapters 5 and 6 were refined
in papers presented at conferences at Fordham Law School and
Stanford Law School. I would like to thank James Fleming and Martin
Flaherty of Fordham and Bob Weisberg of Stanford for their help in
organizing these two events and for advice on a multitude of issues.
Dave Douglas kindly invited me to present my research on St.
George Tucker at William and Mary Law School. Kenneth Katkin of
Northern Kentucky Law School hosted a lively conference on the Second

Amendment, during which several ideas in the book were formulated. Kate Desbarats, Jim Rice, and the members of the St. Lawrence Early American Seminar offered thoughtful suggestions about chapter 4. Andrew Burstein and Nancy Isenberg generously invited me to give the Settle-Cadenhead Memorial Lecture at the University of Tulsa. I profited enormously from their generosity and thoughtful suggestions. A talk on the changing iconography of the armed citizen in American history at Georgetown yielded a host of insights, and I am indebted to Michael Kazin for this opportunity. Jack Censer's invitation to give the Finlay Lecture at George Mason University provided another excellent venue to try out the ideas in this book.

Given the prominence of the Second Amendment in recent legal scholarship I was extremely fortunate to have had the opportunity to present drafts of nearly every chapter in the book manuscript at a series of faculty workshops at some of the nation's premier law schools. I would like to thank the following scholars for providing me with opportunities to try out earlier versions of my argument: Stuart Banner, University of California, Los Angeles; Jim Chen, University of Minnesota; Howard Erlanger, University of Wisconsin, Madison; Gerald Leonard, Boston University; Daniel Polsby, George Mason Law School; Chris Tomlins, American Bar Foundation/Northwestern University. I owe a special debt to Bill Nelson of New York University School of Law, who hosted me for two weeks and whose wonderful legal history seminar read an earlier draft of the entire manuscript and offered innumerable suggestions.

Although this manuscript deals with a host of important issues in American constitutional and legal history—including the right of revolution, popular constitutionalism, the evolution of the common law, federalism, the scope of the early American police power—it would be extremely naive to think that readers will not be curious about the connection between this history and the modern struggle over gun regulation. These issues are dealt with explicitly in the conclusion, which attempts to offer some suggestions about how an appreciation for history can raise the level of public discourse on this issue. In thinking about the contemporary resonances of my work I have benefited from lively exchanges with scholars and activists on both sides of this issue. Among the scholarly proponents of robust gun regulation who have generously shared their knowledge of this topic with me I would like to thank Carl Bogus, Phil Cook, John Donhue, David Hemenway, Jens Ludwig, and Robert Spitzer. Proponents of gun rights have also generously shared their point of view with me, including Randy Barnett, Bob Cottrol, Jim Jacobs, Abigail Kohn, Nelson Lund, Joyce Lee Malcolm, and Eugene Volokh.

The Brady Center to Prevent Gun Violence invited me to participate in a forum at the National Press Club on the subject "Guns and the Second Amendment." I benefited from my discussions with several lawyers at the Brady campaign: Dennis Henigan, Jon Lowy, Tony Orza, and Brian Seibel. Mat Nosanchuk, formerly of the Violence Policy Center (VPC), and Kristin Rand and Josh Sugerman, also of the VPC, took time out of their busy schedules to chat with me about the current state of the debate on this issue. Sue Ann Schiff of Legal Community against Violence was a great source of information about contemporary litigation in this area. An invitation from the Students for the Second Amendment and the National Rifle Association's Institute for Legislative Action to participate in a Second Amendment symposium provided me with another wonderful opportunity to discuss the meaning of this provision of the Bill of Rights. A number of the leading gun rights lawyers in the nation attended that event. In particular I would like to acknowledge David Kopel, Stephen Halbrook, Richard Gardner, Don Kates, and David Hardy for sharing their passionate interest in this issue with me.

Shaping this manuscript into a book that could appeal to an audience beyond the academy required the efforts of many fine editorial pens. Heather Miller and Lauren Osborne gave earlier drafts of the manuscript a close and thoughtful reading. Charlie Finlay, up-and-coming novelist, read the manuscript and offered excellent stylistic advice.

Michele Bové and Lelia Mander at Oxford University Press guided the manuscript through the production process. My brilliant and charming editor at Oxford University Press, Dedi Felman, read so many drafts of this manuscript that I feared this book on the Second Amendment may have violated Dedi's Eighth Amendment rights to be free from cruel and unusual punishment. The unbridled enthusiasm for this project emanating from Niko Pfund, the academic publisher at Oxford University Press, was also a great source of inspiration.

My wife, Susan, and my daughters, Emma and Julia, endured too many hours with me at the computer screen. I appreciate their patience with a project that always seemed to take just a little bit longer to complete than I had hoped. I have dedicated this book to Emma and Julia. I hope that when they start their families someday this issue will no longer be so divisive and America will no longer be plagued by the problem of gun violence. Perhaps with a better sense of the history of this issue Americans can create the kind of society in which schools will no longer need metal detectors in their doorways.

A WELL-REGULATED MILITIA

National Rifle Association President Charlton Heston holding a rifle above his head and inviting gun control supporters to pry it from his "cold, dead hands." This image has become an important icon in the modern gun debate.
(Ric Feld, Associated Press)

INTRODUCTION

A well regulated militia, being necessary to the security of a free State, the right of the people to keep and bear arms, shall not be infringed.
                                                    Second Amendment, U.S. Constitution

Whipping the crowd into a frenzy at the National Rifle Association annual convention, Charlton Heston, the group's charismatic president, raised an antique rifle above his head and challenged gun control proponents to pry his weapon from his "cold, dead hands." This defiant gesture, repeated on numerous occasions by the chisel-jawed actor known for his portrayals of key figures in history, has become a powerful symbol in America's bitter debate over the right to bear arms. To dramatize his rebellious stance, Heston did not wave a modern assault rifle, but a Revolutionary-era rifle, an iconic symbol that adorns pro-gun Web sites, tee shirts, and bumper stickers.

History is at the very heart of the rancorous debate over guns in America, and no issue is more controversial than the original meaning of the Second Amendment. Partisans of gun rights argue that the

Second Amendment protects an individual right to keep and bear arms for self-defense, recreation, and, if necessary, to take up arms against their government. Gun control advocates also claim to have history on their side and maintain with equal vigor that the Second Amendment simply protects a collective right of the states. Both sides have the history wrong.[1]

The original understanding of the Second Amendment was neither an individual right of self-defense nor a collective right of the states, but rather a civic right that guaranteed that citizens would be able to keep and bear those arms needed to meet their legal obligation to participate in a well-regulated militia. Nothing better captured this constitutional ideal than the minuteman. Citizens had a legal obligation to outfit themselves with a musket at their own expense and were expected to turn out at a minute's notice to defend their community, state, and eventually their nation. The minuteman ideal was far less individualistic than most gun rights people assume, and far more martial in spirit than most gun control advocates realize.[2]

Although each side in the modern debate claims to be faithful to the historical Second Amendment, a restoration of its original meaning, re-creating the world of the minuteman, would be a nightmare that neither side would welcome. It would certainly involve more intrusive gun regulation, not less. Proponents of gun rights would not relish the idea of mandatory gun registration, nor would they be eager to welcome government officials into their homes to inspect privately owned weapons, as they did in Revolutionary days. Gun control advocates might blanch at the notion that all Americans would be required to receive firearms training and would certainly look askance at the idea of requiring all able-bodied citizens to purchase their own military-style assault weapons. Yet if the civic right to bear arms of the Founding were reintroduced, this is exactly what citizens would be obligated to do. A restoration of the original understanding of the Second Amendment would require all these measures and much more.[3]

Most Americans no longer live in the small rural communities that nurtured the minuteman ideal. Regulation in modern America is typically seen as antithetical to rights. The opposite was the case for the colonists, who believed that liberty without regulation was anarchy. Without government regulation there would have been no minutemen to muster on the town greens at Lexington and Concord. The state's coercive authority over citizens could be significant. Failure to appear properly armed at a muster resulted in stiff penalties, and government kept close tabs on the weapons citizens owned to meet this vital public obligation. Although ardent in their love of freedom, Americans feared anarchy as much as they dreaded tyranny. An armed body of citizens unregulated by law was a mob, not a militia. The golden mean between the two extremes of anarchy and tyranny was the idea of well-regulated liberty, and nothing better captured this ideal than the militia.[4]

The militia statutes each colony enacted tell only part of the story of how this vital institution was enmeshed in the everyday lives of most colonists. If history taught Americans any lesson, it was that a standing army of professional soldiers presented a perpetual threat to freedom. A well-regulated militia was the only form of defense compatible with liberty. Only when the role of citizen and soldier were united could freedom be preserved. The militia not only protected Americans from external threats such as hostile Indians and rival European powers, but in an era before organized police forces it also provided the only means to protect communities from civil unrest. Before the rise of modern political parties, militia units provided an essential means for organizing citizens for political action. Muster days were important festive occasions that drew citizens together for celebration and revelry.[5]

The Americans who enshrined the right to bear arms in the first state constitutions were haunted by a fear of disarmament, but this fear was quite different than the fears of gun confiscation that cloud contemporary debates over firearms. The Concord minutemen who fired the shots heard round the world had been mustered on that fateful day to prevent British regular troops from confiscating the militia's powder and arms. The first statements of the right to bear arms in American constitutional law were clearly aimed at protecting the militia against the danger of being disarmed by the government, not at protecting individual citizens' right of personal self-defense.

Although most eighteenth-century Americans did not fear that the individual right of self-defense might be threatened, this fear did eventually take hold decades after Americans wrote their first constitutions. In the early nineteenth century some Americans did come to believe this right was under assault. The threat these Americans felt did not come from a despotic monarch or an omnipotent Parliament, but from their own state legislatures. A profound shift in the character of firearms regulation occurred in the early decades of the nineteenth century. In response to widespread fears that handguns and bowie knives posed a serious threat to social stability, legislatures enacted the first comprehensive laws prohibiting handguns and other concealed weapons. Then, as now, the enactment of gun control laws prompted a backlash that led to an intensified commitment to gun rights. One of the many embarrassing truths about the debate over the right to bear arms that neither side wishes to admit is that gun rights ideology is the illegitimate and spurned child of gun control. These early efforts at gun control spawned the first legal challenges to these types of laws premised on the idea of a constitutional right to bear arms for individual self-defense. While most courts upheld gun control laws and continued to assert a civic conception of the right to bear arms, a few courts embraced the new ideology of gun rights. One of the principal confusions in the modern debate over gun regulation, the blurring of the distinction between the constitutional right to bear arms for public defense and the individual right to bear a gun in self-defense, crystallized in the Jacksonian era. Public debate over gun control has stumbled over this issue ever since.[6]

If the debate over the right to bear arms had remained simply a matter of state constitutional law, then the story would be quite straightforward: the growth of an individual rights view and its ongoing struggle against the original civic vision of arms bearing. The only problem with this story is that it tells us nothing about the Second Amendment, which emerged out of the divisive struggle between Federalists and Anti-Federalists over the new Constitution. To understand this history one must deal with the way that this right became embroiled in the bitter debate over federalism. No issue in early American constitutional law was more contentious than the battle between proponents of states' rights and supporters of national power. While the language of the provision on arms bearing that Congress drafted, which eventually became the Second Amendment, was closer in spirit to the civic model embodied in the first state constitutions, Anti-Federalists and their Jeffersonian heirs came to interpret the Second Amendment within an evolving theory of states' rights. The right to bear arms in a well-regulated militia controlled by the states would provide the ultimate check on federal power if such power ran amok. The original Anti-Federalist understanding of the Second Amendment was revolutionary, assigning to the state militias the awesome power to resist federal authority by force of arms.[7]

The modern gun control movement's embrace of the collective rights theory of the Second Amendment is laden with irony. Contemporary gun control theory rests on a strong commitment to a powerful federal regulatory state. Few partisans of this theory realize that its constitutional roots may be found in a radical states' rights ideology that advanced a revolutionary challenge to federal power. Of course the version of states' rights that lies at the heart of modern gun control ideology only faintly resembles its radical ancestor. To understand how states' rights theory was drained of its revolutionary potential we must examine the pivotal role that the Civil War and Reconstruction played in transforming the meaning of the Second Amendment. The foundation for the modern collective rights theory was forged in the carnage of the Reconstruction era.

The evolution of modern Second Amendment theory is closely bound up with the debate over the Fourteenth Amendment. Repub-

lican framers of the Fourteenth Amendment intended to give the federal government the power to incorporate the fundamental liberties
protected by the Bill of Rights. According to incorporation theory,
Congress and the courts would be given the authority to guard basic
liberties, including the right to bear arms. Democrats argued against
incorporation and claimed that the Second Amendment was a right
of the states, not a right of citizens. In the Democrats' narrow states'
rights theory, the amendment did no more than restrain Congress
from disarming the state militias. Ultimately, the courts rejected the
Republican theory of incorporation and embraced the Democratic states'
rights theory of the Second Amendment.[8]

The transformation of this late nineteenth-century states' rights
theory into the modern collective rights theory was accomplished early
in the twentieth century as judges, lawyers, and reformers grappled
with the new problems posed by organized crime and gun violence.
If the Second Amendment was merely a right of the states designed
to prevent federal disarmament of the state militias, then, gun control
proponents claimed, it posed no barrier to state or federal gun
control laws. One additional change in American law and society
facilitated the final transformation of the Second Amendment into
a collective right: Congress replaced the Founding era's universal
militia with the modern National Guard. Ordinary citizens could no
longer make a claim to keep and bear private arms to meet their public obligation to participate in the militia. The connection between arms
bearing and civic participation had been effectively severed. Only the
participants in legally sanctioned military organizations could now make
Second Amendment claims.[9]

Neither of the two modern theories that have defined public
debate over the right to bear arms is faithful to the original understanding of this provision of the Bill of Rights. Previous scholarship
on this history has been warped by the ideological needs of the modern debate over gun control. Only by casting aside the ideology of gun
rights and gun control can one discern the real and previously hidden

history of the great American gun debate. While no scholar writing about this contentious issue can claim to be completely above the fray or entirely neutral, it is possible to approach this issue in a rigorous and balanced manner, focusing on the hopes and fears that drove earlier generations of Americans to venerate the right to bear arms and not confusing these debates with the modern conflict over gun control.

One need not deny gun rights advocates and gun control proponents their history. While each side attacks the other for being a recent invention, the truth is that both sides have a rich history that has much to teach anyone interested in the role of guns in American society. While these opposing theories have deep roots in American history, there is little evidence that either theory was part of the original civic understanding that guided the framers of America's first constitutions. The individual rights and collective rights theories were products of later struggles in American history. Individual rights theory was born in the Jacksonian era as a response to America's first efforts at gun control. Collective rights theory emerged slowly at the end of Reconstruction and only crystallized in its modern form in the early twentieth century. The one theory absent from current debate over the Second Amendment is the original civic interpretation. The virtual extinction of this conception was not inevitable but was a product of a long and complex history. Although the story of the decline of the civic conception of the right to bear arms has never been told, this history is vital to understanding our current predicament over guns in American society.

The tangled history of the struggle to define the right to bear arms ought to serve as a cautionary warning to both sides in this debate. If history seems to provide clear and unambiguous support for one's ideological preferences in the great American gun debate, then the history is likely wrong. While history may not help us chart a clear path toward a solution to America's bitter conflict over the role of guns in American society, some appreciation for how we have arrived at our current deadlock is an important first step to moving forward in this debate.[10]

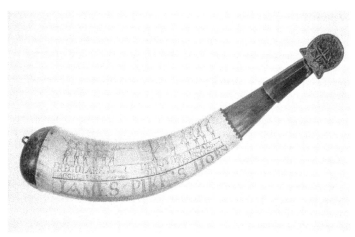

New Hampshire minuteman James Pike's powder horn, carved in 1776, depicts the colonists' well-regulated militia opposing the standing army of Great Britain. Although artistically primitive, the scene carved on this powder horn mirrored the language found in many state constitutions that set the militia and the right to bear arms against the danger of a standing army. (Film negative ICHi-38812, Chicago Historical Society)

CHAPTER ONE

ENGLISH TYRANNY VERSUS AMERICAN LIBERTY

BEARING ARMS IN REVOLUTIONARY AMERICA

In June of 1768 John Hancock's schooner *Liberty* returned to Boston from the Portuguese port of Madeira with its cargo hold laden with wine. Crown officials were eager to make an example of Hancock, whose penchant for smuggling was well known. After inspectors confirmed their suspicions that the appropriate duties had not been paid, customs officials seized the ship. Making an example of the *Liberty* proved to be a grievous error in judgment. "The popularity of her owner, the name of the sloop," and a "general aversion" to customs officials and "parliamentary taxation" worked to "inflame the minds of the people." Hancock was a particularly poor choice to single out for prosecution since he was also an influential member of Boston's branch of the "Sons of Liberty," the group that had sprung up in cities and towns across America during the Stamp Act tax protests three years earlier. An angry crowd soon assembled on Hancock's wharf to protest the seizure. Wielding "clubs, stones and brickbats," Hancock's supporters attacked the revenue officers and drove them from the scene. As word of the Liberty Riot spread throughout the town, large crowds began assembling, and by evening more than a thousand Bostonians had taken to the streets. An angry crowd attacked the homes of crown officials and forced them to seek refuge aboard a Royal Navy vessel anchored in the harbor. Incensed by Boston's defiance and lawlessness, the royal governor, Frances Bernard, requested that British troops be dispatched to the town to restore order. Americans now faced the nightmarish prospect of a standing army garrisoned in their midst, enforcing the dictates of a distant government with little concern for their liberties.[1]

The Liberty Riot was a decisive turning point in American relations with Britain. Samuel Adams, an outspoken champion of American rights and another prominent Son of Liberty, urged Bostonians to "behave like men" and "take up arms immediately and be free." Adams was hardly the only Bostonian to suggest this course of action. Governor Bernard reported that the mob had been harangued by leaders who declared, "We will support our Liberties, depending upon the strength of our own Arms." The use of a standing army without the legislature's consent was a clear violation of British constitutional principles. Such an unconstitutional use of force could have no legal sanction and might legitimately be met with force of arms. Adams and others did not claim to be asserting novel arguments, but rather based their opposition to British policy on well-established English legal principles.[2]

The legal and constitutional arguments made by Adams gained additional force from history itself. The Bostonians who took to the streets to protest the seizure of the *Liberty* were steeped in the lessons of the past, the struggles of the Roman Republic and the more recent battles between English Whigs, the champions of Parliamentary power, and Tories, the supporters of Royal prerogative. History was not simply a subject consigned to the pages of leather-bound volumes detailing the events of bygone days. Americans looked to the past for guidance. An impressive parade of essays signed with the names of historical figures appeared in the press to offer comments on contemporary politics, forging a close link between past and present. Essays signed "Brutus," a hero of the Roman Republic, or "Algernon Sidney," a more recent hero from seventeenth-century English history, filled the pages of newspapers. The use of pseudonyms shielded writers from reprisals and allowed them to affirm their kinship with a host of heroic figures who personified liberty and virtue. Among the favorite pen names adopted by Samuel Adams during this troubled time was "Vindex," a provincial Roman statesman who had opposed the tyranny of the corrupt monarch Nero and denounced the decadence of Imperial Rome. Once again, it was time for virtuous citizens, the modern heirs of Vindex, to step forward to oppose tyranny. One Boston almanac placed an image of Sidney's *Discourses Concerning Government* on its cover. For those readers unfamiliar with this work, the publisher noted that Sidney was a noble martyr to English liberty who had been "beheaded during the Reign of Charles II." Described as the personification of virtue, a man in whom "the spirit of the ancient Republics revived," Sidney's influential treatise became an important political textbook for Americans of Adams's generation. It affirmed a principle that would become the cornerstone of American thinking about the relationship between liberty and arms. "In a popular or mixed government," Sidney wrote, "the body of the people is the publick defence, and every man is arm'd and disciplin'd." When Adams and other Bostonians urged citizens to take up arms to defend their liberty against British tyranny, they did so with a confidence derived from their belief that America had taken Sidney's maxim to heart. In America, the body of the people were armed and well organized.[3]

While Bostonians debated the appropriate course of action to take in response to British policy, the town's selectmen issued an order that their public arms be cleaned and placed on display in the town hall. Governor Bernard viewed the gesture as deliberately provocative, and he informed the Crown that the muskets were placed on view "to remind the People of the Use of them." Despite this assertive gesture, Bostonians had not yet abandoned all hope of seeking a peaceful resolution to their disagreement with the Crown. The town meeting petitioned the governor, stating the colonists' grievances and asserting their understanding of their rights as English subjects. The petition was deemed sufficiently important that copies were printed as a broadside and widely distributed. Colonists asserted three interrelated constitutional principles grounded in their own views of British law. First, a standing army garrisoned among the people without their consent was inconsistent with liberty. Second, colonists had a right to "have Arms for their Defenses." To support these two legal claims they invoked the authority of the English Declaration of Rights of 1689, one of the most influential statements of English constitutional principles. The Declaration of Rights declared that "the subjects being Protestants may have arms for their defense." Bostonians put their own distinctive gloss on this English idea, framing it in strongly collective terms by noting that it was a legal principle that was "well adapted for the necessary Defense of the Community." Finally, colonists anchored their claims by referring to their colony's militia law, describing it as a "wholesome law of the Province" that required each householder to provide himself with a musket to meet his obligation to participate in the militia. Citizens of Massachusetts had done more than simply invoke Sidney's injunction about the necessity of an armed citizenry; they had written its underlying principle into their own laws.[4]

If a standing army symbolized tyranny, a citizens' militia was its antithesis, embodying virtue and liberty. The response of Massachusetts to British policy was decisive and included a call for a colony-wide convention to assemble to discuss the crisis. Towns across the province readily complied with this request. In addition to sending representatives to the convention, individual towns readied their militia for action. Indeed, one week after the Boston town meeting's petition was published, the *Boston Gazette* reported that selectmen in a neighboring town had ordered that a sufficient store of gunpowder be acquired to equip the local militia. The colonel of the local militia in that town "has declared his intention to order a strict Enquiry into the state of his Regiment, respecting Arms, Ammunition, &c." Colonists who bore arms did not act as isolated individuals, but rather acted collectively for the common defense, and did so within a clear set of legal structures established by colonial and British law.[5]

It would be impossible to overstate the militia's centrality to the lives of American colonists. For Americans living on the edge of the British Empire, in an age without police forces, the militia was essential for the preservation of public order and also protected Americans against external threats. One contemporary writer observed that for New Englanders the "near neighbourhood of the Indians and French quickly taught them the necessity of having a well regulated militia." The militia served an important social role as well. Musters were occasions for friends and neighbors to come together to drill and celebrate. Before the development of modern political parties, the militia was one of the central means for organizing citizens. When American colonists spoke about the importance of a well-regulated militia, they were not simply reciting a tired political cliché lifted from the pages of an esteemed political treatise; they defended an institution that was central to their way of life.[6]

THE RIGHT TO BEAR ARMS AS A CIVIC OBLIGATION

Given the centrality of the militia to the everyday lives of the colonists, one can appreciate their horror when they discovered that the British intended not only to foist an oppressive standing army upon them, but also to disarm the colony's militia. Rumors of British treachery spread quickly. A writer for the *Boston Gazette* reported that the royal governor intended to punish Americans in a fashion "more grievous to the People, than any Thing hitherto made known." The governor's plan included three components:

1st that the inhabitants of this Province are to be disarmed.
2d. The Province to be governed by Martial Law.

3d. A number of Gentlemen who have exerted themselves in the Cause of their Country, are to be seized and sent to Great Britain.[7]

On September 28, 1768, two days after the publication of these dire warnings, two regiments of British troops landed in Boston. To prevent colonists from making good on their threats to mobilize their militia, British officials banned the importation of military stores, including gunpowder, and issued orders compelling Boston's citizens to turn in their arms. Americans were outraged and refused to comply with the demand that they disarm.

One of the most incisive attacks on British policy was authored by Samuel Adams. Adams reiterated a point made by the Boston town meeting in its petition that British citizens had a right to maintain arms for their own defense. To support this legal interpretation he quoted the eminent English jurist, Sir William Blackstone, the leading authority on English law. Adams offered the following gloss on Blackstone's interpretation of the English Declaration of Rights: *"Having arms for their defense* he [Blackstone] tells us is 'a public allowance, under due restrictions, of the *natural right of resistance and self-preservation*, when the sanctions of society and laws are found *insufficient* to restrain the *violence of oppression.'"* This ancient right was not exercised by individuals acting unilaterally or in isolation, but rather required that citizens act together in concert as part of a well-regulated militia. Without legal authority, a group of armed citizens acting on their own was little more than a riotous mob.[8]

In defending their right to have arms, Bostonians were acting in strict accordance with the colony's own militia law. "It is certainly beyond human art and sophistry," Adams confidently asserted, "to prove that British subjects, to whom the privilege of possessing arms is expressly recognized by the Bill of Rights, and, who live in a province where the law requires them to be equip'd with arms, &c. are guilty of an illegal act, in calling upon one another to be provided with them, as the law directs." The decision to arm themselves was not an assertion of a new right, but the exercise of an ancient one. The colonists' actions were in accordance with well-established English constitutional principles and were sanctioned by their own militia law. Colonists recognized that the evil they encountered in British policy had a clear political purpose: to sap the colonists' capacity for political resistance.[9]

The right that Adams and Bostonians asserted was described by Blackstone as the "5th auxiliary right" of British subjects, a set of "outworks or barriers" within the British constitutional system that functioned as political safeguards against tyranny. When he described the right as a means of preventing "the violence of oppression" and likened it to other political safeguards such as the right of assembly, Blackstone captured the essentially political nature of this right. Although the right was held by subjects, it was not analogous to other individual rights such as conscience. The right to have arms was linked to a particular civic purpose. It was analogous to the right to petition, another political safeguard protecting English liberty against arbitrary power. The fifth auxiliary right, the right of subjects to have arms, served a public political function and was aimed to prevent the violence of oppression, a term that underscored the right's role as political safeguard.[10]

Blackstone's fifth auxiliary right was legally distinct from the individual right of personal self-defense, and the two were treated separately in his influential legal treatise, *Commentaries on the Laws of England.* The former was a political right embodied in the English Declaration of Rights and was clearly linked to a particular civic purpose. The latter was one of the many natural rights that had slowly evolved under common law, the body of cases that English courts had adjudicated over the course of several centuries and that contained the bulk of English legal doctrine. Most important natural rights, including the right of self-defense, had been modified by the common law. Thus, once men left the state of nature and entered civil society, they renounced the untrammeled right of self-defense. "The law requires," Blackstone declared, "that the person who kills another in his own defense, should have retreated as far as he conveniently or safely can, to avoid the violence of the assault, before he turns upon his assailant." Flight, not armed confrontation, was the legal obligation of English subjects when faced with a threat to personal safety. Indeed, Blackstone contrasted the obligation to stand and fight incumbent upon subjects in time of war, which would have included militiamen bearing arms, with the legal requirement enjoining civilians to retreat to the wall before responding with deadly force to an attack. Another important legal distinction between these two rights related to the power of the state: government could compel individuals to bear arms for public defense but could not force individuals to arm themselves for personal defense.[11]

The constellation of ideas defended by Adams and the Boston town meeting included a set of principles that would come to play a central role in early American constitutional law: an opposition to standing armies and a belief in an obligation to bear arms for the common defense in a well-regulated militia. While there was broad agreement on the importance of these interrelated principles, no single legal model emerged on how to protect them in the first constitutions drafted by Americans. While every state had militia statutes describing the obligation to serve in the militia, the majority of state constitutions drafted during the Revolutionary era omitted any discussion of the right to bear arms. Indeed, the first state constitutions were much more likely to include a prohibition on standing armies than to affirm such a right. Virginia, for example, did not explicitly protect the right to bear arms but included a provision asserting the need for a well-regulated militia. The first state to include such a right was Pennsylvania in its Declaration of Rights, which affirmed that "the people have a right to bear arms for the defense of themselves and the state." Finally, Massachusetts became the first state to protect a right to both "keep and bear arms." In addition to fusing the right to keep and bear arms into a single constitutional principle, the Massachusetts Constitution linked this ideal to an obligation to provide "for the common defense."[12]

In all of these first constitutional documents the right to bear arms was as much a civic obligation as it was a claim against government interference. While today's Americans treat rights as strong claims of citizens against government interference, Adams and his contemporaries believed rights were inextricably bound up with legal obligations. This characteristic of eighteenth-century rights was elaborated by Blackstone when he wrote that "the rights of persons that are commanded to be observed by the municipal law are of two sorts; first, such as are due *from* every citizen, which are usually called civil *duties*; and, secondly, such as belong *to* him, which is the more popular acceptation of *rights*." The learned English jurist then went on to note that allegiance and protection were "reciprocally, the rights as well as the duties of each other." Citizens had both a right and an obligation to arm themselves so that they might participate in a militia.[13]

The clearest example of how different the civic obligation to bear arms was from basic individual rights such as freedom of conscience may be found in the conflict that emerged between these two ideas in the first state constitutions. Quakers and other religious groups committed to pacifism lobbied hard to obtain exemptions from the obligation to bear arms. The state could compel citizens to bear arms, and Quakers sought an explicit constitutional protection not to be forced to bear arms. The problem of religious exemptions also provides another illustration of how different the right to bear arms for the common defense was from the common law of individual self-defense. The state could not force an individual citizen to defend himself; they could force the people to bear arms in defense of the state. Exemptions for conscientious objectors only made sense in the context of the state's right to compel citizens to bear arms for public defense against external threats or internal enemies. None of the early state constitutions adopted language protecting an individual right to keep or carry arms for personal self-defense. Efforts were made to protect such a right in both Virginia and Massachusetts, but in the end neither state chose to adopt an explicit statement protecting the right of self-defense. It would take another four decades before any state would explicitly affirm such a right. The right of individual self-defense would remain a matter of common law, not constitutional law.[14]

THE DEBATE OVER BEARING ARMS IN THE FIRST STATE CONSTITUTIONS: DEFINING A CIVIC RIGHT

The chief architect of Virginia's declaration of rights was George Mason, a wealthy Virginia planter who was one of the largest slaveholders in the state. Contemporaries described him as the modern embodiment of Roman virtue. A leading advocate for colonial independence, Mason also became an outspoken champion of the militia, urging his fellow citizens to enact a law to put the colony's militia in a state of readiness for possible war with Britain. Mason's vision of the militia reflected his own patrician values and the traditional Whig ideas of Sidney and others who praised the militia ideal and believed that social stability required that an armed citizenry be led by "gentlemen of the first fortune and character." Mason's preference for this traditional Whig conception was evident in the following resolve he drafted on January 17, 1775, for the Fairfax County Committee of Safety, an important institution responsible for coordinating the colony's military efforts.[15]

> Resolved, That this Committee do concur in opinion with the Provincial Committee of the Province of Maryland, that a well regulated Militia, composed of gentlemen freeholders, and other freemen, is the natural strength and only stable security of a free Government.

Mason's emphasis on the need for the militia to be composed of property holders reflected a view common among members of Virginia's gentry elite that it was dangerous to arm the "rabble." Without the guidance of gentlemen, an armed population might easily become a mob, not a well-regulated militia.[16]

Mason took a leading role in drafting Virginia's declaration of rights, and his efforts reflected ideas he had developed in his earliest public writings about the need for a well-regulated militia. Edmund Randolph, another influential figure in Virginia politics, remarked that Mason's proposal "swallowed up all the rest, by fixing the grounds and plan, which after great discussion and correction, were finally ratified." Mason's first draft did provoke some controversy among Virginians because it affirmed "that all Men are born equally free and independent." Some members of the Virginia convention opposed such language, fearing that it might undermine the institution of slavery and incite slaves to rebel. Edmund Randolph recollected that such objections were easily satisfied by reminding delegates that "with arms in our hands, asserting the general rights of man, we ought not to be too nice and too much restricted in the declaration of them." The connection between the militia and the slave patrols that protected Virginians against the threat of slave insurrections was well understood by Mason and others. Although the committee followed Mason's language closely, the affirmation of the need for a well-regulated militia departed from his earlier statements in one important respect. It abandoned any reference to a militia composed or officered by gentlemen. The final language adopted by Virginia asserted that the militia was "composed of the body of the people."[17]

When the committee charged with producing the declaration of rights revised Mason's original draft, they settled on the following language:

That a well regulated militia, composed of the body of the people, trained to arms, is the proper, natural, and safe defence of a free state; that standing armies, in time of peace, should be avoided, as dangerous to liberty; and that, in all cases, the military should be under strict subordination to, and governed by, the civil power.[18]

Not all Virginians were satisfied with Mason's militia-focused language. Thomas Jefferson, perhaps the most forward-looking and innovative legal thinker involved with the framing of the Virginia Constitution, wished to include an expansive statement of the right to keep arms. Jefferson's formulation would have severed the connection between such a right and any obligation to bear them in a well-regulated militia. An admirer of the Italian Enlightenment theorist Cesare Beccaria, Jefferson endorsed Beccaria's observation that laws prohibiting individuals from carrying firearms only worked to the benefit of criminals. In essence, Beccaria was the first modern theorist to argue that when firearms are outlawed, only outlaws will have firearms. Jefferson copied Beccaria's discussion of this matter into his legal commonplace book in a section dealing with government policy. In an alternative constitutional proposal that Jefferson circulated among members of the convention, he sought the inclusion of a provision protecting a more robust individual right to keep and carry firearms outside of the context of the militia. Had Jefferson succeeded, the Virginia Declaration of Rights would have asserted that "no free man shall be debarred the use of arms." This language proved too bold for his contemporaries, and Jefferson quickly emended his draft language to narrow the scope of this right, effectively eliminating the right to carry arms. The revised proposal suggested that the Virginia Declaration of Rights include language asserting that "no free man shall be debarred the use of arms [within his own lands or tenements]." This modified Beccarian model affirmed an individual right to keep arms for private purposes. Yet neither the expansive Beccarian model nor the more limited modified model of keeping arms was ultimately included in the Virginia Declaration of Rights. The convention chose instead to retain Mason's formulation of this right, which focused on a well-regulated militia.[19]

Virginia's constitution was crafted by members of a planter elite who were often compared to the great leaders of the Roman republic, men such as Brutus or Cato. Pennsylvania's constitution, by contrast, owed far more to plebeian ideas than to patrician ones. The colony was often described by contemporaries as the "best poor man's country," and its constitution was framed by men of humble origins who spoke on behalf of the laboring classes and the industrious middling sorts, such as tradesmen and small farmers. One prominent group who took a leading role in crafting the Pennsylvania Constitution hailed from the western part of the state. These men were animated by long-standing grievances against the eastern Quaker elite who had dominated the legislature for most of the colonial period. For more than a decade prior to American independence, backcountry Pennsylvanians pressed for a militia law to help them protect their communities against threats from Indians along the frontier. The Quaker-dominated assembly rebuffed these appeals, preferring to negotiate, not fight, with the Native population. The most notorious incident in this decade-long struggle was the Paxton Boys' Uprising, the massacre of a group of defenseless Conestoga Indians by backcountry Pennsylvanians in 1763. "The Apology of the Paxton Volunteers" framed their grievances against the Pennsylvania government in the following terms:

> When we applied to the Government for Relief, the far greater part of our Assembly were Quakers, some of whom made light of our Sufferings & plead Conscience, so that they could neither take Arms in Defense of themselves or their Country, nor form a Militia law to oblige the Inhabitants to arm.[20]

The text of the Paxton apology anticipated the language eventually included by Pennsylvanians in their Declaration of Rights, which asserted that the people had a right to "bear arms in defense of themselves and the state." There is no evidence from the pre-Revolutionary era that Pennsylvanians were concerned about threats to the common-law right of individual self-defense. The Quaker-dominated legislature had not disarmed backcountry inhabitants, nor had it passed laws that prevented them from defending their homes against intruders. What the assembly had refused to do was enact a militia law or provide arms for frontier communities to mount a concerted collective defense, including retaliatory raids on Indian communities. The language eventually incorporated into the Pennsylvania Declaration of Rights reflected this bitter struggle over public safety, and had little to do with public concern over an individual right to keep arms for self-protection.[21]

Although they had dominated colonial politics for much of the previous century, Quaker influence was on the decline by the onset of the American Revolution. Many Quakers opposed independence, a choice that further weakened their position. Although the Quakers' influence in Pennsylvania politics was greatly diminished, they were able to obtain one important concession from the framers of the state constitution. As religious pacifists opposed to bearing arms, Quakers won a religious exemption that would allow them not to bear arms:

> That every member of society hath a right to be protected in the enjoyment of life, liberty and property, and therefore is bound to contribute his proportion towards the expence of that protection, and yield his personal service when necessary, or an equivalent thereto: But no part of a man's property can be justly taken from him, or applied to public uses, without his own consent, or that of his legal representatives: Nor can any man who is conscientiously scrupulous of bearing arms, be justly compelled thereto, if he will pay such equivalent: Nor are the people bound by any laws, but such as they have in like manner assented to, for their common good.[22]

By including a right to bear arms and a right not to be forced to bear arms, the Pennsylvania Declaration of Rights struck a compromise position between the opposing demands of the backcountry residents and the Quakers.

Only after asserting the civic obligation to bear arms did the constitution then affirm:

That the people have a right to bear arms for the defence of themselves and the state; and as standing armies in the time of peace,
are dangerous to liberty, they ought not to be kept up: And that
the military should be kept under strict subordination, to, and
governed by, the civil power.

As was invariably true in most Revolutionary-era constitutions, the
right to bear arms was also set against the danger posed by standing
armies, a juxtaposition that only underscored the military civic character of the right.[23]

While the right to bear arms was articulated as a civic right inextricably linked to the civic obligation to bear arms for public defense,
the constitution did deal with the private use of arms in one other context. The Pennsylvania Constitution explicitly protected the right to
hunt in a separate provision from the right to bear arms. In contrast
to England, where game laws made hunting the exclusive province of
the wealthy, in Pennsylvania "the inhabitants of this state shall have
liberty to fowl and hunt in seasonable times on the lands they hold,
and on all other lands therein not inclosed; and in like manner to fish
in all boatable waters, and others not private property." The formulation of this right implied a right of government regulation, since hunting might be limited as to time, place, and manner. Still, protecting
the right of all citizens to hunt made clear an opposition to the kinds
of restrictions that the English game laws had codified and that had
been used to effectively disarm a significant portion of the English
population.[24]

The Massachusetts Constitution maintained the emphasis on collective defense found in the Virginia and Pennsylvania declarations of
rights, but it added one crucial new word:

The People have a right to *keep* and bear arms for the common
defence. And as in time of peace armies are dangerous to liberty,
they ought not to be maintained without the consent of the

legislature; and the military power shall always be held in exact subordination to the civil authority, and be governed by it. (emphasis
added)[25]

The convention's inclusion of the word *keep* built on an assumption
implicit in the state's militia statute that most citizens, apart from the
poor, would provide their own weapons for militia duty and would
therefore keep those weapons in their homes.[26] In contrast to
Jefferson's alternative formulation of the right to keep arms, which did
not link this right to bearing arms, Massachusetts forged a tight link
between the two. A single constitutional principle emerged, linking
the right to keep arms with the obligation to bear them for the common defense.

One of most remarkable features of the framing and ratification of
the Massachusetts Constitution was the decision to submit the draft
constitution to towns for comments. The towns' responses to the
various provisions of the constitution provides a rare glimpse into popular constitutional ideas in the Founding era, including arms bearing.
Although individual towns produced dozens of detailed responses to
the proposed constitution and identified many flaws in the new frame
of government, the clause on the right to keep and bear arms did not
prompt extensive commentary. Only two western towns expressed any
reservations about the wording: Both towns sought something closer
to Jefferson's modified Beccarian model, which would have severed the
connection between the right to keep arms and the obligation to bear
them for the common defense.

A response from the town of Northampton suggested that "the
people have a right to keep and bear arms as well for their own as
the common defense."[27] Williamsburgh, another town in western
Hampshire County, echoed these protests:

1st. that we esteem it an essential privilege to keep Arms in our
houses for Our Own Defense and while we Continue honest and

Lawfull Subjects of Government we Ought Never to be deprived of them.

Reas. 2 That the legislature in some future period may Confine all the fire Arms to some publick Magazine and thereby deprive the people of the benefit of the use of them.[28]

Williamsburgh sought an explicit statement of a right to keep arms for personal defense.[29]

The fear that the state might insist on the collective storage of arms had been voiced two years earlier when the state rejected the first proposed constitution. These apprehensions demonstrated how American thinking about the right to bear arms was powerfully influenced by a fear of British-style disarmament of the militia. The march of British Regulars on Concord to seize colonial military stores in 1775 left an indelible imprint on citizens of the commonwealth. Backcountry residents were especially anxious about ceding too much power to a distant government. For those who feared centralization of power, the state government in Boston was as much to be feared as the government of King George III had been during the Revolution. All governments were liable to become corrupt and oppressive if citizens failed to watch them with a jealous eye. Although as a practical matter Williamsburgh probably had little to fear about the dangers of centralized storage of weapons, the possibility was not completely beyond the pale. The state enjoyed enormous powers to regulate its internal police and enact laws consistent with the common good. In military matters the state's power was even greater since it could seize weapons or compel military service. It was precisely because they recognized the enormous power of the state's authority over firearms that Williamsburgh town residents sought to affirm a right to keep and bear arms in more expansive terms. Despite their protests, no other town in the commonwealth followed their lead, and the language included in the Massachusetts Constitution remained unchanged.[30]

A WELL-REGULATED RIGHT

The meaning of the Massachusetts Constitution's provision on keeping and bearing arms was clearly understood by contemporaries to provide explicit constitutional protection for weapons associated with militia service. The status of weapons with no connection to the militia posed a different set of issues. The scope of the right to keep or carry arms outside of the militia prompted a fascinating newspaper exchange less than a decade after Massachusetts towns had debated the merits of their constitution. One writer, adopting the Roman persona of Senex, argued that constitutional protection for the right to bear arms was limited by the purpose of the provision, which was to provide for the common defense. Following a well-established principle of legal construction and constitutional interpretation that would have been easily understood by Americans, Senex reminded his audience that in "defining this article, we ought to consider the evil intended to be remedied." In Senex's view, the right to bear arms was included in the Massachusetts Constitution as a means of preventing the disarmament of the militia. As Senex noted, "The idea, that Great Britain meant to take away their arms, was in the minds of the people."

Another writer, who cloaked himself in a more popular literary style, adopting the less pompous name of Scribble-Scrabble, conceded "the people's right to keep and bear arms for a particular purpose is secured to them against any future acts of the legislature." As far as the personal right to use arms was concerned, "the legislature have a power to control it in all cases, except the one mentioned in the bill of rights, whenever they shall think the good of the whole require it." Until the legislature acted, either to regulate or prohibit the particular use of firearms, the people retained the right to use firearms for any lawful purpose. Asserting a basic principle of common law, Scribble-Scrabble informed his readers that "the other purposes for which they might have been used in a state of nature, being a natural right, and not surrendered by the constitution, the people still enjoy, and must continue to do so till the legislature shall think fit to interdict." Senex and Scribble-Scrabble's interpretations of the Massachusetts Constitution were consistent with the fears expressed by Williamsburgh and Northhampton residents less than a decade earlier. While militia weapons owned for the purposes of meeting a specific legal obligation were constitutionally protected, other weapons were not. Although the scope of legislative authority over nonmilitary weapons was considerable, it was certainly not unlimited. Laws enacted regarding firearms had to serve a legitimate public purpose and have a rational basis. Within those constraints the state was free to enact any type of regulation the legislature deemed necessary to promote public safety.[31]

The right of the people to govern themselves and legislate their "internal police" was a bedrock principle of American constitutionalism. Pennsylvania's Declaration of Rights made this explicit when it asserted that "the people of this State have the sole, exclusive and inherent right of governing and regulating the internal police of the same." While many in modern America have come to view regulation as somehow antithetical to liberty, this was not how Americans in the Revolutionary era viewed the matter. The ideal that Americans venerated was not the unrestrained liberty of the state of nature, but the ideal of well-regulated liberty. As one contemporary noted, "Well regulated liberty of individuals is the natural offspring of laws, which prudentially regulate the rights of whole communities." By contrast, "all liberty which is not regulated by law, is a delusive phantom." Outside of a well-regulated society governed by the rule of law, liberty was nothing more than licentiousness and anarchy.[32]

The lengthy militia statutes enacted by the individual colonies and then revised by the states after they gained independence constituted the largest body of law dealing with firearms. These regulations could be quite intrusive, allowing government not only to keep track of who had firearms, but also requiring citizens to report to muster or face stiff penalties. The individual colonies used their broad police powers to regulate the nonmilitary use of firearms in a variety of ways.

Regulations governing the storage of gunpowder were among the most common. States also prohibited the use of firearms on certain occasions and in certain locations. A good example of the breadth of the state's police powers is provided by a regulation forbidding Boston residents from storing loaded firearms in any domestic dwelling. The 1786 statute, "An act in addition to the several Acts already made for the prudent Storage of Gun Powder within the Town of Boston," empowered the town's fire wardens to confiscate weapons and impose stiff fines for violating this law.[33]

The state also retained the right to disarm groups deemed to be dangerous. While the state could not pass English-style game laws that unilaterally disarmed the entire population, it could use loyalty oaths and enact discriminatory legislation to disarm particular groups in society that posed a risk to public safety. Although the language of Pennsylvania's constitutional provision on arms bearing was among the most expansive, the state also adopted one of the most stringent loyalty oaths. The Test Acts, as they were known to contemporaries, barred citizens who refused the oath from holding public office and serving on juries. These individuals were also to be disarmed, as "persons disaffected to the liberty and independence of this state."[34] The acts thus stripped many but not all the essential rights of citizenship from a large segment of the population, perhaps as much as 40 percent of the citizenry. Individuals who failed to take the oath could still publish, assemble, and seek petition for redress of grievances, but they were not full participants in the civic life of their state. Their status fell somewhere between full citizens and resident aliens. Although loyalty oaths were enacted in other states, the Pennsylvania Test Acts were not repealed until long after the treaty of Paris was signed in 1783 and formal hostilities with Britain ended. The oaths did more than address the special situation faced by the state during wartime; they reflected a more fundamental belief that citizenship was tied to a set of legal obligations and demanded a certain level of public virtue. One other type of systematic disarmament policy was common. Laws disarming groups such as slaves, freed blacks, Indians, and those of mixed-race ancestry were common. Thus, Pennsylvania prohibited "any Negro" to "carry any Guns, Sword, Pistol, Fowling-Piece, Clubs, or other Arms or Weapons whatsoever" without "his Master's special Licence." Since blacks were ineligible to bear arms, the prohibition was phrased as a limit on carrying weapons.[35]

The legal difference between laws regulating civilian gun use and laws pertaining to bearing arms was an important one. The state enjoyed far greater authority over the former type of activity. A good illustration of this principle may be found in a bill introduced by the young James Madison during his time as a legislator in Virginia. In a "Bill for the Preservation of Deer," Madison proposed a stiff penalty for individuals who hunted out of season. The most interesting features of this law penalized persons who "shall bear a gun out of his inclosed ground, unless whilst performing military duty." The language of this provision provides a remarkable window into the way Madison understood the differences between bearing a gun for personal use and for the common defense. The state clearly retained the right to regulate the use of firearms and differentiated between the level of restrictions that might be placed on bearing a gun and bearing arms.[36]

Even in the absence of any legislation regulating the right to keep or carry firearms, there were a variety of constraints embedded in the common law. The common law also provided some modest protection for a right to keep or carry firearms for personal protection. The nature of the common law made it particularly well suited to deal with the complex problem of regulating firearm use. The genius of the common law was that it was an organic entity, capable of evolution and growth. The meaning of self-defense was an excellent illustration of this dimension of the common law. The natural right of self-defense had evolved slowly into the more limited right embodied in the common law. These changes reflected the accumulated wisdom of countless judges who had struggled with the difficult task of balancing the right of self-defense with the need to protect public safety.[37]

The right to travel armed was severely constrained under common law. The author of *English Liberties, of the Free-born Subject's Inheritance*, a popular English legal text reprinted in the colonies, defined an affray as a crime against the king's peace and that "constables may take away the Arms of them who ride or go armed in Terror of the People." Another influential legal text, *The Conductor Generalis, the Office, Duty, and Authority of Justices of the Peace*, noted that "in some case there may be an affray, where there is no actual violence; as where a man arms himself with dangerous and unusual weapons, in such a manner as will naturally cause terror to the people." Under British law armed travel was regulated, and mere possession of arms likely to provoke a public panic was also punishable. Popular guides to the law published after the Revolution continued to devote considerable space to the subject of affrays. The nature of the common law provided considerable flexibility in deciding exactly what constituted an affray. Context was crucial to making these kinds of determinations. In America, where legal restrictions on hunting were far more lax and gun ownership more common, the crime of affray was more narrowly defined than in England. A party of men hunting in season in Pennsylvania would not under most circumstances have been viewed as committing an affray, while an armed assembly riding into town might well be viewed as such and could be legally disarmed by a justice of the peace.[38]

SHAYS'S REBELLION

While the framers of America's first constitutions struggled to craft documents that preserved the ideals of well-regulated liberty, there were those who felt that the new state governments were themselves potential threats to liberty. In the period between the 1760s and 1780s, popular protest movements emerged in backcountry regions of North and South Carolina. As one contemporary observed, the protestors described themselves as "Regulators" because they attempted "to regulate the administration of justice in the remote settlements." Regulator movements were an expression of a species of popular constitutionalism in which the people took direct action themselves and thus bypassed the courts or the legislature. Perhaps the most dramatic action of Regulators was the closing of courts to protect debtors from creditors. The notion that the people might assemble in arms and defend their liberty posed a potential challenge to the new state governments' authority. During the Revolution, popular assemblies, including mobs, had played an important role in the movement for independence. During the Liberty Riot in 1768, citizens invoked a right of constitutional resistance. In 1786, embattled farmers in western Massachusetts sounded an alarm and mustered, asserting their right to take up arms to defend their liberty against the tyranny of a distant government that seemed unresponsive to their needs. This time that distant government was not far across the sea, but sitting in Boston. The very same logic that led Samuel Adams to invoke the fifth auxiliary right in the aftermath of the Liberty Riot was used by farmers in western Massachusetts to challenge their own state government's authority. Shays's Rebellion, the largest violent uprising in the new nation's history, would become the first test of the radical potential of the militia and the right to bear arms in post-Revolutionary America.[39]

The western farmers' grievances were serious. Funding the war against Britain had placed a severe strain on the American economy. The individual states adopted different strategies to deal with the burden of war debt. Massachusetts adopted a tight fiscal policy, including high taxes. Farmers in the western part of the state were particularly hard-hit by these policies. As the number of farm foreclosures rose, and popular frustration mounted, events took a dramatic turn when a contingent of Revolutionary War veterans mustered themselves and marched in military array on the town of Northampton to shut down the local courts and prevent further foreclosures. Although the protestors did not have the legal authority to act as a state-sanctioned militia, their behavior imitated the rituals and organization of the militia. The insurgents, many of them armed with muskets, marched behind a fife and drum and assembled in the center of town. The judges of the court, dressed in formal judicial attire—long black robes and gray wigs—were prevented from entering the courthouse by the assembled protestors. The men who marched on the courthouse in western Massachusetts did not call themselves rebels or insurgents, but Regulators. As had been true for earlier Regulator movements in the Carolinas, the Shaysites cast themselves as champions of the "good of the commonwealth" and framed their protests in a distinctly collective idiom, invoking the metaphor of the "Body of the People." Shays and his followers claimed to be exercising "the first principles of natural self preservation." Thus, in choosing to arm themselves, the Shaysites did not invoke the right to bear arms protected by their state constitution; instead they claimed a natural right that superceded any written constitutional text. The voice of the people spoke not through written constitutional texts, but directly through popular assemblies, including the militia.[40]

The Regulators who took up arms against the government of Massachusetts went to extraordinary lengths to dispel the idea that they were a mob. Their actions and rhetoric self-consciously drew on symbols associated with the Revolutionary militia. Citizens were urged to emulate the minutemen and "turn out at a minute's notice." Regulators organized themselves into regiments and kept track of participants on muster rolls. The goal stated by these Regulator units was to suppress the "tyrannical government in the Massachusetts State." Regulators acted as if they were simply carrying forward the heritage of the Revolution and even adopted the practice of adorning their hats with green boughs, a symbolic gesture that had been used on ceremonial occasions by troops during the Revolutionary struggle.[41]

Proponents of Regulation denied that they intended to "subvert all Government, and throw all things into a State of Anarchy and confusion." The governor of the commonwealth, James Bowdoin, saw matters differently. In a proclamation condemning the actions of the Northampton insurgents, he asserted that their behavior was "fraught with the most fatal and pernicious consequences" and "must tend to subvert all law and government." In short, Bowdoin denounced the rebellion for undermining the security provided by a "well-regulated society" and threatening life, liberty, and property.[42]

A few days after the events in Northampton, another crowd of farmers closed the courts in Worcester. This time Governor Bowdoin took decisive action and called out the militia. Rather than follow the orders of the governor and disperse the insurgents, however, a large number of the town's militia refused to march against the protestors. Some members of the militia even joined ranks with the rebels they had been sent to quell. A similar scenario played out in Great Barrington. Once again the government dispatched the militia to liberate the court from the mob. When the militia met up with the Regulators, a member of the crowd suggested putting the matter to a vote: supporters of opening the court stood to one side of the road while those opposed crossed the highway. Nearly eight hundred of the thousand militia members who had been sent to protect the courts voted with their feet to join the rebels and keep the courts closed.[43]

For Shays and his supporters, the actions of those citizens who had refused to take up arms against the Regulators were a living proof of the superiority of a citizens' militia over a standing army. In contrast to professional soldiers, who would have had few scruples about opening fire on an assembly of citizens, a militia composed of the body of the people would never be party to such an act. For the Friends of Order, the supporters of government authority, the refusal of the western militia to muster against the Regulators only confirmed the weakness and inadequacy of the militia as a bulwark against anarchy. Shays's rebellion exposed a tension in American constitutional theory: was the militia an agent of government authority, or was it a popular institution that might serve as a check on government? The notion that the militia might effectively nullify an unjust law by refusing to enforce it, or in extreme situations actually take up arms against the government, were two of the most radical ideas to emerge out of the intellectual ferment of the Revolutionary era. Both of these ideas had been put into practice during Shays's Rebellion.[44]

Regulators defended their actions in a language that reflected a strong corporate sensibility that was itself rooted in their desire to defend their local communities against outside threat. Men did not act alone as isolated individuals, but acted in concert with one another as a public body. In the view of the Shaysite Luke Day, the Regulators were literally "the body of the people assembled in arms." Shays and his followers were not radical individualists, but strongly communitarian and localist in their outlook. For backcountry radicals such as the Regulators, the militia was an expression of the locality, not a creature of the state.[45]

Opponents of the rebellion, Friends of Order, attacked the Regulators as insurgents, "levellers," "bandetti," or simply "the mob." In their view, American Independence had banished the right of armed resistance against constitutional government. As one Congregational minister from western Massachusetts noted, "Our government is so constituted that publick oppressions may be soon removed without force, either by remonstrance against the measures of rulers, or by a change of the rulers themselves." The right of revolution was a natural right that individuals ceded as a prerequisite for creating political society. The only justification for taking up arms was when "rulers usurp a power oppressive to the people, and continue to support it by military force in contempt of every respectful remonstrance." Shaysites enjoyed representation and had access to the courts. Indeed, their decision to close the courts only underscored their lawlessness. Rebellion against duly constituted authority demanded a forceful response by government. "If a part of the people attempt by arms to controul or subvert the government, the rulers, who are the guardians of the constitution, have a right to call in the aid of the people to protect it." Even Samuel Adams, the firebrand of the Revolution, denounced the Regulation. In a situation in which representative institutions and courts of law were functioning, the rule of law, not arms, was the primary guarantee of life, liberty, and property.[46]

When the Continental Congress learned of unrest in Massachusetts, including the refusal of western militia units to quell the rebellion, they used the pretext of raising troops to combat Indians in the Northwest Territory as the justification for raising additional troops to aid Massachusetts. Eventually the state raised an army, turning to Boston's business community to underwrite the effort. The prospect of an army marching westward prompted the Regulators to make a bold decision: they moved to seize the federal arsenal at Springfield. When word of the Regulators' plan reached Boston, troops headed west to Springfield to cut them off and defend the arsenal. The better-equipped troops loyal to the government easily routed the Regulators, and the movement collapsed.[47]

The leaders of the movement, Daniel Shays and Eli Parsons, fled the state. The government of Massachusetts passed the Disqualification Act and required Shaysites to take a new oath of allegiance. Those who refused to take the oath were denied the right to serve on juries, hold public office, or vote. The law also disarmed individuals. While the Disqualification Act prevented Regulators from serving on juries or possessing firearms, they were not stripped of all their rights. The state clearly distinguished between rights associated with citizenship, civic rights such as participation in juries and bearing arms, and rights that were genuinely individual in character such as freedom of conscience or "the liberty of the press."[48]

In the view of Massachusetts poet, playwright, and historian Mercy Otis Warren, "the turbulent spirit" in western Massachusetts "awakened all to a full view of the necessity of concert and union in measures that might preserve their internal peace." The Boston merchant Stephen Higginson commented, "I never saw so great a change in the public mind on any occasion as has lately appeared in this state as to the expediency of increasing the powers of Congress." Beyond the borders of Massachusetts similar responses were articulated by a variety of leading political figures. No one was more shaken by the events than General George Washington. When news of the uprising reached him at Mount Vernon, he fired off letters to several of his former Continental Army aides and inquired about the "cause of all these commotions." Was the rebellion the outgrowth of "licentiousness," or was it instigated by "British-influence disseminated by the Tories," or was it possible that this tumult sprang from some "real grievances"? Washington's alarm reflected a genuine sense of fear about America's future. History taught that all republics were fragile and could be destroyed by popular licentiousness as well as by conspiracies hatched by corrupt leaders. To steer a course between the threats of anarchy and tyranny was no easy matter. Decisive action was necessary to avert the contagion from spreading. In a letter to Henry Knox, Washington worried that "there are combustibles in every state, which a spark might set fire to."[49]

While in general there was little support for the rebels among the nation's elite, there was one notable exception, Thomas Jefferson. In a letter to his friend James Madison, Jefferson offered his own assessment of the "the late troubles" in Massachusetts. "I hold it," Jefferson wrote, that "a little rebellion now and then is a good thing." Jefferson's response to Shays's Rebellion, like his rejected proposal on the right to keep arms, demonstrated again that on most constitutional matters he stood well outside the mainstream in Revolutionary America. Yet, his ideas about an individual right to have arms tapped into a strain in American constitutional thought that would gain strength, not diminish, in the coming decades.[50]

Despite the quick collapse of Shays's Rebellion, the Regulator movement did have an important impact on American constitutional development. It provided additional impetus for a growing movement to reform the Articles of Confederation, America's first constitution. Delegates from each of the states were dispatched to Philadelphia to attend a constitutional convention. The problem of military reform would be critical to their deliberations. Providing some means to coordinate the individual state militias under a centralized authority was deemed essential to protect the nation from internal and external threats. The problem was how to accomplish this goal without undermining the power of the states and alarming a population that was still fearful of standing armies and devoted to the idea of state control of the militia.

The original draft of the Bill of Rights produced by the Congress in 1791. What became the Second Amendment was originally the fourth amendment (see detail) submitted to the states for ratification. (Courtesy of U.S. National Archives and Records Administration)

CHAPTER TWO

A WELL-REGULATED MILITIA

THE ORIGINS OF THE SECOND AMENDMENT

The delegates who traveled to the Constitutional Convention in Philadelphia had good reasons to be apprehensive about the future of the new United States. America's fledgling experiment in republican government faced a host of dangers from within and without. Shays's rebellion had frightened many of the nation's leaders who feared that the young republic was drifting toward anarchy. Moreover, debt-ridden farmers were hardly the only group in America whose grievances might lead them to rebellion. Southern delegates to the Constitutional Convention, most of whom were planters, feared a different threat to civil order, enslaved Africans. External threats to the new nation also weighed heavily on the delegates' minds. The nation's borders needed to be rendered secure from potential Indian attack. British troops continued to be garrisoned along the frontier, and Spain was tightening its control of the Mississippi River and the port of New Orleans. Many Americans, particularly those who traveled to Philadelphia, had become convinced that the nation needed a strong national government that could deal with these multiple threats to its security. If America was to survive these challenges, military reform was essential. The question of what to do about the militia was placed at the center of constitutional debate.

At the start of the American Revolution there had been widespread agreement that a well-regulated militia was the only form of defense compatible with republican liberty. The militia's mixed performance during the War for Independence caused many to lose faith in this ideal. Dissatisfaction with the militia was particularly keen among convention delegates. Many of them had served in the Continental Army's officers corps and had experienced the difficulties of waging a war against a well-trained professional fighting force firsthand. The Revolution had kindled the flame of nationalism in these officers. If America was to survive as a nation, it would have to forego reliance on the militia as the nation's primary means of defense and create a standing army. In addition to diminishing the nation's reliance on the militia, some nationalists sought to transform the militia itself. One group at the convention wished to transfer control of the militia from the states to the federal government. Other reformers wished to abandon a universal militia and replace it with a smaller select militia drawn from the ranks of an elite group of militiamen.[1]

Not everyone in attendance at the convention embraced this nationalist agenda. A small minority of the delegates feared tyranny more than anarchy. Opponents of the nationalist agenda feared that if state authority over the militia were undermined and the federal government were given the ability to raise a standing army, there would be no way to check the designs of ambitious and corrupt rulers. If history had taught any lesson to these Americans, it was that if power was unchecked, it inevitably led to despotism.

The movement to revise the Articles of Confederation and substitute in their place a new powerful national government dramatically altered the terms of debate over the meaning of the militia and the right to bear arms. The debate over including the right to bear arms in the first state constitutions had been relatively muted. No one doubted that the militias were creatures of the individual states. The only issue that prompted some minor protest was the failure to provide explicit protection for an individual right of self-defense. Most Americans were not troubled by this omission and were content to leave such a right a matter of common law. The dominant model that emerged from America's first great wave of constitution writing was the civic conception of the right to bear arms, which tied the exercise of this right to participation in the militia. The debate over the federal constitution would change all of this as the arguments over the meaning of the right to bear arms and the militia became embroiled in the larger dispute over federalism. Control of the militia became a crucial issue in defining the future balance of power between the states and the new national government. The issue of federalism had not been on the minds of Americans when they drafted their first state constitutions. The new constitution proposed by the Philadelphia convention forced Americans to ponder a different question: would the militia continue to be an agent of state power or would it become a tool of a powerful national government?

The development of a states' rights theory of the militia and the right to bear arms occurred slowly as opponents of nationalism struggled to define a constitutional theory that would provide the states with an effective check on federal power. Building on the civic conception of the right to bear arms, proponents of states' rights argued that an armed citizenry organized as a well-regulated militia controlled by the states could take up arms against the federal government and thereby act as the final check against government tyranny.

FEDERALISTS, ANTI-FEDERALISTS, AND THE CONSTITUTION: THE GREAT DEBATE BEGINS

The Philadelphia convention began its work with a limited mandate to revise the Articles of Confederation. Led by delegates from Virginia who advocated abandoning the Articles of Confederation's model of a league of perpetual friendship, the convention accepted the Virginia Plan as the basis for a radical reworking of American constitutionalism. The new government would be a hybrid with both federal and national features. Under the new government the states would continue to be sovereign in most internal matters while the new national government would be supreme in areas such as foreign affairs. The problem of national defense figured prominently among the concerns that led the delegates to take this bold step.[2]

The new constitution that emerged from the convention's work was a compromise that included elements of the Virginia Plan and a host of other concessions and compromises that reflected the concerns of small states such as Connecticut and New Jersey and the interests of slaveholding states such as South Carolina. The convention's wide-ranging debates, conducted under a veil of secrecy, allowed the delegates to offer frank assessments on a variety of issues, including the relative merits of a standing army and a citizens' militia. Few delegates were as bold as South Carolina's Charles Pinckney, who declared he had little "faith in the militia." James Madison stated the nationalist concern over the issue of control of the militia when he argued that "the Discipline of the Militia is evidently a *National* Concern, and ought to be provided for in the *National* Constitution."[3]

The convention failed to resolve the thorny issue of who would constitute this new militia. Some delegates adhered to the traditional idea of a militia composed of the body of the people while others rejected this notion as impractical and inefficient. In place of a universal militia, some delegates pushed for a select militia drawn from a smaller body of citizens who would be better trained and equipped. A few delegates even rejected the idea of the militia entirely, arguing that America could no longer depend on citizen soldiers and ought to follow the European model and create a professional standing army. Rather than fix the meaning of the militia in the text of the

Constitution, the convention decided to give the new congress the authority to determine the future composition of the militia.

Proponents of states' rights defended the traditional idea of the militia and opposed the growing demand for the creation of a powerful federal standing army. Elbridge Gerry of Massachusetts captured this view when he warned the delegates that "the people were jealous on this head." Gerry urged the delegates to emulate the many state constitutions and include a ban on standing armies. Without such a ban, the people would view the Constitution as a threat to their liberty. Gerry's qualms proved prescient: the failure to include such a prohibition would inspire a vigorous opposition once the convention's work was made public and the new Constitution was submitted to the states for ratification. Even among those sympathetic to the idea of strengthening the national government there was a recognition that the individual states would not easily give up control of their militias.[4]

Ultimately, the convention arrived at a compromise between the extreme nationalist and states' rights positions. The Constitution gave the federal government the authority "to call forth the aid of the militia, in order to execute the laws of the Union, enforce treaties, suppress insurrections, and repel invasions." The new national government was given the authority to organize, arm, and discipline the militia. The states would maintain some measure of control by retaining the power over the "appointment of the officers, and authority for training the militia according to the discipline prescribed." In so doing, the convention made the militia a creature of both the states and the new national government.[5]

As the convention was finalizing the language of the new frame of government, Virginia's George Mason proposed adding a declaration of rights similar to the one he had helped draft for Virginia. The convention rejected Mason's suggestion. Some delegates believed a declaration of rights was unnecessary in a document of strictly limited powers, all of which had been specifically enumerated in the body of the Constitution. Others may have been too worn out to take up the issue and were confident the document could easily be amended at a future date if necessary. The decision to brush off Mason's suggestion was a serious miscalculation. Indeed, the absence of a bill of rights would emerge as one of the most serious objections to the Constitution.

Three days after the Constitutional Convention adjourned, the Continental Congress debated the merits of the new Constitution. Some congressional delegates criticized the convention for exceeding its authority and violating their specific instructions to revise the Articles of Confederation. Virginia's Richard Henry Lee suggested a list of possible changes, including a prohibition on "standing armies in times of peace" and a provision that would have required the consent of two-thirds of each house of Congress before such an army could be raised. Congress rejected Lee's suggestions and decided to send the original unamended Constitution to the states for ratification. The issue of the right to bear arms was not among Lee's short list of crucial amendments.[6]

The Philadelphia Convention's decision to submit the Constitution to popularly elected state ratification conventions ushered in one of the most wide-ranging public debates over politics and law in Western history. Less than a week after the Constitution appeared in print, a Philadelphian reported that "the new plan of government proposed by the Convention has made a bustle in the city and its vicinity." A commentator in Virginia noted that "the plan of a Government proposed to us by the Convention—affords matter for conversation to every rank of beings from the Governor to the door keeper." Discussion of the new document's merits was not restricted to the pages of the nation's newspapers. The Constitution was discussed in town squares, on the steps of courthouses, and in taverns across America. In some cases, supporters and opponents of the Constitution took to the streets in celebration or protest. Supporters, who took the name Federalists, could count on the support of many of the nation's most esteemed political leaders, including George Washington, Alexander

Hamilton, and James Madison. Opponents were saddled with the name Anti-Federalists, a name that ill suited them since they claimed to be the true supporters of a confederation whereas their opponents seemed to be intent on consolidating the union into a single powerful national government. Anti-Federalists also boasted an impressive lineup of spokesmen including George Mason, Patrick Henry, and Samuel Adams, as well as a host of powerful state politicians such as George Clinton, governor of New York, and William Findley, Pennsylvania's powerful backcountry spokesman.[7]

Opposition to the Constitution did not take long to coalesce. Mason's fear that the absence of a bill of rights posed a threat to liberty was widely echoed in the press. Gerry's prediction that the absence of a ban on a standing army would become a common complaint also came to pass. Federalists wasted little time in formulating responses to each of these criticisms. One of the most forceful and influential replies was framed by the Pennsylvania Federalist James Wilson, an esteemed lawyer who had himself been a delegate to the Constitutional Convention. Delivered within a month of the Constitution's publication, Wilson's influential State House speech was reprinted in newspapers across America. In response to the first charge, Wilson affirmed that the new government was one of delegated authority alone; since the grant of power was of a limited nature, there was no need for a bill of rights. The people and the states retained all powers not delegated to the new government. The issue of a standing army was even simpler. No nation could long survive without an effective military, and there was little danger to be apprehended from such a force when it was controlled by a government in which the people enjoyed full representation.[8]

Recognizing the importance of Wilson's speech, Anti-Federalists subjected it to a barrage of attacks. One Anti-Federalist critic who mocked Wilson's aristocratic pretensions and styled himself "A Democratic Federalist" invoked the memory of the brave minutemen of Concord and Lexington who had faced down the most powerful army in the world. He posed a simple question to his readers: "Is not a well regulated militia sufficient for every purpose of internal defense?" Another author, "Brutus," invoked the ideals of Roman virtue and recommended that the Constitution emulate the Virginia Declaration of Rights' provision on the militia. By invoking ancient republican stalwarts such as Brutus and valorizing America's own heroic minutemen, Anti-Federalists sought a noble pedigree for their critique of the Constitution. History painted a grim portrait of nations that abandoned the militia in favor of a standing army.[9]

Anti-Federalists did more than invoke well-known historical precedents. To these stock arguments, Anti-Federalists added a new idea that linked control of the militia to the problem of federalism. Without their militias to protect them, the states would be at the mercy of a strong government, which would soon consolidate all power within its orbit. No Anti-Federalist author was more effective at developing the logic of this states' rights argument than Luther Martin, an influential Maryland lawyer. Martin had participated in the Philadelphia Convention and had refused to sign the Constitution in protest. For Martin, state control of the militia was necessary to prevent encroachments by the national government on the rights of the states, which were the true guardians of citizens' rights. Martin went further than most Anti-Federalists in pursuing the logic of this states' rights theory, asserting that "the time may come when it shall be the *duty* of a *State*, in order to preserve itself from the oppression of the general government, to have recourse to the sword." For Martin, the militia was the final structural check in America's system of federalism.[10]

Federalist Noah Webster, the author of a popular guide to American spelling and the future author of the most important dictionary of American English, took on the Anti-Federalist argument directly. Writing as "A Citizen of America," Webster advised Americans to "forget their apprehensions from a British standing army, quartered in America." While such fears had been justified during the Revolution, America had cast off the yoke of British tyranny and established a new republican system of government. Whereas the chief danger America had faced in 1776 came from a government too powerful, the threat to America now came from a government too weak. Webster reminded Americans that many of their own esteemed state constitutions did not bar standing armies; and that in those states that had included explicit prohibitions, the creation of such a force merely required the legislature's consent. Webster believed that Anti-Federalist demands for assurances about the viability of the militia reflected pre-Revolutionary habits of mind and were ill suited to post-Revolutionary American life.[11]

There was little danger to the militia from the Constitution. "Before a standing army can rule," Webster observed, "the people must be disarmed; as they are in almost every kingdom in Europe. The Supreme Power in America can not enforce unjust laws by the sword; because the whole body of the people are armed." It was precisely because the militia was such a central institution in American life that Americans had little to fear from a standing army. The militia would continue to serve as a bulwark against tyranny under the new government. In short, the new argument propounded by Anti-Federalists that the Constitution would disarm the state militias was absurd.[12]

The intensity of Anti-Federalist opposition forced other Federalists to join the fray and defend the Constitution. In the process of rebutting Anti-Federalist criticism, the supporters of the Constitution were forced to refine their ideas and in some cases concede some ground to their opponents. The debate over the militia was an excellent illustration of the dynamic quality of ratification. Although many Federalists had expressed grave reservations about the militia in private, their public statements reassured Americans that this institution would continue to serve as a bulwark of liberty.

The appearance of *The Federalist*, a set of newspaper essays authored by John Jay, Alexander Hamilton, and James Madison, marked a new level of sophistication in public debate on the Constitution. *The Federalist* not only rebutted Anti-Federalist criticisms of the Constitution, but it eloquently defended the idea of a powerful government that would strengthen liberty, not threaten it. Adopting the pen name Publius, a hero of the Roman Republic, the authors offered the most philosophical meditation on government published during ratification. The essays first appeared serially in newspapers across America and were eventually gathered together into a book as the ratification struggle was winding down.[13]

The authors of *The Federalist* accepted that the new government was a novel mixture of federal and national elements. This hybrid nature was evidenced in the way control of the militia was divided up between the states and the central government. Publius reminded readers that it was unwise to put too great a reliance on the militia, a misplaced faith that nearly "lost us our independence." The performance of the militia in the Revolution demonstrated that "the great body of yeomanry" were unwilling to submit to the level of regulation necessary "to acquire the degree of perfection which would intitle them to the character of a well regulated militia." Experience had demonstrated that most Americans were reluctant to sacrifice their individual liberty to the collective good and take on the burdens necessary to create an effective militia. Given this reality, Publius concluded that it was best to leave the future composition of the militia up to Congress, though he hoped that Congress would recognize the need to create an elite group of select militia drawn from the ranks of those citizens with the greatest aptitude for military exercises.[14]

Having disarmed the Anti-Federalists' argument that the militia was the best defense for a republic, Publius challenged their suggestion that the new government's authority over the militia posed a threat to the states or citizens. Any danger was effectively neutralized by the structure of checks and balances in the new frame of government. Publius acknowledged that if all of the many safeguards built into the new system failed, the final check on tyranny would be "that original right of self defense which is paramount to all positive forms of government." Americans would not lose the natural right of revolution that always existed as the ultimate check on tyranny. Publius cleverly used this extreme situation, a dissolution of government and a return to a state of nature, to show just how unlikely such a turn of affairs would be under the new Constitution.[15]

Although it is hard to imagine Publius or any other Federalist conceding a right of the states to take up arms against the federal government at the start of the ratification battle, the persistent criticism of the Anti-Federalists did force Federalists to adapt their arguments to deflect those of their opponents on this issue. Following the same rhetorical strategy he had used to demonstrate that the Constitution would not deprive Americans of the natural right of revolution, Publius cast such an occurrence as an extreme situation, an option of last resort that was almost unthinkable. In the unlikely event that this radical option had to be exercised, the Constitution would pose no barrier to this ultimate check on despotism. Yet, even in this unlikely scenario, Publius took great pains to point out that if this nightmare state of affairs presented itself and the nation were plunged into a civil war, then the exercise of the right of revolution would have to proceed in an orderly manner to enjoy legitimacy and have any chance of achieving its goal of restoring liberty and order. Thus, while Publius conceded that in extreme situations the states might have recourse to use their militias against the national government in the defense of liberty, he denied that individuals or localities were ever justified in a resort to arms. Indeed, as a practical matter the notion of individual or local resistance was likely to lead to disaster. To illustrate this point Publius contrasted the effectiveness of the orderly and coordinated actions of the militias under state authority with the futile efforts of individuals and localities that might "rush tumultuously to arms, without concert, without system, without resources." A well-regulated militia, he reminded his readers, was not an armed mob.[16]

While Publius briefly considered the cataclysmic turn of events that could lead to the dissolution of government, he confidently asserted that this was a "phantom" conjured up by the most paranoid opponents of the Constitution. Building on a line of argument developed by Webster and other Federalists, Publius boasted that the very strength of the militia in America meant that a despotic federal government could never tyrannize the people. America, he reminded his readers, was unlike any other nation in the world because it boasted "a militia amounting to near half a million of citizens with arms in their hands, officered by men chosen from among themselves, fighting for their common liberties, and united and conducted by governments possessing their affections and confidence." The existence of a well-armed population organized into state militias guaranteed that America would never succumb to tyranny. To counter the radical states' rights theory of the militia championed by Anti-Federalists such as Luther Martin, Publius offered his own more limited and measured defense of the role of the state militias as a check on the power of the federal government.[17]

THE RIGHT TO BEAR ARMS BECOMES AN ISSUE: "THE DISSENT OF THE MINORITY" AND THE FEDERALIST RESPONSE

Although the issue of a standing army and the vexing question of federal control of the militia emerged as contentious issues from the outset, demands for some type of explicit protection for the right to bear arms did not figure prominently early in the ratification process. The first proposal for amendments drafted by Richard Henry Lee in the Confederation Congress had not even mentioned the right to bear arms. Nor had James Wilson bothered to address this concern in his widely reprinted State House speech. The right to bear arms did not emerge as an issue until the end of December at the very close of the Pennsylvania state ratification convention when delegate Robert Whitehill presented a list of fifteen recommended amendments to the delegates. Echoing earlier criticism of the Constitution, the list insisted on a ban on a standing army and a restoration of state control of the militia. In addition to these frequently voiced concerns, Whitehill added a new demand: an affirmation of the right to bear arms. The Federalist-dominated convention dismissed these demands, and the convention accepted the new constitution without any qualifications. Still seething over their defeat, the Anti-Federalist minority resolved to take their appeal directly to the people. Whitehill's list of amendments was hastily assembled and appended to a somewhat rambling critique of the Constitution and published as "The Dissent of the Pennsylvania Minority." The Dissent asserted the following claims:

7. That the people have a right to bear arms for the defense of themselves and their own state, or the United States, or for the purposes of killing game; and no law should be passed for disarming the people or any of them, unless for crimes committed, or real danger of public injury from individuals; and as standing armies in the time of peace are dangerous to liberty, they ought not to be kept up; and that the military shall be kept under strict subordination to and be governed by the civil powers.

8. The inhabitants of the several states shall have the liberty to fowl and hunt in seasonable times.

11. That the power of organizing, arming, and disciplining the militia (the manner of disciplining the militia to be prescribed by Congress) remain with the individual states, and that Congress shall not have authority to call or march any of the militia out of their own state, without the consent of such state and for such length of time only as such state shall agree.

Whitehill's seventh proposal cobbled together two different provisions from the Pennsylvania state constitution, a right to bear arms and a right to hunt. Curiously, the Dissent repeated the right to hunt twice in its list, a fact that testifies to the essay's slapdash draftsmanship. The term *bear arms* was traditionally approached as a legal term of art that clearly implied arms used for public defense. As was sometimes true of technical legal concepts, the term was occasionally used more loosely in popular discourse, and the Dissent's usage of the term *bear arms* in the context of hunting fit this latter nonstandard usage. Although other writers picked up on the Dissent's call for explicit protection for the right to bear arms, no other author employed its unique formulation of a right to hunt or bear arms for nonmilitary purposes.[18]

Additional evidence about how the Dissent was read at the time may be found in Federalist responses to it. While Anti-Federalist concern over the future of the right to bear arms as part of a well-regulated militia prompted some comment, Federalists did not feel a need to devote much intellectual energy to refuting the suggestion that the constitution would deprive citizens of a right to hunt or use guns for civilian purposes.

One vocal critic of the Dissent, Tench Coxe, authored two separate attacks on its arguments. Coxe focused his attack on the Dissent's exaggerated fears about threats to the militia. As was true for all Federalists, Coxe viewed such alarmist ramblings as entirely unfounded. "Who are these militia?" Coxe asked readers. *"Are they not ourselves?"* In his view, the strength of the militia in America meant that there was no danger to be apprehended from the Constitution's authority over it. In essence Coxe argued that the civic conception of arms bearing was so deeply embedded in American culture that there was little to fear from the Constitution's power over the militia. Coxe went further, declaring that Congress had no power to disarm the militia because "their swords, and every other terrible implement of the soldier, are *the birthright of an American."* The right to bear arms was, in Coxe's view, clearly intended to preserve a right to keep and bear military weapons intended for militia service. As was true of other Federalist authors who responded to the Dissent, Coxe did not take the problem of hunting or civilian firearms use as a serious issue meriting any attention.[19]

THAT EVERY MAN MAY BE ARMED: THE VIRGINIA RATIFICATION DEBATES

Although the danger of a standing army and the threat to the militia were discussed in virtually all of the state ratification conventions, the issue figured most prominently in Virginia. The group of delegates who assembled in Richmond included an impressive cast. The Anti-Federalist forces were led by George Mason and Patrick Henry. The Federalists had James Madison and the future chief justice of the Supreme Court, John Marshall, to plead their case. Eight states had already ratified the Constitution when Virginia debated its merits. If the Anti-Federalists were victorious, they might yet secure substantial amendments.

Virginians had experienced the danger of disarmament firsthand during the Revolution. Lord Dunmore's attempt to seize the colony's gunpowder and vandalize the militia's muskets more than a decade earlier left an indelible imprint on the minds of leading opponents of the Constitution such as Patrick Henry and George Mason.[20] Virginia Anti-Federalists were equally mindful that the disarmament of the militia might be achieved by less bold measures than those chosen by Lord Dunmore. The new powerful federal government created by the Constitution could accomplish the same goal by simply failing to act. Refusing to enact effective regulations and neglecting to supply the militia with arms were in some ways even more insidious since the process of slow disarmament could be accomplished by more stealthy means. "The great object is, that every man be armed," Henry lamented, but experience had taught that while "our Assembly has, by a succession of laws for many years, endeavored to have the militia completely armed, it is still far from being the case." The primary responsibility of arming and disciplining the militia, Henry argued, belonged to the states and should only be exercised by the federal government when states failed to fulfill their obligations.[21]

In response to these concerns, Federalists picked up an argument that had been made elsewhere. The states and the people would be represented in Congress, which would be responsible for enacting laws governing the militia and would not act against the people's own interests. The states would continue to train the militia according to the rules established by Congress, a representative body elected by the people of the states. Madison also disputed the claim that the militia had been effectively nationalized. "The power of arming the militia," Madison asserted, was "concurrent, and not exclusive."[22]

As far as the danger of a standing army was concerned, Federalists maintained that Congress would tightly control such an army through the power of the purse. Madison captured the view of many Federalists when he noted the greatest threat to civil liberty came not from the national government but from "internal dissensions." Madison confidently asserted that under the new constitution the militia would not only continue to serve the vital function of providing states with a means to deal with riots and insurrections but would also allow the states to deal more effectively with internal conflict by drawing on the resources of other states and, if necessary, the federal government. When Patrick Henry warned that Virginians might be robbed of the means to deal with slave rebellions, Federalist George Nicholas observed that the new constitution provided additional security for slave owners by making it "the duty of the General government to aid them with the strength of the Union."[23]

Anti-Federalists fought valiantly and doggedly, but when the final vote was tallied, the Federalists emerged victorious. Virginia Anti-Federalists failed to secure prior amendments to the Constitution. Anti-Federalists did, however, manage to obtain assurances that a list of recommended amendments would be taken up by the First Congress. Among the many concerns listed in these proposed amendments were demands for assurances about the militia and the right to bear arms. In fact, all of the provisions suggested by the Virginia Convention focused on the militia. No one stepped forward to suggest that the Constitution ought to include something similar to Jefferson's failed proposal for the Virginia Declaration of Rights on keeping arms. Nor did anything like the Dissent of the Pennsylvania Minority's demand for a right to hunt figure in the recommended amendments proposed by the Virginia Convention. The focus of the debate in Virginia was on the militia, not a private right to keep arms for civilian use.[24]

THE PEOPLE IN ARMS: BACKCOUNTRY VIOLENCE AND THE CHALLENGE OF POPULAR RADICALISM

Although the rhetoric of ratification had been intense, the debate over the merits of the Constitution had been on the whole remarkably peaceful. Most Anti-Federalists accepted defeat gracefully and turned their attention to securing seats in the upcoming elections for the First Congress, where they could work on securing amendments. A small but vocal minority, however, refused to concede defeat or accept the legitimacy of the Constitution. Opposition to the Constitution in backcountry Pennsylvania, the Carolinas, and New England had always been intense. The Carlisle Riot in western Pennsylvania provides a rare glimpse into how the militia and the right to bear arms were understood by the most radical voices among the Anti-Federalists. The radical potential latent in the militia that emerged during Shays's Rebellion once again surfaced as western Pennsylvanians organized themselves and prepared to oppose the federal government with force of arms if necessary.[25]

Violence in Carlisle erupted when local Federalists decided to celebrate Pennsylvania's adoption of the Constitution in late November of 1787. When Anti-Federalists encountered celebrants in the streets of Carlisle, a harsh exchange of words between the two sides quickly escalated into a small riot. Several of the Anti-Federalists responsible for instigating this altercation were jailed. The imprisoned rioters refused bail, expressing their contempt for lawyers and state courts alike. Instead, they placed their faith in the local militia who acted without state authority, marched on the jail, and liberated the rioters. Carlisle Anti-Federalists believed that local communities might assemble in arms and oppose tyranny. The imprisonment of the rioters provided a pretext for asserting this right. The assertion of this right did not require a formal legal process and was not subject to the approval of either the state or the federal government. For Federalists and many Anti-Federalists, including the signers of the "Dissent of the Minority," the armed body that liberated the prisoners was not a militia, but little more than a mob.

The actions of the Carlisle militia, like those of Daniel Shays and his followers, rejected the states' rights theory of the militia that mainstream Anti-Federalists had championed throughout ratification. The Carlisle rioters cared little for states' rights and instead championed a more radical populist conception of democracy, rooted in the will of the local community, not the states. To these plebeian populists, events in Carlisle, including the release of the prisoners from jail, vindicated their radical localist ideology.[26]

William Petrikin, one of the rioters, became a spokesman for radical Anti-Federalists in Carlisle. He accused Federalists of trying to disarm "farmers, mechanics, [and] labourers." Rather than accept defeat, Petrikin advocated armed resistance.[27] Carlisle was hardly the only place in the Pennsylvania backcountry where radical ideas found a receptive audience. As one anonymous author noted, "the counties of Cumberland, Dauphine, and Franklin, appear to take the lead, and have been long since repairing and cleaning their arms, and every young fellow who is able to do it, is providing himself with a *rifle* or musket, and ammunition." Echoing Petrikin's rhetoric, the author of this essay attacked the Constitution, charging that "the *lawyers*, &c." had "precipitated with such fraud and deception the new system of government upon us." The conspiracy against the people was destined to fail because the Federalists "did not recollect, that the militia had arms." Plebeian populists put their faith in an armed population and did not flinch from the prospect of armed resistance. "A *civil war* is dreadful, but a little blood spilt now, will perhaps prevent much more hereafter." For those who followed Petrikin's advice, the right to bear arms was a genuinely insurrectionary right of revolution. Similar ideas were articulated in other parts of the new nation. In the pro-Shaysite regions of backcountry Massachusetts, one enthusiastic Anti-Federalist attacked the Constitution as a tool of "great men & lawyers." The Constitution was part of a Federalist conspiracy in which the "people will be disarmed" and "a standing army will be immediately formed."[28]

Ironically, the rumblings in the backcountry actually facilitated the acceptance of the Constitution by demonstrating that continued opposition would only lead to instability and mob rule. Rather than inspire moderate Anti-Federalists to join with them in an ongoing struggle against the Constitution, popular radicalism drove mainstream Anti-Federalists toward an accommodation with Federalists. The irony of popular radicalism is evident in the outcome of the Harrisburg Convention, a meeting of delegates from Pennsylvania in late September 1788 that took up the radical Anti-Federalist demand for a new constitutional convention. The meeting included Robert Whitehill, original author of the list of amendments that had formed the core of the "Dissent of the Minority." The meeting also attracted the fiery delegate from Carlisle, William Petrikin. The delegates at Harrisburg betrayed Petrikin's hopes for the emergence of an anti-Constitution movement. Instead, they focused on the practical problems of winning seats in the First Congress and creating a viable list of amendments that would accomplish their states' rights agenda. The list of recommended amendments produced by the Harrisburg delegates focused squarely on the issue of states' rights and included a ban on a standing army and a restoration of state control over the militia. It made no mention of the right to bear arms or the right to hunt. The fear that the federal government might use its power over the militia to disarm the states prompted two other novel proposals: a ban on the use of martial law to coerce the militia except during time of war or rebellion and time limits on federal use of the militia, a provision that prevented the potential use of the militia of one state against that of another. The prospect that the Harrisburg Convention might create the core of a new anti-Constitution movement collapsed. Reform of the Constitution would proceed in an orderly legal fashion through the amendment process, which would focus on the Anti-Federalist states' rights agenda. Petrikin saw the exclusive focus on states' rights as a betrayal, and he advised backcountry residents to continue to train as local militia units and counseled that they be prepared to defend popular liberty by arms against the potential threat the new federal government posed.[29]

The popular constitutionalism of the Carlisle Rioters set them apart from the nationalist-minded Federalists and states'-rights-oriented Anti-Federalists. While elites on both sides of the constitutional struggle were divided on many issues, leading Anti-Federalists and Federalists were in accord on one thing: the conception of the militia defended by Petrikin and other radicals led to Shaysism and anarchy. Amendment, not armed resistance, was the appropriate remedy to any lingering problems with the Constitution.

THE BILL OF RIGHTS AND THE ORIGINS OF THE SECOND AMENDMENT

While Federalists had achieved an impressive victory over their opponents during ratification, the presence of lingering Anti-Federalist anxiety over the Constitution posed a potential threat to the new government. Federalists had blocked efforts to make ratification conditional on prior amendments. The most politically savvy Federalists realized that amendments were necessary to assuage moderate Anti-Federalists and help broaden support for the Constitution. The job of digesting the many proposals for amendments made by the various state ratification conventions and stewarding them through the First Federal Congress fell to James Madison.[30] Madison focused his attention on the official recommendations that had been made by the ratification conventions of Virginia, Massachusetts, New York, Maryland, and New Hampshire. He did not acknowledge the more strident calls for a return of authority to the states found in texts such as the "Dissent of the Minority." All five state conventions had recommended that the Constitution include a prohibition on standing armies in peacetime; four demanded some type of explicit protection for the right to bear arms; two affirmed the principle of state control of the militia; and two proposed limits on the use of the militia outside the state. The right to keep or use firearms arms outside the context of the militia, including the right to hunt recommended by the "Dissent of the Minority," did not appear on Madison's comprehensive list of possible amendments.[31]

One of the most interesting and novel proposals on Madison's list was one suggested by New Hampshire that recommended an amendment that would have limited congressional authority to "disarm any citizen, unless such as are or have been in rebellion." Decisions about which citizens might be disarmed were something properly left to the states. Many had used their police powers to impose loyalty oaths and enact other types of firearms regulations. New Hampshire's provision would have limited the federal government from enacting similar oaths that might disarm the people. The framing of the prohibition suggested that the primary concern was federalism, not a right to protect the use of guns for private purposes. Had New Hampshire sought such a personal right, the state could have easily followed the model provided by the Pennsylvania Dissent and included a provision on hunting.[32]

Madison's initial formulation of the right to bear arms read:

> The right of the people to keep and bear arms shall not be infringed; a well armed, and well regulated militia being the best security of a free country; but no person religiously scrupulous of bearing arms, shall be compelled to render military service in person.[33]

Some Federalists were dismissive of the proposed amendments, including the provision on bearing arms. Fisher Ames was particularly scathing in his denunciation of this provision, noting that he could barely contain his laughter when contemplating the absurdity of this concern. While some Federalists ridiculed the amendments, the most ardent Anti-Federalists were equally dismissive of the project for its failure to curtail federal power. One prominent Anti-Federalist described them as being "like a tub thrown out to a whale," a mere diversion.[34]

Madison had hoped simply to weave the various amendments into the body of the Constitution. He intended to place the right to bear arms in Article I, Section 9, next to other restraints on federal power. Congress rejected this approach and decided instead to append a series of amendments after the text of the Constitution. The House revised Madison's original formulation, placing the affirmation of a well-regulated militia before the right to keep and bear arms. The decision to recast the language had enormous constitutional significance. Preambles, the introductory clauses of statutes, were commonly understood by eighteenth-century lawyers to hold the key to the "design and meaning" of a law. Framing the right to bear arms as a corollary of a preamble focusing on the need for a well-regulated militia clearly signaled that the purpose of the amendment was to protect the militia. The House also added a clause describing the militia as "composed of the body of the people" and changed a semicolon to a comma, an editorial decision that linked the clauses containing the militia and the right of the people more closely.[35]

Further evidence on the military focus of the debate in the House is provided by the debate over how to treat religious pacifists. Elbridge Gerry, one of the few Anti-Federalists elected to the House, objected to the way in which the clause about conscientious objection status might allow the new government to disarm state militias. "This clause would give an opportunity to the people in power to destroy the constitution itself. They can declare who are those religiously scrupulous, and prevent them from bearing arms." Gerry did not, however, use this opportunity to bemoan the threat this power might pose to the rights of individuals to use guns outside militia service. Gerry warned that "whenever government means to invade the rights and liberties of the people, they always attempt to destroy the militia." Gerry evoked memories of British efforts to disarm the colonists, a set of policies aimed at the militia. The British had "used every means in their power to prevent the establishment of an effective militia to the eastward." The inclusion of an amendment protecting the right to keep and bear arms was designed to prevent future efforts at disarming the militia.[36]

Records of the Senate's deliberations do not survive, so it is more difficult to sort out how the debate over the right to bear arms played out in that body. Federalists, particularly the more nationalist minded among them, were eager to reduce state control and if possible nationalize as many of the militia's functions as was politically feasible. The primary issue in the Senate was federalism: who would have control of the militia? The Senate struck out the phrase that described the militia as composed of the body of the people, a move that restored Madison's original formulation and gave Congress authority to determine who in the future would be included within the ranks of the militia. Additional evidence that the Senate's main focus was on control of the militia may be found in an unsuccessful attempt to include a prohibition on peacetime standing armies, a suggestion the Senate also rejected. Anti-Federalists in the Senate scored one important victory when they deleted language affirming that the purpose of the militia was to provide for the common defense. For those who feared federal power, inclusion of such language would have seemed ominous. If placed in the Bill of Rights this phrase might have provided unscrupulous leaders with a pretext for prohibiting the militia from defending the states or localities from external or internal threats. This phrasing would have struck both of the ardent states' rights senators from Virginia as a dangerous concession to the federal government. Virginians were especially worried that federal control of the militia would threaten their state's ability to put down insurrections, a particularly frightening prospect for a state with a large slave population. The militia existed for local, state, and common national defense.[37]

One of the few surviving letters describing the character of the Senate debate over this issue confirms the centrality of federalism to the discussion over the wording of the amendment. Virginian John Randolph wrote to St. George Tucker, the eminent Virginia jurist, informing him that a faction in "the Senate were for not allowing the militia arms." Randolph explained his reasoning to Tucker, noting that Federalists feared an armed citizenry who might "stop their full Career to Tyranny & Oppression." A well-armed militia controlled by the states was necessary to provide the states the ultimate check on potential federal despotism.[38]

The Senate edited the House list of seventeen provisions, paring it down to twelve provisions, which were then submitted to the states for ratification. When the states failed to ratify the first two amendments, which dealt with apportionment of representatives and congressional salaries, the Fourth Article became the Second Amendment. The final text read: "a well regulated militia, being necessary to the security of a free State, the right of the people to keep and bear arms, shall not be infringed."[39]

Public reaction to the proposed Bill of Rights is difficult to gauge. During the debate over ratification of the Constitution, the press teemed with essays extolling and denouncing the new government.

The drama within Congress over the Bill of Rights, however, did not garner much press attention. One of the few essays to address Madison's proposed amendments was authored by Tench Coxe, who described his effort to Madison as slapdash. "I have therefore taken an hour from my present Engagement," Coxe confided to Madison, and "thrown together a few remarks upon the first part of the Resolutions." The essay was not widely reprinted and prompted no commentary by contemporaries, two facts that suggest that it did not have much of an impact at the time. Writing about Madison's initial proposal, the version without the preamble asserting the need for a well-regulated militia, Coxe asserted that the proposed Bill of Rights affirmed "the right of the people to keep and bear their private arms." Using language consistent with his earlier essays attacking the "Dissent of the Minority," Coxe argued that citizens would not be deprived the "implements of the soldier" but would continue to enjoy the right to keep and bear those arms needed to meet their civic responsibility to participate in a well-regulated militia.[40]

It is difficult to know with precision how the Second Amendment was understood by the vast majority of Americans at the time it was proposed. In all likelihood there was no single original understanding that united Federalists and Anti-Federalists. The most ardent Anti-Federalists were bitterly disappointed by the amendments proposed by Congress. One of the most vociferous critics of the Constitution, Samuel Bryan (using the pen name "Centinel"), lamented the ineffectual nature of these changes, which did not restrain "the absolute command vested by other sections in Congress over the militia." For other champions of states' rights the language of the Second Amendment provided little solace. For supporters of states' rights the Bill of Rights was inadequate. Anti-Federalist Thomas Tudor Tucker confessed his disappointment with the final form of the amendments that emerged from Congress, which was "calculated merely to amuse, or rather to deceive." Not every former opponent of the Constitution was so negative. George Mason confessed that he had "received much

Satisfaction from the Amendments to the Federal constitution, which have lately passed the House of Representatives."[41]

If one moves below the ranks of the elites who shaped the debate in Congress and the individual state houses, there are tantalizing suggestions that the ideas that animated popular Anti-Federalist opposition in Pennsylvania had taken root elsewhere. Writing from the Maine frontier to his Federalist Congressman George Thatcher, Anti-Federalist Samuel Nasson expressed his desire that the amendments Congress was contemplating would protect "the right to keep Arms for Common and Extraordinary Occasions such as to secure ourselves against the wild Beast and also to amuse us by fowling and for our Defense against a Common Enemy." Nasson believed in the civic responsibility to bear arms for common defense, and he also articulated a desire to see some type of explicit protection for keeping guns for personal use. Unfortunately for Nasson and others who shared his point of view, the constitutional views of Harvard-educated Federalists such as Thatcher shared little with the perspective of an untutored Anti-Federalist from the Maine frontier. Nasson's polite inquiries fell on unresponsive ears.[42]

Others within the ranks of the former Anti-Federalists were not content to simply write their congressmen and adopted a more militant posture. The outspoken populist from Carlisle, William Petrikin, captured these festering resentments when he wrote, "We are determined to die hard." "Our Volunteer company," he boasted "is very large, well armed and Equipped, parades often and exercises very well." Rather than seek peaceful reform through the system, Petrikin and other populist radicals in the backcountry prepared themselves for armed resistance to the new government. Charles Pettit, a prominent Pennsylvania Anti-Federalist, confessed his own fears that popular radicalism posed a serious threat to the future of the young republic. The existence of these pockets of popular discontent encouraged leading Anti-Federalists to accept the amended Constitution.[43]

The adoption of the Second Amendment did not settle the meaning of the right to bear arms, nor did it end the widening disagreement over the appropriate role of the militia. Rather than establish a single monolithic original understanding, the bitter and divisive debate over ratification gave rise to several competing interpretations of the Second Amendment's meaning and its role in the federal system. The dominant view of the Second Amendment reflected its origins in the various state arms bearing provisions. According to this view, the right to keep and bear arms was a civic right inextricably linked to the public responsibility to participate in a well-regulated militia. Although they had been defeated at virtually every turn, Anti-Federalists clung tenaciously to their states' rights view of the Second Amendment as providing the foundation for state resistance to the federal government.

CONGRESSIONAL DEBATE OVER THE MILITIA

The framers of the Second Amendment left open the question of the future composition of the militia. It was up to Congress to decide if the militia would continue to be drawn from the entire white male population or some smaller select group. Anti-Federalists feared that Federalists were committed to abolishing the universal militia and creating a select one. To blunt Anti-Federalist criticism, a number of Federalists offered fulsome praise of a well-regulated militia. Charles Nisbet, president of Dickinson College, observed somewhat cynically that "our leaders flatter the People by declaiming against Standing Armies, and pretending to believe that the Militia is the best Security of a Nation," but "they are not in earnest." Federalist disenchantment with the militia was succinctly captured by Gouverneur Morris, another participant in the Philadelphia Convention, when he confessed that "to rely on militia was to lean on a broken reed."[44]

Given their disappointment with the militia's performance, it is hardly surprising that Federalists would press ahead with their desire for military reform, including changes to the militia. President George Washington, who had been a witness to the problems of utilizing the militia against professional troops, urged Congress to enact legislation to reform the militia almost immediately upon assuming office in 1789. Congress appointed a committee, but a host of other pressing matters delayed action until Congress convened in 1790. Washington worked closely with Secretary of War Henry Knox to draft a comprehensive plan for militia reform. Introduced on January 21, 1790, the Knox plan used a system of classification that would divide the militia into an "advanced corps," a "main corps," and a "reserved corps." The Knox plan would have effectively nationalized the militia. The federal government was to determine the organization of units, train the militia, and take charge of almost every detail apart from declaring exemptions and appointing officers, powers the Constitution expressly reserved for the states.[45]

Knox's plan provoked a storm of protest, prompting young New Yorker De Witt Clinton to remark that it was both "absurd and impolitic." The enormous cost of the plan led some to decry its extravagance while others felt the classification system would unduly burden urban and manufacturing interests, which could ill afford to have such a large percentage of potential apprentices plucked away for extensive military training. The plan was resoundingly defeated. Congress temporarily put aside the issue of the militia while it debated Hamilton's scheme for funding state debts and creating a national bank. Although there was broad agreement on the need for militia reform, there was little consensus on how to achieve that goal. As would be true for virtually every issue debated in the First Congress, the issue of the militia was hopelessly entangled with the larger struggle between those who sought to endow the new federal government with greater power and those who continued to believe that individual state governments had to be protected if liberty were to survive.[46]

When American forces were decisively defeated by Native Americans in the Ohio Territory in 1790, the issue of militia reform took on a new sense of urgency. New Jersey Federalist Elias Boudinot attacked a universal militia and declared that he "disapproved of making a soldier of every man between 18 and 45." James Jackson of Georgia defended the ideal of a more inclusive militia, noting, "The people of America would be highly displeased at being debarred the privilege of carrying arms." He argued further that "every man in a republic ought to be a soldier—if it was only to prevent the introduction of that greatest of all evils, a standing army." Jackson cast the right to bear arms as a civic obligation, describing it as one of the "most important duties we owe society."[47]

The continuing importance of the civic conception of arms bearing as an obligation emerged again during the vigorous debate over the issue of religious exemptions from militia service. The plight of the Quakers prompted extensive commentary. Some in Congress worried that if Quakers were given exemptions "the whole nation" would "turn quakers" and leave the nation defenseless. Others scoffed at the notion that Americans would abandon their obligations by feigning false religiosity. A middle position was staked out by those who favored exempting the religiously scrupulous from bearing arms by allowing them to pay a fee instead. This compromise satisfied no one since Quakers would still be taxed for military preparation they opposed. Finally, there were others who believed that such matters were best left to the states to decide.[48]

The passage of the Uniform Militia Act by a narrow margin was a victory for those who opposed the idea of a select militia. Indeed, the final vote, on March 5, 1792, was extremely close: 31 to 27. In this act, the militia was defined as all "free able bodied white male" citizens between the ages of 18 and 45. Although a number of congressmen had complained that a significant portion of this group of potential militiamen, particularly younger men such as apprentices, might not be able to afford a musket, as the bill required, Congress opted to place the burden of arming the militia on individual citizens and the states.[49]

Federalists' public response to the Militia Act was predictably negative. *The Gazette of the United States*, published by John Feno, a close associate of Alexander Hamilton, derided the law.

> The Militia Law will probably seem a feeble system to many persons versed in military affairs. The great difference of the militia laws of the several states is such, that some will improve, and others perhaps run retrograde in consequence of this law of the United States.

The *National Gazette*, a paper opposed to the Federalists, offered a more balanced view, conceding that the bill had experienced almost "insurmountable obstacles" in Congress before being signed into law. Although the law was not perfect, it deserved praise for creating "a militia system, the true and equal guardian of freedom and a free country."[50]

One final piece of legislation on the militia awaited congressional approval. To address the issue of when the militia might be used, a concern that had prompted considerable alarm during ratification, Congress passed the Calling Forth Act of 1792. This law prompted a less protracted debate than the Militia Act. While Article I, Section 8 of the Constitution explicitly empowered the president to call forth the militia to "Suppress Insurrection, and repel Invasion," it was up to Congress to create a legal mechanism to facilitate this process. The bill Congress finally approved was a compromise between those who feared the potential for executive tyranny and those eager to enhance the power to respond to insurrection and rebellion. In spite of the Constitution's clear grant of authority in this area, the idea of giving so much power to the executive alarmed some members of Congress. One member objected that "it was an insult to the majesty of the people to hold out the idea that it may be necessary to execute the laws at the point of the bayonet." The appeal of the states' rights theory of the militia had not been dampened by the protracted debates in

Congress over the Second Amendment and the Uniform Militia Act. Indeed, the belief that the states might use their militia against the federal government was so alarming that one Federalist congressman felt impelled to denounce the idea that the militia existed "to enable the individual States to oppose the encroachments which may be made on them by the General Government!"[51]

When Americans drafted their first state constitutions, they had included a right to bear arms in a well-regulated militia. The essence of this civic conception of the right to bear arms was captured in an oration delivered before the Society of Black Friars in 1793 by Samuel Latham Mitchill, a chemistry professor at Columbia College. After discussing freedom of the press and freedom of religion, two other rights protected by the Bill of Rights, Mitchill turned his attention to the constitutional function of the militia. Mitchill's oration focused on the militia, not the right to bear arms, as the primary principle protected by Bill of Rights. A well-regulated militia existed to "suppress any mob or insurrection" and provide the first line of defense against foreign attack. Mitchill was mindful that firearms had come to occupy a unique role in American society. Comparing the role of firearms in British society with their function in America, he noted that the English game laws had effectively disarmed the people while American law had encouraged a militia drawn from the broad ranks of the citizenry. "The Establishment of a Militia, in which most able bodied and middle aged men are enrolled and furnished with arms, proceeds upon the principle, *that they who are able to govern, are also capable of defending themselves.*" It followed logically from this principle that "the keeping of arms, is, therefore, not only not prohibited, but is positively provided by law." To achieve the goal of having a well-regulated militia meant that government would encourage citizens to acquire military-style firearms and attain a basic competency with them. In America, he opined, arms "shall not rust for want of employ, but shall be brought into use from time to time, that the owner may grow expert in the handling of them." Mitchill did not equate the right to bear arms with a right of individual self-defense. The Second Amendment did not alter the legal distinction between bearing a gun for self-defense and bearing arms for public defense. His emphasis on the civic purpose of the amendment was unmistakable. Mitchill did, however, state a point that would have seemed obvious to Americans of his day. The fact that Americans were well armed delivered an extra personal security dividend to society. Weapons owned for militia service also "serve for the defense of the life and property of the individual against violent or burglarious attacks of thieves."[52]

Although there was still broad support for the civic conception of the right to bear arms described by Mitchill, the struggle over the Constitution had transformed the debate over the meaning of this right by embroiling it in the debate over federalism. Proponents of states' rights viewed the militia as a creature of the states while supporters of a powerful federal government sought to effectively nationalize the militia. Neither of these views was shared by radical localists who carried forward the heritage of Shays, viewing the militia as an instrument of the will of the local community. Rather than put an end to debate over the meaning and scope of the right to bear arms, and the proper constitutional function of the militia, the Second Amendment's adoption raised more questions than it answered. The deepening divisions in American society and the political and constitutional crisis of the next decade intensified the debate over the appropriate constitutional function of the militia. Within a decade of ratification it became clear to many that the original fears expressed by Anti-Federalists could no longer be dismissed as "visionary supposition" or "the incoherent dreams of a delirious jealousy." The system of checks and balances created by the framers of the Constitution appeared to be failing, and many Americans wondered if the time had not arrived when a resort to armed resistance might be needed to prevent Federalist despotism from destroying liberty. To prevent such a dire fate, Americans would have to take seriously the radical potential latent in the Second Amendment.[53]

GENERAL GEORGE WASHINGTON.
Reviewing the Western army at Fort Cumberland the 18th of octob 1794

President Washington reviews the well-regulated militia used by the federal government to put down the Whiskey Rebels in 1794. (Courtesy of the Winterthur Museum)

CHAPTER THREE

"THE TRUE PALLADIUM OF LIBERTY"

FEDERALISTS, JEFFERSONIANS, AND THE SECOND AMENDMENT

The first systematic effort to explore the role of the Second Amendment in America's new constitutional system was undertaken by the learned Virginian judge St. George Tucker. These observations were made in a series of lectures at the College of William and Mary, where Tucker held the prestigious chair in Law and Police. Tucker believed that *The Federalist* provided a superb analysis of the theoretical foundations of the Constitution, but he lamented that "Publius" had not treated the defects of the Constitution candidly, something that Tucker resolved to do in his lectures. The other impetus for organizing his thoughts about the Constitution in a systematic manner was the recent adoption of the first ten amendments to the Constitution. Tucker believed it was vital to provide his students with a detailed guide to the new law of the land.[1]

Tucker's analysis reflected his own moderate Anti-Federalism. Although he had initially opposed ratification, he appreciated that a Federalist victory was likely and revised his views accordingly. He came to believe that, with proper amendments, the Constitution could effectively protect both the rights of the states and individual liberty.

Admittedly, Tucker was not entirely pleased with the final shape of the Bill of Rights, which, in his opinion, did not sufficiently scale back the powers of the federal government. Still, he expressed guarded optimism that America's new constitutional system could weather any future storms on the horizon.[2]

Tucker described the Second Amendment as a necessary concession to Anti-Federalists who feared that the state militias might be disarmed by the federal government. In his account, the Second Amendment was cast as a right of the states, and he explicitly connected it with Article I, Section 8's discussion of the concurrent authority over the militia enjoyed by the states and the federal government. Tucker went even further, arguing that the Second Amendment gave the individual states the awesome power of "resisting the Laws of the federal Government, or of shaking off the Union." Tucker anticipated the criticism of those who felt such a stance would inevitably lead to anarchy and disunion.

> To contend that such a power would be dangerous for the reasons above-mentioned, would be subversive of every principle of Freedom in our Government; of which the first Congress appear to have been sensible by proposing an Amendment to the Constitution, which has since been ratified and has become a part of it, viz. "That a well regulated militia being necessary to the Security of a free State, the right of the people to keep & bear Arms shall not be infringed."

To underscore the fact that the Second Amendment functioned as a check within the federal system, Tucker explicitly linked the Second Amendment to another provision that dealt with federalism, the Tenth Amendment. In his earliest gloss on the Second Amendment, drafted shortly after its adoption, Tucker interpreted the right to bear arms within the context of federalism as a right of the states to arm their militia, and if necessary use them against the federal government.[3]

The idea that the Constitution gave the states the power to use force of arms to resist potential federal tyranny was alarming to many Federalists. In a grand jury charge delivered at roughly the same time that Tucker was lecturing on law at William and Mary, Judge Alexander Addison reminded jurors in Pennsylvania that "if one law is repealed, at the call of armed men, government is destroyed: no law will have any force." In Addison's view, an appeal to arms was in essence "a declaration of independence." Addison clearly struggled with this issue because he returned to the theme again in another grand jury charge and refined his analysis somewhat. While firmly rejecting the notion that armed resistance was ever legitimate in cases of an obnoxious law, he conceded that armed resistance might be theoretically justifiable in the case of an unconstitutional law, hastening to add that such actions were "highly dangerous." Echoing the sentiments articulated by Alexander Hamilton in *The Federalist*, Addison stressed that all legal means had to be exhausted before an appeal to arms could be made. Addison sought to cloak the assertion of this right in some type of constitutional legitimacy by attempting to define how one might legally identify acts or policies qualifying for such treatment. He implicitly rejected the right of the individual states to make such determinations. In his view it was the province of the courts, not individuals or states, to determine when a law violated the constitution. Although he failed to explore the logic of his argument in detail, Addison seemed to imply that a law declared unconstitutional by a court might justify the use of arms to prevent its enforcement. Endorsing a limited right of the courts to sanction the use of force of arms to prevent an unconstitutional act was a far cry from either the popular belief in the right of the local militia to make such decisions or the Anti-Federalist view that the states retained this right.[4]

Addison was hardly the only person in the new nation struggling to make sense of the new Constitution and the limits of its authority. Inevitably, Americans were forced to ponder the nightmare scenarios that Federalists and Anti-Federalists had each bandied back and forth during the debate over the Constitution. What, if any, role might armed resistance play in preserving America's new constitutional system? The answer to this question forced Americans to ponder the meaning of their own revolutionary heritage. While few would have doubted the continuing legitimacy of a natural right of revolution, there was far less agreement over the possibility that there was a constitutional right of revolution built into the structure of American law. The issue was sufficiently important to be formally debated by New York's Tammany Society, a fraternal organization that met regularly to engage in forensic discussions on the most pressing issues of the day. William Pitt Smith, a member of the medical faculty of Columbia College and one of the participants in that debate, took up this issue in earnest and concluded that the exercise of such a right was ultimately not compatible with constitutional government, but signaled the end of government. "A Convention in arms, supposes a people disorganized, or just emerging from a state of nature lately assumed, and claiming the rights of freemen." While the natural right of revolution could never be parted with, the notion that there could be a constitutional appeal to arms was antithetical to the idea of constitutionalism itself.[5]

THE WHISKEY REBELLION: THE CHALLENGE OF POPULAR RADICALISM

The question that William Pitt Smith addressed in formal debate and St. George Tucker pondered in his lectures soon proved to be a subject of more than mere academic interest. The right of revolution was tested in practice in western Pennsylvania, where farmers took up arms against the federal government as part of a protest against the whiskey excise tax.

Federalists sought to create a powerful fiscal and military state on the British model. This economic program included a plan for funding the national debt and chartering a national bank. To finance this ambitious program, Federalists followed the recommendations of George Washington's brilliant secretary of the treasury, Alexander Hamilton, who pushed for higher taxes. The tax on whiskey fell particularly hard on backcountry farmers from Pennsylvania and Kentucky. Western farmers distilled their grains into hard spirits, which not only fetched a higher price than grain but were easier to transport to eastern markets. Angered by the government's policy, distillers harassed excise collectors. Local whiskey distillers who complied with the tax were warned that their stills would be "mended" by "Tom the Tinker," a pseudonym used by opponents of government policy whose preferred form of tinkering was shooting at the stills of those who paid their taxes. The use of violence and intimidation to oppose the tax did not coalesce into systematic opposition at first. Anger over the tax simmered for three years before organized resistance erupted. In the summer of 1794 a group of angry protestors marched to the home of tax collector General John Neville. When the assembled crowd refused to disperse, Neville fired on the crowd, injuring several and killing one of the protestors. About a month later angry citizens assembled in arms at Braddock's Field near Pittsburgh, declaring their willingness to oppose the government policy by force of arms. What had begun as a tax protest had escalated into an armed rebellion.[6]

President Washington received conflicting advice from his cabinet about how to handle the Whiskey Insurrection. Hamilton was an early advocate for using force to put down the rebellion, but others with the president's ear were more cautious. Secretary of State Edmund Randolph counseled moderation. Washington sided with Hamilton, believing that anything less than "firm measures" would mean an "end to our Constitutions & laws." While Washington and Hamilton viewed the events in western Pennsylvania as a serious threat to federal authority, representatives from Pennsylvania saw the situation less ominously. Washington met with leading Pennsylvanians, including the governor, the chief justice of the state Supreme Court, the attorney general, and the secretary of state, to discuss the growing unrest in western Pennsylvania. The chief justice of the Pennsylvania Supreme Court was confident that the state courts were more than competent to deal with the civil unrest occasioned by opposition to the whiskey excise. Indeed, he argued, "the employment of a military force, at this period, would be as bad as anything that the Rioters had done—equally unconstitutional and illegal." There was widespread agreement among the state officials present at the meeting that federal action was unnecessary.[7]

Washington went forward with a two-prong strategy, appointing a group of federal commissioners to meet with the rebels and issuing an order to call out the militia. Simultaneously, he sought a ruling from Associate Justice of the U.S. Supreme Court James Wilson that the protest was an uprising "too powerful to be suppressed by the ordinary course of judicial proceedings." Washington mobilized more than twelve thousand troops from Pennsylvania, Maryland, New Jersey, and Virginia. Hamilton enthusiastically supported this strategy; others within Washington's cabinet feared that the federal government might do more damage than good by resorting to force.[8]

Few Federalists were more scathing in their denunciations of the rebels than Hamilton, who was emphatic that "there can therefore be no such thing as a 'constitutional resistance' to laws constitutionally enacted." While citizens might pursue "the repeal of a law," the actions of the rebels "to obstruct the operation of it presents a contradiction in terms." Similar attitudes were expressed in a grand jury charge delivered by a Federalist judge in Berks County, Pennsylvania, who reminded jurors that "one successful instance of a *forcible opposition* to law, will naturally generate others." Taking the argument a step further, he argued that the structure of American constitutionalism had rendered the right of revolution effectively obsolete. He confidently asserted that "there can be no oppression in a government constituted as that of the United States."[9]

Hamilton's policies not only alienated backcountry farmers, but the strongly nationalist agenda of Federalists also led many who had supported the Constitution in 1788 to join with former Anti-Federalists to create the Republican movement. Mainstream opposition to Hamilton and the Federalist agenda stopped well short of sanctioning their resort to extralegal measures. Rather than support the insurrectionary popular ideology of the rebels, the Republican and former Anti-Federalist William Findley found himself adopting a stance that ultimately placed him much closer to his Federalist opponent Hamilton than to the men who assembled in arms in Braddock's Field. "All men of discretion," Findley concluded, realized that "if they permitted government to be violently opposed, even in the execution of an obnoxious law, the same spirit would naturally lead to the destruction of all security and order," a situation that would lead to "a state of anarchy." While opposing the tax with peaceful measures was entirely appropriate, he did not countenance "riots or any thing that might tend to promote any unconstitutional exertions." Those who took up arms against government were in Findley's view little more than "armed banditti."[10]

The Whiskey Rebels, following in the tradition of Shays, believed that the people might spontaneously assemble in arms to defend liberty. For these plebeian populists, the militia was an agent of the local community. The rebels regarded their own state government with no greater deference than they did the oppressive federal government responsible for the whiskey excise. The adoption of the federal Constitution and Bill of Rights had done little to dampen the ardor of those who believed that the will of the community expressed directly through the jury or the militia might supersede the acts of legislatures, or even written constitutions. From the Whiskey Rebels' point of the view, their current situation under the federal Constitution was little better than that of the colonists prior to the Revolution.

As had been true for the Shaysites before them, the Whiskey Rebels appropriated the rituals and rhetoric of the militia muster to organize themselves and give their actions legitimacy. Indeed, another Republican critic of the rebellion, Hugh Henry Brackenridge, was struck by how the rebels couched their actions in the language of the militia and consciously tried to make it seem as if they "were called out by authority, as in the case of the reviews of the militia." The rebels went to great lengths to adopt the legal forms of a militia and to persuade the outside world that "we are no mob" but had assembled in arms in an orderly manner.[11]

In a "circular letter" calling on western Pennsylvanians to oppose the excise, the Whiskey Rebels reminded citizens of their moral obligation to render their "personal service" and muster. A note by "Tom the Tinker" admonished those "delinquents" who did not "come forth, on the next alarm" to defend "the virtuous principles of republican liberty." The rebels not only utilized the rituals, forms, and institutional framework of the militia, they also borrowed its potent language of political obligation. Thus, the rebels did not speak in an idiom of individual rights, but used the language of civic obligations and republican liberty. They chose to assert their claims not as individuals "bearing arms," but as a community "assembling in arms," a phrasing that underscored the public and collective nature of their action. Although the rebels did not invoke the language of the Second Amendment to justify their actions, their behavior implicitly embodied the principles of the preamble, whose language asserted the ideal of the militia as the guardian of popular liberty.[12]

Among the most radical voices supporting the rebels were people like William Petrikin, the ardent Anti-Federalist who had led the Carlisle Rioters during the struggle over ratification. While Findley and Brackenridge refused to support the rebels' appeal to arms, Petrikin "applauded and supported" the actions of "the Glorious Sons of Liberty to the West." Petrikin, one contemporary reported, "sd a great deal agst the excise law" but also attacked "the Constitution." Robert Whitehill, another Republican from Pennsylvania who had also been a signer of the Anti-Federalist "Dissent of the Minority," opposed

Petrikin and warned "it would be better to submit" since continued opposition could "bring on a revolution." Petrikin did not dispute Whitehill's reasoning, but welcomed such an outcome. "All Revns began by force and that it was as well it should begin," reasoned Petrikin, adding, "It was time there should be a Revolution—that Congress ought either to Repeal the Law or allow these people to set up a government for themselves—& be separated from us." The right of revolution, Petrikin argued, had not been cast aside with establishment of the Constitution, and he believed that western Pennsylvanians were in exactly the same relationship to the new government as American colonists had been with Britain. Resistance against the Whiskey Tax was therefore just and legal.[13]

While Republicans sympathized with the grievances of the Whiskey Rebellion and opposed Hamilton's economic program, they rejected the idea that the people might assemble in arms spontaneously outside of their role as part of a well-regulated militia under state authority. Others not quite willing to sanction armed resistance were willing to contemplate a different form of passive resistance. Implicit in the idea of the militia was the idea that citizen soldiers were not passive tools of government, but retained a right to refuse to muster and thereby exercise a form of passive veto on government policy. Although this theory had never been fully theorized, it enjoyed broader popular support than the radical ideology of the Whiskey Rebels. Pennsylvania's Governor Thomas Mifflin believed that Pennsylvanians would act "as Freemen," which meant that "they would enquire into the cause and nature of the service proposed to them, and I believe that their alacrity in performing, as well as accepting it, would essentially depend on their opinion of its justice and necessity." This type of passive resistance was akin to the right of juries to refuse to convict a citizen under an unjust law, effectively nullifying the law at issue. Jury nullification reflected the strong tradition of popular constitutionalism in Anglo-American law. While these notions have atrophied in modern American law, they were a vital part of eighteenth-century law. In essence, local juries would act as a minilegislature or even a mini–constitutional convention, spontaneously evaluating the justice of a particular law or particular constitutional provision. During Shays's Rebellion the militia simply refused to muster and march against their fellow citizens. Militia nullification occupied a constitutional middle ground, somewhere between the categorical Federalist rejection of the idea of constitutional resistance and the Whiskey Rebels' assertion of a continuing right of revolution.[14]

Even among those who rejected the legitimacy of militia nullification there was some concern that this idea enjoyed considerable popular support and would present a serious obstacle to any effort by the federal government to call out the militia. Thus, Secretary of State Edmund Randolph was deeply worried that using force to crush the rebellion might trigger resistance to government action, either active or passive. After noting that "a radical and universal dissatisfaction with the excise pervades the four transmontane counties of Pennsylvania," Randolph remarked, "Several counties of Virginia, having a strong militia, *participate in these feelings.*" Randolph echoed the concerns voiced by Mifflin, noting that not only was it possible that Pennsylvania's militia might refuse to respond to the governor's request, but also that "if the militia of other States are to be called forth, *it is not a decided thing that many of them may not refuse.*" Furthermore, the Whiskey Rebels and Pennsylvania militia might find common cause if confronted by an invading force of militia drawn from neighboring states. Either type of resistance to federal authority would precipitate a major constitutional crisis. Randolph was especially worried about the potential consequences of a civil war for the South. *"There is another enemy in the heart of the Southern States,"* Randolph reminded Washington, *"who would not sleep with such an opportunity of advantage."* As had been true during the debate over ratification of the Constitution, the problem of slave rebellion was never far from the minds of leading southern politicians. Randolph's warnings demonstrate the tenuous nature of federal control over the militia in the years immediately after the adoption of the Constitution and the unresolved nature of American thinking about the constitutional function of the militia as a possible check on federal tyranny. Washington ultimately rejected Randolph's more cautious approach, siding with Hamilton's preference for a firm display of force. Randolph's dire prognostications about the militia refusing to muster proved unfounded, and the nation thus averted a major constitutional crisis.[15]

The musings and reservations expressed by Mifflin and Randolph demonstrate the fluidity of American constitutional thought in the years immediately following ratification about the constitutional function of the militia. Questions about the limits of resistance within the new legal system created by the Constitution had not yet been worked out. In his initial response to Washington, Mifflin conceded that members of the militia enjoyed considerable independence and would deliberate on the legality and justice of a summons to arms. Yet, when units of the militia failed to heed a call to muster and prepare to march against the insurgents, Mifflin was mortified. The governor soon retreated from his earlier recognition of some measure of autonomy among individual units of the militia. Within six weeks of expressing some doubts to Washington in private, Mifflin stood before the militia of Lancaster, Pennsylvania, and delivered a rousing call to arms to support the president. The shift in tone and attitude toward the role of the militia was profound. Abandoning even a vague hint that a right of militia nullification existed, Mifflin now argued that militiamen were legally and duty bound to follow orders, even if members harbored personal reservations about the government's policies. Mifflin's views now appeared almost indistinguishable from those of Hamilton. The only constitutionally legitimate response for unjust laws was for them to be "amended if they are imperfect, or they may be repealed if they are pernicious." The notion of some type of popular nullification was no longer viable in Mifflin's view. "The oath of affirmation of every public officer, and the duty of every private citizen" required that laws legally enacted "cannot be disobeyed, or obstructed, or resisted."[16]

Government forces easily crushed the rebellion. The trial of the leaders of the rebellion provided the government with another opportunity to assert its authority and firmly squash the notion that the Constitution had somehow incorporated a right of revolution into American law. Two of the Whiskey Rebels were indicted for treason. Neither of the defendants claimed a constitutional right of revolution, nor did they invoke their Second Amendment rights to keep and bear arms. Instead they readily conceded that their actions left them open to prosecution for rioting. Having conceded this fact, however, they strenuously denied that their actions met the Constitution's narrow definition of treason, which required proof of treasonous intent. Although the court did convict them, Washington was not eager to create any martyrs and quickly pardoned them.

The triumph of the forces of order over the Whiskey Rebels occasioned an outpouring of public sentiments in favor of the government's decision to use force to put down the rebellion. Federalists found a particularly sympathetic audience among many of the nation's clergy, who heeded Washington's call for a national day of thanksgiving to commemorate the suppression of the rebellion. Ministers chose to "commemorate the blessings of our new government, now more firmly established by the suppression of a late unnatural, ill-advised insurrection." The defeat of the rebels was cast as a blow to anarchy and a triumph for "liberty with order." Samuel Kendal, a minister from Massachusetts, reminded his parishioners that

> there cannot exist any reason, or cause, which will justify the rising of a part of the people in arms against a government, like our federal government, which is supported by the will of the majority, and may at any time be altered by the same will; especially as there are constitutional means for the redress of any grievances, resulting from its administration.

Other sermons denounced events in Western Pennsylvania as "commotions" and compared the rebels to Shays and other fomenters of "anarchy and disorganization." The rebels' actions were counter-posed to the "patriotick militia" that crushed the rebellion. Once again, supporters of ordered liberty attacked the notion that Americans were entitled to a constitutional right of revolution against their government. Similar sentiments were expressed in the popular press. As one writer noted, "The late insurrection in the western counties and the alacrity of the militia, in rising for its suppression, demonstrate the propriety of a free people keeping arms in their own hands." The right to keep and bear arms and participate in the militia was intended to provide the people with the means to put down rebellions, not foment them.[17]

While the defeat of the Whiskey Rebels was certainly a setback for the opponents of the Federalist agenda, the states' rights conception of the militia and the radical localist view had not been extirpated from American constitutionalism. The ideas that led citizens to assemble in arms in Braddock's Field, and assert a right to challenge federal authority, continued to exert a strong appeal to many opposed to the Federalists' centralizing agenda, particularly in the volatile backcoun-try. The notion that the states might use their militia to interpose between the federal government and its citizens also continued to attract adherents within the ranks of Republicans. Whether framed as a direct challenge to federal power or conceptualized as a veto, the notion that the militia might actively or passively protest unjust federal policies remained a latent force to be reckoned with in American constitutionalism.[18]

VOLUNTEERS AND STREET FIGHTING MEN

The years following the Whiskey Rebellion did not usher in an era of political good feelings. Indeed, political tempers and partisan fervor only intensified after the uprising. Political divisions in America were exacerbated by the polarization of European politics after the French

Revolution. Federalists rallied to the side of Britain, while Republicans embraced the cause of the French Revolution. British order and French liberty represented the twin lodestars of American politics. Quite apart from their roles as political symbols, support for Britain and France had important economic consequences. Unfortunately for Americans, hostilities between the two European powers erupted into armed conflict. It became increasingly difficult for America to avoid entanglements in European affairs, particularly given Americans' desire to trade with both Britain and France. By 1797 the simmering conflict with France over America's assertion of neutrality had led to a marked deterioration in diplomatic relations between the two nations; naval skirmishes between the two escalated into an undeclared quasi war. Americans, Federalists feared, were living in a dangerous time with enemies everywhere. Given the strong French sympathies of Republicans, Federalists also worried about the dangers of domestic subversion.[19]

Washington's successor, John Adams, resisted the most ambitious Federalist calls for a larger standing army and chose to concentrate his attention on building America's navy and creating the U.S. Marine Corps. Other Federalists wished to pursue a more aggressive policy. Hamilton proposed the creation of a provisional army of twenty thousand men who could be enlisted when the president judged it necessary. The president would also be allowed to accept volunteer companies, which were generally composed of wealthy Federalists, into the nation's military forces. Republicans countered with a proposal to mobilize eighty thousand militiamen to meet any military threat that might arise.[20]

The Federalist proposal to expand the nation's army revived an issue that had been vigorously debated since the founding of the nation. Republicans opposed efforts to create a large army, clinging to the traditional Whig ideal that viewed standing armies as a threat to liberty. Federalists disparaged the performance of the militia on the battlefield and argued that a professional force was needed to meet the threat posed by the French. Quite apart from their general lack of faith in the militia, Federalists questioned whether or not there were enough arms in the hands of the militia to make it an effective force. Republicans disputed the claim that America was insufficiently armed, arguing that there were enough weapons in state arsenals to outfit individuals unable to provide their own weapons. In addition to these points of disagreement, Republicans argued that giving the president power to raise a provisional army effectively undermined the constitutional separation of powers that gave Congress the legislative authority to organize the armed forces. The proposal to use volunteers struck Republicans as a particularly ominous development. Albert Gallatin, one of the most articulate spokesmen for the Republican opposition, attacked the plan for violating the Constitution, which recognized only two types of troops: army and militia. This type of select militia was especially dangerous since these units would be drawn from a particular class, the wealthy, and might easily become a tool of Federalist policy. Federalists took umbrage at the suggestion that troops under presidential control might somehow threaten the liberty of the nation. The only people who had reason to fear the provisional army and volunteers were the "turbulent and seditious" and "insurgents," they argued. The charge that they were enemies of government in turn angered Republicans, who denied that any group in America was bent on the kinds of lawlessness Federalists described.[21]

During this wide-ranging debate over military policy, the meaning of the Second Amendment and its relevance to the constitutional function of the militia came up only once in a brief aside by Gallatin. The militia, Gallatin argued, included all citizens capable of bearing arms. "Whether a man be rich or poor, provided he has a common interest in the welfare of the community, he had an equal reliance upon him. And this is a constitutional idea; for the Constitution says, 'the rights of the people to bear arms shall not be questioned.'" A universal militia in which citizens bore arms would provide the states with a vital check on despotism. The Federalists' volunteer militia, by contrast, was intended to create an armed faction that would effectively undermine this constitutional check on federal power.[22]

Political tensions only intensified as the quasi war dragged on. Federalists rallied around John Adams's presidency and attacked French treachery on the high seas. Suspicion of France was exacerbated by the XYZ Affair, a notorious and widely reported attempt on the part of French diplomats to solicit a bribe from America's envoys in France. Although the incident was an embarrassment for Republicans, they continued to protest the Anglo-monarchical tendencies of their opponents and tried to remain as supportive of France as possible under the circumstances.[23]

While America and France were engaged in a quasi war at sea, Federalists and Republicans were engaged in a different sort of battle in the nation's newspapers and in some cases in the streets of America's cities and towns. Philadelphia, the nation's capital, was bitterly divided. One newspaper reported, "The streets of Philadelphia were filled with crowds of people, who wanted nothing but the firing of the first musket to precipitate Pennsylvania, and perhaps the continent, into the horrors of civil war." Thomas Jefferson recalled an incident when a group of Federalists wearing the black cockade encountered Republicans sporting the French tricolored cockade. A riot ensued between the two groups. "The city was so filled with confusion," Jefferson recollected, "that it was dangerous going out." Recognizing that politics rendered the streets dangerous, Republicans urged their supporters to form their own volunteer militias. "As men intent upon hostility have associated themselves in military corps, it becomes your duty to associate likewise. Arm and organize yourself immediately —Make yourself acquainted with military discipline, be ready, and you will be at peace." In this tense political environment the greatest threat to individual safety was not crime, but political violence. The political animosities engendered by partisan politics reached such a fervid pitch that Governor Thomas Mifflin thought it prudent to have cavalry and militia patrol the streets of Philadelphia. President Adams felt sufficiently threatened to "order Chests of Arms from the War Office to be brought through bye lanes and back doors" to his personal residence.[24]

The quasi war and partisan political violence spurred Federalists to enact a series of laws designed to strengthen the federal government's ability to respond to threats from domestic and foreign radicals. Immigration was one area Federalists viewed as a potential source for radical infiltration. Three Alien Acts were passed to restrict immigration into the United States and place those already resident in America under greater scrutiny. To deal with the danger of domestic threats to public order, Federalists passed the Sedition Act. This act created a federal law of seditious libel and provided stiff punishments for those convicted of criticizing the government.[25]

One of the most dramatic protests against the Alien Act occurred in Philadelphia at St. Mary's Catholic Church in February 1799. William Duane, editor of the antiadministration *Philadelphia Aurora*; Dr. James Reynolds; and two resident aliens set out to collect signatures on a petition against the Alien Acts. The petitioners posted notices on the gates leading into the churchyard and waited for congregants to leave the church. Angered by this profane and "seditious meeting" on church property, irate Federalists exiting the church fell upon Duane, Reynolds, and their companions. A small riot ensued, and Reynolds pulled a pistol from his coat and brandished it to fend off the angry mob. The crowd overpowered Reynolds, knocked him to the ground, and disarmed him. The four men were charged with riot, and Reynolds faced an additional charge of assault with a deadly weapon.[26]

The trial provides a remarkable window into contemporary attitudes about constitutional liberty and the right of individual self-defense. The meaning of the right of assembly and the scope of the right of individual self-defense were discussed at great length during the trial. The involvement of Duane, a leading publisher and prominent Republican, meant that the case attracted some of the leading legal minds of the day and drew considerable attention in the press. Indeed, the case was significant enough to justify publishing the entire trial transcript in pamphlet form. The arguments used by the defense and the prosecution provide one of the clearest expressions of how lawyers conceptualized the right to use firearms for self-defense in the generation immediately following the adoption of the Second Amendment and the first state constitutional provisions on arms bearing.

Although occasioned by a protest against the Alien Acts passed by Congress, the criminal charges against the defendants were filed in state court for violations of Pennsylvania law. Accordingly, the arguments in the case focused on issues of state constitutional law and common law. Speaking on behalf of the defendants, noted attorney Alexander Dallas expressed his dismay that anyone could find fault with his clients' actions. "To denounce as riotous a constitutional right, the obtaining of signatures to a respectful memorial addressed to the proper organ of government," was astonishing in a republic. The right to petition to seek redress of grievances was explicitly protected by the Pennsylvania Constitution.[27]

Although the attorney general conceded that assembly was a basic constitutional right explicitly protected by the Pennsylvania Constitution, and a bedrock principle of American law, he took exception to two of the defense's claims. First, the right was not, strictly speaking, an individual right, but rather was one associated with citizenship. The resident aliens who assisted Duane could not claim a constitutional right of assembly. Second, government might still legitimately regulate this right by imposing certain reasonable limits on the time, place, and manner in which it might be exercised.[28]

Reynolds's use of a firearm posed a different set of legal issues. While the defense and prosecution had different ideas about the constitutional right of assembly, neither side believed that the use of a gun for personal self-defense had any connection to the constitutional right to bear arms protected by the Pennsylvania Constitution. The argument over the right to use firearms touched no constitutional question but did raise an issue under common law. The prosecution argued that Reynolds's decision to arm himself was not justified by traditional common-law principle and provided evidence of his criminal intent. Eyewitness testimony produced by the prosecution asserted that Reynolds acted not in self-defense, but merely to defend himself against insult and minor injury. While self-defense was a well-accepted principle under common law, defending ones' honor against insult was not. Similarly, the right to stand one's ground and fend off attackers was not protected by common law. Indeed, even if Reynolds had feared for his life, his decision to stand his ground rather than flee meant he had forfeited the right of self-defense guaranteed by the common law. The prosecution asserted an extremely limited Blackstonian conception of self-defense, which required a "retreat to the wall" before resorting to deadly force.[29]

The defense agreed that the constitutional right to bear arms was not at issue in the case. Instead, they focused on the meaning of the common law right of self-defense. Dallas made a simple argument: "There is no law in Pennsylvania to prevent it; every man has a right to carry arms who apprehends himself to be in danger." In the absence of any law against carrying a firearm, the prosecution could not infer any criminal intent from Reynolds's decision to arm himself. Given the depth of political animosities in Philadelphia, Reynolds's actions were not indicative of criminal intent, but simple prudence. "Party spirit" had reached such a fervid pitch and personal animosities grown so intense that Reynolds had been obliged to arm himself as a means of self-protection. Interestingly, there was widespread agreement that Reynolds's choice of weapon, a pistol, was unwise. Given the likelihood of a pistol's misfiring, a dirk or sword cane were better choices.[30]

The Reynolds case provides a rare and remarkable glimpse into how leading lawyers of the early republic viewed carrying firearms outside of the context of bearing them as part of a well-regulated militia. The distinction between a constitutional right to bear arms and a common-law right to keep or carry arms for self-defense was accepted by both sides. Although the defense attorneys had readily resorted to constitutional arguments to support their clients' right to assemble, they relied on common-law doctrine to sanction the use of a pistol for self-defense.

The fact that the prosecution and defense viewed the scope of the right of individual self-defense in such radically different terms demonstrates the uncertain state of the law of self-defense in the new republic. In the Reynolds case, a more traditional and limited Blackstonian conception of self-defense was pitted against a newer, more aggressive notion of standing one's ground. One of the most intriguing arguments hinted at in the case dealt with a right to use force to defend one's honor, a conception that would come to play an even more crucial role in the evolution of American thinking about the right of self-defense in the coming decades. Although it is difficult to disentangle the case from the bitter political conflicts of the day, the jury obviously found the defense's case more compelling. They acquitted the accused on all charges.[31]

TESTING THE CONSTITUTIONAL RIGHT OF RESISTANCE

Opposition to the Alien Acts was mild when compared to the scope of protests against the Sedition Act. By criminalizing public criticism of the government, Federalists appeared to be striking at freedom itself. Newspapers teemed with denunciations of the legislation. Public meetings drew large crowds of protestors, petitions were collected, and liberty poles were raised in many cities and towns. America faced a full-blown constitutional crisis, one that forced Republicans to think hard about the option of constitutional resistance.

During the debate over the Constitution, Federalists had assured their opponents that there were ample protections for liberty built into the structure of the new federal system. Although they opposed the Anti-Federalists' states' rights conception of the Constitution, Federalists had been forced to concede that in the event of an unconstitutional usurpation of power by the federal government, states would rally to protect liberty. The exact mechanism by which the states would exercise this role had not been spelled out with any precision in 1788. Ten years later, the heirs to the Anti-Federalists, the Republicans, were faced with a serious constitutional problem: how could the states exercise this vital role as the guardians of liberty? Would the agents of this be the state judiciaries, the state legislatures, or the state militias? Republicans considered all of these possibilities in the course of their spirited opposition to the Sedition Act.

The initial goal of the opposition was the repeal of the law. This strategy foundered for want of political support in heavily Federalist areas of the nation such as New England. Opponents next looked to the courts. In theory juries might have protected those accused of seditions libel by refusing to convict them. Jury nullification of the Sedition Act was stymied by the Federalist-dominated judiciary, which refused to allow juries to exercise this function. When it became clear that ordinary political and legal means had failed, opposition thinkers began to theorize in a more systematic fashion how they might justify some type of constitutional resistance.[32]

In a letter to Thomas Jefferson, John Taylor, a leading southern voice within the Republican alliance, suggested that the states might exercise a check on the government. Taylor's states' rights constitutional theory was taken up and elaborated more fully in Jefferson's "Kentucky Resolutions" and James Madison's "Virginia Resolutions." Jefferson and Madison asserted that the protection of individual liberty depended on preserving the balance of power between the states and the federal government and that states might interpose between the federal government and individuals. The mechanism for enforcing this interposition was only vaguely outlined, and language of the two resolutions implied that moral suasion, not legal action or military force, was the appropriate means of accomplishing some type of nullification of unconstitutional laws.[33]

While most mainstream Republicans adhered to this peaceful defense of states' rights, the radical ideology that had inspired protests such as the Whiskey Rebels' produced a different response among local militia units and local communities scattered across the nation. The militia of Amelia County, Virginia, resolved "that any 'Act' violating the Constitution, is, we conceive a nullity." Moreover, it was "the duty of every citizen to oppose by all constitutional means every attempt to violate the Constitution." Citizens ought to refuse to "aid in carrying the said acts into effect." Although they were less bold, the Freemen of Rutland County, Vermont, declared a similar principle when they contrasted the willingness of a standing army to enforce acts contrary to the Constitution with the actions of a well-regulated and virtuous militia who would never feel compelled to enforce such acts. Similarly, a Kentucky broadside issued by citizens from Lexington warned Federalists that free citizens would defend the Constitution "at the hazard of their lives and fortunes" against any enemy but would never support "acts that are unconstitutional." The explicit affirmations of the Amelia County militia and the veiled threats emanating from Kentucky and Vermont voiced a rough-hewn theory of constitutional resistance that relied on popular nullification of unjust laws. The militia was key to this function and would achieve its role by refusing to muster or carry out orders to enforce unconstitutional acts.[34]

The possibility of some sort of armed clash between the state militias or local units and the federal government was taken very seriously by contemporaries. Nathaniel Pope, a Republican from Virginia, warned that efforts to enforce the Alien and Sedition Acts would "compel the people forcibly to resort to first revolutionary principles." Rather than embrace violence, Pope counseled opponents of the acts to employ a "mild and constitutional mode of obtaining a redress of our grievances." Despite the efforts of such moderate voices, Federalist newspapers reported rumors that a resort to arms might be made to prevent enforcement of the Alien and Sedition Acts. These reports were given additional credence because of the Virginia state legislature's unprecedented actions to reform the militia in the midst of the crisis. Legislators raised taxes by a staggering 25 percent, an enormous sum for a state that had previously protested loudly about excessive Federalist taxes. The Virginia plan for militia reform included ample funds for procuring additional arms and ammunition and an ambitious plan to create a new state armory. Did Virginians really contemplate using the militia as the final check on federal tyranny in 1799? It is difficult to be certain, but Federalists certainly felt that such a threat was credible. Virginians may well have been engaged in some dramatic saber rattling, using a long-overdue plan to overhaul the militia for maximum political effect. Still, the effect of such posturing on their opponents is undeniable.[35]

Federalists not only rejected armed resistance, but they attacked popular nullification and the doctrine of state nullification as well. "The Address of the Minority of the Virginia Legislature," a response to Madison's and Jefferson's theory of nullification, declared that it was not only within the "legitimate powers of the government" to enact laws "punishing open resistance," but that government might legitimately act preemptively to prohibit actions that might constitute "the germ from which resistance springs." The official response of the state of Rhode Island to the Virginia and Kentucky Resolutions was no less hostile. The logic of Virginia and Kentucky led to "civil discord" and would inevitably result in "each state having in that case, no resort for vindicating its own opinion, but to the strength of its own arm."[36]

FRIES'S REBELLION, THE REVOLUTION OF 1800, AND THE RIGHT OF ARMED RESISTANCE

The quasi war with France fueled a military buildup, and to fund this effort Federalists passed a series of taxes on houses, land, and slaves. Opposition to the new taxes turned violent in the German communities of southeastern Pennsylvania. The tax on land seemed particularly intrusive since it required assessors to enter citizens' homes to complete their evaluations. The assessors were harassed and threatened. As had been true during Shays's and the Whiskey Rebellion, opposition was organized through local units of the militia. When a federal warrant was issued for the protestors and arrests made, the local militia sprang into action. Three local companies of armed citizens mustered and marched to the jail to release the prisoners. Once again the radical potential of the militia had been unleashed in response to government actions deemed despotic by some Americans. President Adams acted decisively and called out the Pennsylvania state militia to put down the rebellion. As had been true during the Whiskey Rebellion, the well-regulated militia controlled by the federal government was used against local units of the militia. The leader of the uprising, Jacob Fries, was apprehended and charged with treason.[37]

As had been true during the Whiskey Rebellion, the rebels had turned to the forms and symbols of the militia to frame their protests. The insurgents, one witness testified, "damned the house-tax" and "the alien and sedition law, and finally all the laws: the government and all the laws the present Congress made. They damned the Constitution also. They did not mention what constitution, whether of this state or of the United States." Rebels fell back on a potent populist constitutional tradition that looked to local community institutions. Thus, one federal marshal recounted how an insurgent described both the Alien Act and the house tax as unconstitutional and railed against the practice of bringing violators to Philadelphia for trial. "They had no objection," he recalled, against being "tried in their own courts, and by their own people." The defense of local juries was consistent with the decision to use the local militia as a means of nullifying a law deemed obnoxious and unconstitutional. Some rebels invoked the legacy of 1776 while others cited the more recent example of the French Revolution. At one meeting, a witness testified that he saw about a dozen armed men in uniform marching in military fashion with a flag with the word "liberty" written on it. After the law was explained to the group, one man exclaimed, "We don't want any of your damned laws, we have laws of our own." To drive home his point, the rebel "shook the muzzle of his musket in my face, saying 'this is our law, and we will let you know it.'" When rebels denounced one government official as a Tory, the federal marshal replied that such an epithet "could not apply to me; that I had a share in the Revolution: and I was as fond of liberty as any of them." When the insurgents "huzzaed for liberty; I told them that I should join them in that, if they would huzza for liberty of the right kind; but this was licentious liberty." The invocation of liberty by the rebels underscored the disjunction between these two opposing visions of constitutional law.[38]

The prosecution in Fries's case followed the model set out in the trial of the Whiskey Rebels. The government argued that the Constitution defined treason as "levying war against the United States, and aiding the enemies of the United States." U.S. Attorney William Rawle insisted that treason did not require a full-scale rebellion, but could consist of assembling "with force of arms, or by numbers sufficient for that purpose, to cause an impression of terror" intended to prevent the exercise of federal law. Rawle drew a distinction between acts aimed at a particular individual in his private capacity, which would be punishable as riot, and those directed at public officials and intended to promote a general resistance to the laws of the United States, which would be treasonous.[39]

Alexander Dallas, who had so ably defended Duane and Reynolds against the charges of riot and assault, represented Fries in his trial. This time Dallas was presented with a much more difficult task. His strategy was similar to the one employed in the trial of the Whiskey Rebels. While conceding that the rebels had engaged in criminal activity, Dallas insisted that there was an important legal distinction between rioting and rebelling. The law recognized a wide gulf between acts of "riot and folly" and those of "deliberate treason." Despite the defense's best efforts to persuade the jury that Fries was a rioter and not a rebel, the jury convicted Fries of treason and sentenced him to death. Eager to avoid creating a Republican martyr, John Adams pardoned Fries and the other insurgents.[40]

Federalists not only believed there was no right of revolution protected by the Constitution, but they approached the common-law right to carry arms in narrow terms as well. Thus, in his charge to the jury during Fries's trial, Judge Richard Peters made it clear that federal marshals had been justified in disarming citizens who were planning to join the insurgents. Indeed, Peters went on to suggest, "a constable has a right to restrain and confine, under strong circumstances of suspicion, persons whose conduct or appearance evidence an intention to commit illegal and violent acts." Guns were clearly not like words; they were subject to some forms of prior restraint. Even the detested Sedition Act did not allow government to place prior restraints on publications.[41]

Although Republicans opposed the Federalist decision to call out the militia to put down the rebellion, they did not sanction the protesters' use of violence. Both Federalist and Republican elites decisively rejected the notion that individuals or local communities might exercise a right of armed resistance. The gulf separating popular constitutional culture, which continued to accept the idea of local nullification and even armed resistance, and elite ideas about constitutional resistance remained wide. Fries's conviction was another serious setback for the populist vision of the militia. Despite this defeat, this ideology continued as a powerful underground current in American culture. Two powerful forces in American life sustained it: the strong centripetal pull of localism and the emotionally resonant language of American revolutionary rhetoric.[42]

While Republican elites may have abandoned the notion of an individual or communal right of armed resistance, a state's prerogative to exercise such a right was still very much alive in Republican thought.

In its least controversial form, state governors could simply refuse to call up their militia to enforce federal policy. The more radical notion that states might actually use their militias against the federal government under extraordinary circumstances, while still controversial, gained additional support when Republicans faced another constitutional crisis and another example of Federalist despotism, the electoral college deadlock of 1800.[43]

This crisis was a dramatic example of an unanticipated flaw in the Constitution's design. No provision had been made to distinguish between votes cast for president and vice president in the Electoral College. In 1800, Federalists had wisely arranged to divert one vote from vice presidential candidate Thomas Pinckney to assure presidential candidate John Adams more votes than his running mate. Republicans, fearful of possible defections that might cost them the election, made no such plans. When the final votes were counted, Thomas Jefferson, the candidate for president, received the same number of votes as his running mate, Aaron Burr. The Constitution specified that in cases of a tie the House of Representatives would decide the election. Although the choice was now between two Republican candidates, some Federalists believed anyone was preferable to Jefferson and threw their support to Burr, who became the Federalist favorite. Behind the scenes, both sides engaged in a frenzy of activity to resolve the electoral dispute peacefully. Each side feared that the other might use force to steal the election. The Federalist *Gazette of the United States* posed the question bluntly: Were Jefferson and his supporters "ripe for civil war, and ready to imbrue their hands in kindred blood?" Hugh Henry Brackenridge wrote to Jefferson to voice his concern that Hamilton would act the part of Oliver Cromwell, backed by his own "New Model Army" composed of Federalist volunteers. Were Federalists to draw "the bayonet," Brackenridge was confident they would encounter a Republican resistance distinguished by its "valor, virtue, and numbers." In any such contest, he concluded, the Federalists would certainly be vanquished.[44]

The crisis once again forced Americans to ponder the role of the militia and the scope of the right of armed resistance under the Constitution. One of the most remarkable documents produced during this tense situation was drafted by Albert Gallatin, one of Jefferson's leading advisors, who outlined the various options available to Republicans should Federalists block Jefferson's election. The larger question Gallatin posed was simple: "If they shall usurp, for unconstitutional assumption is usurpation, are we to submit or not?" In Gallatin's view, "usurpation must be resisted by freemen whenever they have the power of resisting." If Federalists tried to steal the election from Jefferson, the normal constitutional mechanisms for protecting liberty would have been cast aside and Americans would be thrust into a revolutionary situation akin to that of 1776. The difficult issue for Gallatin was not the legitimacy of resistance, but the correct "mode of resisting."[45]

Gallatin took great pains to frame a response that sought to avoid anarchy and utilize those structures of constitutional government that remained uncorrupted. The key to preventing anarchy was to block "every partial insurrection, or even individual acts of resistance." The only legitimate mode for collecting the voice of the people was through individual state governments. Resistance was acceptable when the "laws of the particular states" sanctioned it. Gallatin discussed the notion of the individual state militias refusing to obey the orders of any usurper. The militias were still creatures of the states, and although they had supported the government during the Whiskey Rebellion and Fries's Insurrection, they might legitimately decide to oppose the federal government at this juncture.[46]

To many, the prospect of civil war appeared all too real. Governor Thomas McKean of Pennsylvania and Governor James Monroe of Virginia each prepared to ready their states' militia in the event that Federalists attempted to seize power. Samuel Tyler informed Monroe that Pennsylvania "had 22 thousand prepared to take up arms in the event of extremities." Rumors of the alliance between Pennsylvania and Virginia leaked to the press. One Federalist newspaper boasted that the militias of Massachusetts, New Hampshire, and Connecticut were "united almost to a man, with half the number of at least the citizens of eleven other states ranged under the federal banner in support of the Constitution." Against such numbers, "what could Pennsylvania do aided by Virginia"? The author of this essay went on to deride the quality of the Virginia militia, describing them as "untrained and farcically performing the manual exercise with corn stalks instead of muskets." Monroe took several extraordinary steps to ready his state for a possible conflict. Fearing that arms stored in a federal arsenal at New London, Virginia, might be used against the state government by Federalists, Monroe set in play a plan to transfer the munitions to the state militia. He dispatched a loyal officer to the arsenal to determine the state of the weapons. The arms, many of which had been captured during the Revolution and had recently been refurbished, included "4000 excellent muskets and bayonets with about 3000 cartridge boxes," powder, ball, and "two good brass field pieces with their carriages." Using the fear of a possible slave insurrection as his justification, Monroe ordered a detachment of state militia to guard the weapons and ammunition.[47]

The willingness of Governors McKean and Monroe to mobilize their militias may have helped resolve the crisis by convincing Federalists to accept Jefferson's claim on the presidency. As Jefferson observed, "We thought it best to declare openly and firmly, one & all, that" in the event of an act of usurpation, "the middle states would arm, & that no such usurpation, even for a single day, should be submitted to." The effect of such resolve was unmistakable in Jefferson's view: "This first shook them; and they were completely alarmed at the resource for which we declared." The actions of McKean, Monroe, and Jefferson took the states' rights theory of the militia, first articulated by Anti-Federalists a decade earlier, and made it orthodoxy among Republicans.[48]

AN AMERICAN BLACKSTONE PONDERS
THE SECOND AMENDMENT

In his law lectures at William and Mary, delivered shortly after the adoption of the Bill of Rights, St. George Tucker had defended the Second Amendment as an essential part of the structure of checks and balances that protected the rights of the states and the integrity of the federal system. The Second Amendment, in his view, had been included so that the states might have the awesome power of resisting federal tyranny by force of arms. Tucker revisited the role of the Second Amendment in American constitutionalism in his multi-volume study of Sir William Blackstone, published three years after the peaceful resolution of the electoral crisis of 1800.[49]

Tucker dealt with the Second Amendment in several places in his monumental treatise. His first discussion was coupled with a denunciation of Federalist use of volunteer militias during the quasi war with France (1797–1800). In essence, Federalists had created a select militia that was neither representative of the people nor properly controlled by the states. Rather than serve as a check on federal power, this new institution was likely to become an engine of federal despotism.[50]

Tucker reiterated his earlier view that the Second Amendment and the Virginia Declaration of Rights each had to be read in conjunction with the Constitution's discussion of the militia in Article 1, Section 8 of the Constitution. The adoption of the Second Amendment was a direct response to Anti-Federalist concerns over the future of the state militias. Tucker interpreted the amendment as a strong affirmation of states' rights, one that dispelled "all room for doubt, or uneasiness upon the subject."[51]

One of the most novel features of Tucker's Second Amendment analysis was his belief that the right to bear arms in a well-regulated militia was judicially enforceable by federal courts. This issue provided an opportunity to illustrate the larger danger posed by Federalist constitutional theory and defend the concept of federal judicial review. The issue that concerned Tucker was how to respond when "the legislature should pass a law dangerous to the liberties of the people." In Tucker's view,

> The judiciary, therefore, is that department of government to whom the protection of the rights of the individual is by the constitution especially confided, interposing its shield between him and the sword of the usurped authority.

Congressional disarmament provided an excellent illustration of this point:

> If for example congress were to pass a law prohibiting any person from bearing arms, as a means of preventing insurrections, the judicial courts, under the construction of the words necessary and proper, here contended for, would be able to pronounce decidedly upon the constitutionality of these means.

The underlying constitutional theory that made such developments possible was the Federalist theory of loose construction of the Constitution. "If congress may use any means, which they choose to adopt" to achieve their goal of preventing insurrections, Tucker complained, they could easily transform "the provision in the constitution which secures to the people the right of bearing arms" into "a mere nullity."[52]

Tucker's fears about potential federal disarmament of the militia were not entirely groundless. Federalists had already created volunteer militias and had hinted that some sort of preemptive legislation aimed at preventing insurrections might be necessary. Although Federalist use of the doctrine of seditious libel had stopped short of enacting prior restraints on publication, Tucker feared that Federalists would have had few constitutional scruples about using federal law to prevent citizens from bearing arms. If Federalists tried to enact similar restrictions on the right to bear arms, Tucker believed that it would be appropriate for federal courts to strike down such laws as unconstitutional. Tucker's treatise was published after Jefferson was safely ensconced in the presidency, and his discussion of constitutional resistance was less militant than his musings on the subject a decade earlier. Tucker did not disown his earlier avowal of a states' rights view of the Second Amendment, but his later elaboration of the civic conception of bearing arms and bold claim that federal courts could protect this right broadened his understanding of the potential role of the Second Amendment as a vital part of the federal system.[53]

THE RIGHT TO BEAR ARMS AT THE ONSET OF THE NINETEENTH CENTURY

In a Fourth of July oration delivered two years after the publication of Tucker's *Commentaries*, John Danforth Dunbar reiterated the importance of the dominant civic conception of the Second Amendment in succinct terms. He reminded his fellow citizens that "the patriots of '75 considered the right to keep and bear arms as one of our dearest privileges." The roots of the Second Amendment, according to Dunbar, were to be found in the patriots' fear of standing armies and their belief in the superiority of the militia. Dunbar wove together a patriotic recitation of the Revolutionary era's conception of the militia and the right to bear arms with a cautionary tale about recent threats to this ideal during the Federalist era. During their decade-long domination of the national government, the Federalists had advanced a military program that included plans for a large standing army and a volunteer select militia. Although this agenda had not been fully realized, Americans could ill afford to relax their guard. The defeat of Federalists in 1800 and the election of Jefferson to the presidency had not banished Federalist ideas entirely. Still, Jeffersonians could take pride in the fact that the "militia" continued to be a scourge to "tyrants at home and invaders from abroad." In Dunbar's view, the right to keep and bear arms as part of a well-regulated militia was a foundational principle of American constitutionalism. Samuel Dana articulated the same civic conception of arms bearing in "An Address on the Importance of a Well Regulated Militia." Dana's civic discourse was delivered in Concord, Massachusetts, a location closely associated with the minuteman ideal. After noting that the federal constitution had given the responsibility of "organizing, arming, disciplining the Militia" to the national legislature, Dana reminded his audience that "the right of bearing arms for the common defense, is recognized among our unalterable laws." Picking up on a theme sounded by Samuel Mitchill in an oration delivered less than a decade before, Dana noted that to achieve this ideal "these arms must not be suffered to rust in our houses." The notion that the right to bear arms for the common defense posed a burden and an awesome responsibility on citizens continued to define public discourse on the Second Amendment.[54]

Although the civic conception of the right to bear arms continued to enjoy widespread support, by the end of the era of Federalist domination, the states' rights conception of the Second Amendment had gained a strong foothold. Throughout the 1790s, Federalists had consistently sought greater federal control of the militia and denounced the idea of a constitutional right of resistance, either passive or armed. Republicans had defended state control of the militia and were more receptive to the idea of militia nullification or, in extreme cases, state resistance to federal tyranny. The notion of the militia exercising a passive check on the federal government enjoyed broader support than the more assertive view that the states might actually take up arms against the government in defense of liberty. While the 1790s helped elevate to prominence the states' rights view of the Second Amendment, the defeat of the Whiskey Rebels and Fries's Rebels was another setback to those Americans who believed in a continuing right of revolution and clung to their faith that people assembled in arms, organized as local militia units, might defend their communities against state and federal tyranny. Leading Republicans distanced themselves from this radical formulation of the militia's role and clung to the idea of a well-regulated militia under state control. Despite the outcomes of the Whiskey Rebellion and Fries's Rebellion, this popular constitutional tradition remained latent within American culture.

The publication of Tucker's work did not end the debate over the meaning of the right to bear arms or the constitutional role of the militia. Surprisingly, the states' rights view of the militia would soon be embraced by Federalists eager to oppose the policies of Thomas Jefferson and his successor, James Madison. Although the political animosities of the 1790s led some to reconsider the meaning of the right of self-defense, the new theory enunciated by the defense in the Reynolds case would continue to gain ground as some Americans began to doubt the more limited Blackstonian conception of the right of self-defense. Ultimately, this critique would lead some to fuse the common-law right of bearing a gun in self-defense and the constitutional right to bear arms into a single principle.

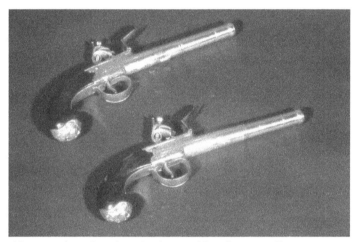

This screw barrel pocket pistol owned by Thomas Jefferson was similar to the type used by Thomas Selfridge in the most notorious murder case of the Jeffersonian era, the shooting of Charles Austin in 1807. (Courtesy of the Monticello, Va.: Thomas Jefferson Foundation, Inc.)

CHAPTER FOUR

MILITIAS, MOBS, AND MURDER

TESTING THE LIMITS OF THE RIGHT TO BEAR ARMS

Reflecting on the state of politics in his own state of Massachusetts after Jefferson's election to the presidency, John Adams wryly noted that "we in this commonwealth are making great advances, if not in the perfectibility of human nature, yet in the great arts of lying and libeling and the other arts which grow out of them, such as wielding the cudgel and pistol." The ultimately peaceful transfer of power from the Federalists to the Republicans had done little in Adams's view to dampen partisan rancor. The best-known example of political violence in the Jeffersonian era was the fatal duel fought between the Federalist Alexander Hamilton and his political opponent Aaron Burr. While duels, including the one that took Hamilton's life, were among the most formal and stylized type of political violence in Jeffersonian America, they were hardly the only occasions when partisan rivalries or animosities led to violence, or even death. Heightened political tensions, as Adams observed, led many to arm themselves as a precaution against political assault. Indeed, the most notorious murder case of the new republic was occasioned by a political feud that turned deadly. The murder of the Jeffersonian Charles Austin by

Federalist Thomas Selfridge shocked the nation and altered the traditional common-law understanding of the right of self-defense.[1]

The Jeffersonian era not only helped transform the meaning of the law of self-defense, but it also tested the limits of the revived states' rights theory of the Second Amendment that had helped secure Jefferson the presidency. In 1800 Virginia and Pennsylvania had each come dangerously close to mobilizing their militias and using them against the federal government. Ironically, Jefferson's successor in the presidency, James Madison, another supporter of states' rights, would have this ideology turned against him on two separate occasions, by Federalists opposed to his policies.

The Jeffersonian era also produced the first Supreme Court decision in the new nation's history to cite the Second Amendment. It was not an auspicious debut for this provision of the Bill of Rights before the high court. The issue was not only consigned to a minor aside in the decision, but Justice Joseph Story also misidentified it as the Fifth Amendment, even as he disdainfully dismissed the states' rights theory of the amendment. Story's curt rejection did little to dampen the ardor of those who continued to believe that the Second Amendment provided the states with a means to exercise the ultimate check against federal tyranny. The debate over the meaning of the right to bear arms and its role in American constitutionalism was only just beginning.

POLITICAL MURDER

A scant two years after Hamilton and Burr had faced one another on the field of honor, partisan political acrimony resulted in yet another fatality that galvanized the nation's attention. The site for this tragedy was not an isolated field in New Jersey, but the crowded streets of Boston. The victim, Charles Austin, a Harvard student and the son of Benjamin Austin, one New England's most prominent Jeffersonians, was shot down in cold blood in front of a crowd of onlookers. Thomas Selfridge, the man charged with Austin's murder, was one of the city's most respected lawyers and a leading light of New England's Federalist establishment.[2]

The deadly encounter between Austin and Selfridge was the culmination of a complex chain of events shaped by the bitter partisan rivalries that divided Boston in the Jeffersonian era. In this highly charged climate, revelry itself was not only highly political, but took on an added competitive edge as well. Jeffersonians and Federalists vied to hold the most lavish political celebrations. Benjamin Austin had organized a Fourth of July banquet intended to entertain his fellow Jeffersonian supporters and impress his enemies. To add an exotic element to the occasion, Austin had invited the Tunisian ambassador, who arrived in "his showy oriental costume" and brought with him "a number of his attendants in rich Turkish and Moorish dresses."[3]

The lure of good food and the exotic entourage attracted many who had not purchased tickets for the event. The gate-crashers consumed far more than the Republican committee had allocated for the cost of the event. The tavern owner demanded payment in full. Since the cost for the event ran well over the agreed-upon fee, Austin balked at paying the difference. The owner of the tavern sought the advice of a Federalist lawyer, Thomas Selfridge. When Austin learned that he would be sued for the difference, he denounced the suit as the work of party spite, instigated by the tavern's Federalist attorney. Selfridge, a respected member of the city's legal establishment, charged Austin with having "circulated an infamous falsehood concerning my professional conduct." The aggrieved lawyer demanded "the satisfaction due to a gentleman." With no apology forthcoming from Austin, Selfridge followed the rules established by the code of honor. Before meeting on the field of honor, an exchange in print was usually customary. Selfridge "posted" Benjamin Austin in the *Boston Gazette*, declaring him to be "A COWARD, A LIAR, and A SCOUNDREL." Austin posted his response in the Republican *Independent Chronicle*, asserting that he would not debase himself by responding directly to Selfridge's "insolent and false publication."

When the print exchange did not resolve the matter, the chances of some sort of violent encounter increased. Rumors circulated that Austin had recruited a "bully" to give Selfridge a sound thrashing. Determined to protect himself from attack or intimidation, Selfridge armed himself with two pistols. Even as Selfridge resolved to defend himself with deadly force, young Charles Austin fulminated at the assault on his father's honor and resolved to avenge the family name. Charles often carried a walking stick, but on the day that he encountered Selfridge in the streets of Boston he had equipped himself with a "stout hickory cane." When Austin confronted Selfridge and attempted to beat him with the cane, Selfridge drew his pistol and fatally wounded his attacker.[4]

The death of the young Charles Austin convulsed the city of Boston. Selfridge confessed that Austin's unfortunate death "has excised the prejudices, awakened the passions, and agitated the feelings of the community, in a manner which has neither precedent nor parallel." Onc observer noted in his diary that it was a "most interesting trial, it seems, to the whole Continent." The trial was widely reported in the contemporary press. One newspaper compared the significance of the event to the Boston Massacre and the duel between Hamilton and Burr. Public interest in the case prompted the *Boston Gazette* to observe that "the feelings of the public have been deeply agitated by this melancholy event, beyond what we recollect them to have been by any occurrence within the compass of some memory." Anticipating the public's interest in the case, the *Gazette* undertook to publish a pamphlet containing the proceedings of the trial. Believing that there would "be an immense demand for the volume," the publisher surmised that the central legal issue in the case, "the right of self defense with a mortal weapon," would be an issue of wide interest to the reading public.[5]

The repercussions of the case echoed well beyond Boston. Republicans denounced the assassination as a "Federalist murder."

Selfridge was vilified in the Republican press, prompting his attorney to caution the jury in the case that "the democratic presses throughout the country, have teemed with publications, fraught with appeals to the passions, and bitter invective against" his client. As one contemporary observer noted, "the great political parties in the State" were "arranged under their respective standards on the simple question of the guilt or innocence of an individual under criminal investigation."[6]

Attorney General James Sullivan argued the commonwealth's position, asserting that Selfridge had not been justified in arming himself and had a clear duty to retreat. There was an important difference between the situation one faced when confronted by an attacker "in the highway and an assault in a town." On a crowded city street where one might seek refuge or call on assistance, the right to arm oneself and use deadly weapons in self-defense was severely circumscribed. While the attorney general conceded that "there may be such a time in which a man may thus arm; but it could not be necessary at noon day, and when going on so public a place." Even if arming himself had been his only recourse, a view that the state rejected, then Selfridge should have not concealed his weapon. His decision to do so suggested that he was intent on playing the part of an assassin and was not simply an innocent citizen defending himself. For the prosecution, the case of Selfridge provided a clear example of the limited scope of the right to carry arms for personal protection. "All men are bound to surrender their natural rights upon entering into civil society, and the law become the guardians of the equal rights of all men." Selfridge had other options to save himself, and he had been legally bound to exhaust those before using deadly force.[7]

The issue of the right to bear arms was mentioned in passing by Selfridge's lawyer, who conceded that "every man has a right to possess military arms" and "to furnish his rooms with them." The case of Selfridge presented a different problem, however: the use of non-military weapons for individual self-defense. Rather than assert a constitutional claim that his client was simply exercising a right to bear arms in self-defense, Selfridge's attorney used the same two-prong strategy employed by lawyers in the Reynolds case less than a decade earlier. First, the defense contended that "there is no law written or unwritten, no part of the statute or common law of our country which denies to a man the right of possessing or wearing any kind of arms." Secondly, "in every free society a man is at liberty to do that which the law does not interdict, nor can the doing that which is not forbidden be imputed as a crime." Selfridge had not broken any law, and his decision to arm himself was not only entirely legal, it was also prudent.[8]

In the course of framing its arguments, the defense acknowledged that Selfridge may not have chosen his weapon wisely. Given the likely chance that a pistol might misfire, it was a notoriously poor choice for personal self-defense. Indeed, the unreliability of a handgun was used by the defense as further proof that Selfridge's actions were not criminal, but were both sensible and necessary. Given the chances of misfiring or not firing at all, Selfridge could simply not afford to fire a warning shot or aim to wound his attacker. An individual wielding a dirk, sword cane, or other edged weapon might have had the luxury of attempting to ward off an attacker by merely threatening to use the weapon or by delivering a nonlethal blow. Selfridge had no choice and had acted as any rational man would have if faced with a similar situation.[9]

The case turned on the meaning of the common-law right of self-defense. In a decision that proved to be extremely controversial, the court recast the traditional Blackstonian theory in a more expansive fashion. According to this new doctrine, one did not need to be in actual danger; one need only have had reasonable cause to fear for one's life to use deadly force in self-defense. This new standard, reasonable cause to fear for one's life, proved to be the most controversial legal issue in the case and had a profound impact on the subsequent development of the law of justifiable homicide.[10]

The *Independent Chronicle*, Benjamin Austin's paper, denounced the court's new standard. To allow an individual to respond with deadly force if he had a "reasonable ground for believing that the person slain had a felonious design against him" imperiled every citizen and was, in the view of the *Chronicle*, "calculated to disturb, rather than promote the peace of society." By effectively lowering the threshold for using violence from an actual threat to a reasonable belief that such a threat existed, the judges risked turning "every trifling fracas" into a conflict that might "end in death."[11]

The use of a concealed weapon also prompted extensive comment. The *Chronicle* printed a number of articles critical of this practice. One acerbic commentator mocked the upper-class pretensions of Federalists and attacked the "knights of the concealed pistol," a group that he predicted would soon be provoking controversies so they could dispatch their opponents with the help of their favorite weapons of choice. Republicans linked Selfridge's pistol with class privilege and painted the Federalists as a murderous elite.[12]

The Federalist press returned fire with equal intensity. The *Port Folio*, a leading Federalist magazine, praised Selfridge, who had acted in self-defense and attacked his Jacobin enemies, partisans of the excesses of the French Revolution. In the view of Federalists, the common law, both in England and America, justified Selfridge's actions. Indeed, Selfridge's actions were not only legal, but were also justified by Christian teachings that accepted the legitimacy of self-defense. Interestingly, the one legal source that the *Folio* did not choose to invoke was the constitutional right to keep and bear arms. The discussion in the press, including Jeffersonian and Federalist papers, saw the issue as one of common law, not constitutional law.[13]

The jury accepted the argument that Selfridge acted in self-defense. While Federalists breathed a collective sigh of relief, Jeffersonians were outraged. Dr. Nathaniel Ames, a contemporary observer and supporter of Austin's cause, remarked in his diary about the intensity of the public's anger over the acquittal.

Jan. 1, 1807. Selfridge's effigy hanged in Boston.

Jan. 10. Selfridge still hung in effigy various places.

Jan. 31. Selfridge and Chief Justice Parsons hung in effigy in divers parts of continent, New York, Salem, etc.[14]

Benjamin Austin did not passively accept the outcome of the trial. Within a year of the trial's conclusion Austin presented a memorial to the legislature, imploring them to take action to correct the court's expansive definition of the right of self-defense. Austin claimed that the expansive notion of self-defense actually violated several provisions of the state's constitution. The preamble to the state constitution affirmed that the purpose of government was to "furnish the individuals who compose it with the power of enjoying, in safety and tranquility, their natural rights and the blessings of life." Austin also quoted from the state's bill of rights, which affirmed that "no individual shall be deprived of his *life*, but by the judgment of his Peers, or the law of the land." Similarly, the provision of the constitution asserting that "each individual of the society has a right to be protected by it in the enjoyment of his life, liberty and property, according to standing laws" was undermined if the judiciary were free to reinterpret the meaning of the right of self-defense unilaterally.[15]

The legislature considered Austin's appeal but concluded that this was a matter best left to the courts to apply on a case-by-case basis. The meaning of self-defense had evolved under the common law in response to myriad changes in society. It was simply impossible for any legislature to define with the requisite precision a body of criminal law to deal with every case that might arise. It was precisely the genius of the common law to develop by the slow accumulation of wisdom a set of rules that might help guide judges on how to construe the meaning of murder, manslaughter, and excusable homicide. Legislatures could never hope to create a body of statutes sufficiently flexible or comprehensive enough to deal with so complicated an issue.

The impact of the Selfridge case could still be felt decades later. The notorious events of "Bloody Monday" were "long remembered" for years after the trial. In 1842, the *Boston Law Reporter* included the Selfridge case among its list of America's most "remarkable trials." In his influential treatise on homicide, published in the middle of the century, the eminent jurist Francis Wharton devoted considerable attention to

Selfridge's case, and he even went to the trouble of including long excerpts from the trial transcript in an appendix to his volume. According to Wharton, the key issue had been the one that Austin and the *Independent Chronicle* had fastened on and tried to dispute: the notion that one had only to have a reasonable fear for one's life to respond with deadly force. After Selfridge, the law of justifiable homicide gave greater latitude to defendants to plead that their response had been premised on a potential threat, not an actual threat. Although Wharton believed the law had been interpreted properly, he did express some skepticism about the claim that Selfridge's fear had been reasonable under the circumstances. As Wharton noted, "He had not retreated to the wall, for he fired instantaneously, at the first encounter," and "It cannot be said that a man of thirty, armed with a pistol, can be reduced to desperate danger by the onset of another of eighteen, with a cane in his hand, of which he was holding the heavy butt-end, in a street in which there were a dozen spectators." Thus, Wharton applauded the underlying legal principle elaborated in the case even as he doubted whether the facts had justified the outcome.[16]

THE SIEGE OF FORT RITTENHOUSE: TESTING THE STATES' RIGHTS THEORY OF THE MILITIA

Less than a decade later, after Jefferson had threatened to use the Pennsylvania militia to prevent Federalists from stealing the election of 1800, the militia of the Keystone State was mobilized to fend off a threat posed by the federal government. In 1809, members of the Pennsylvania militia stood poised, bayonets at the ready, to prevent the federal government from executing a legal writ issued by the U.S. Supreme Court. The state of Pennsylvania had ordered out its militia to prevent a federal marshal from serving a court order against two old ladies, the heirs to the disputed estate of David Rittenhouse, former treasurer of the state of Pennsylvania. The cause of the conflict was not a weighty matter of constitutional law, but an argument over the proceeds from the sale of a ship captured during the American Revolution.[17]

The confrontation in the streets of Philadelphia was the final chapter in a long and bitter quarrel over the ship *Active*, a British vessel seized during the American Revolution. Gideon Olmstead, one of the litigants, had commandeered the ship and claimed exclusive right to the proceeds from its sale. The state of Pennsylvania disputed this claim. Olmstead, they argued, had not completely secured control of the ship before it had been boarded by a ship outfitted by the state of Pennsylvania. The prize money had been the subject of protracted litigation, and the funds had eventually been deposited in the personal account of the state treasurer, David Rittenhouse, pending resolution of the lawsuit. After Rittenhouse's death the money became the property of his estate and passed on to his heirs, two elderly daughters.[18]

Olmstead sued Rittenhouse's estate in federal court in 1803 and won a favorable judgment. Unfortunately, his efforts to collect were stymied by the state of Pennsylvania, which passed a law that directed the governor "to protect the just rights of the state" and to use whatever "means and measures that he may deem necessary" to prevent the court from enforcing its judgment against Rittenhouse's daughters. The formal resolution adopted by the General Assembly echoed the language of the Virginia and Kentucky Resolutions, proclaiming that "the causes and reasons which have produced this conflict" should be made public for the benefit of "her sister states, who are equally interested in the preservation of the state rights." Governor Simon Snyder believed that Madison's well-known support for states' rights would lead him to back Pennsylvania's claims. Indeed, the governor described the president as a man who was both "intimately acquainted with the principles of the Federal Constitution, and who is no less disposed to protect the Sovereignty and independence of the several States." Unfortunately for Snyder, President Madison was no

longer the leader of an opposition battling against a strongly nationalist and entrenched Federalist administration. He was in fact embroiled
in a states' rights challenge from New England Federalists. During
the Napoleonic wars, Jefferson restricted American trade with bel-
ligerent nations as a means of avoiding war. Madison had inherited
this unpopular embargo policy, and by 1809 frustration with the
policy had grown so intense in parts of New England that the region
was nearly in a state of open rebellion. Pennsylvania's ill-timed appeal
to states' rights was not very likely to win much sympathy from the
president.[19]

The federal courts' decisions in favor of Olmstead placed the
Madison administration on a collision course with Pennsylvania.
Federal marshal John Smith was dispatched to serve the writ against
the Rittenhouse heirs. As he approached their elegant home, Smith
was accosted by a group of armed Pennsylvania militiamen. One eager
militiaman pressed his bayonet to the chest of the startled marshal,
ordering him to cease and desist. Smith demanded to speak to the officer
in charge. General Michael Bright was quickly summoned to the
scene. The marshal informed Bright and his men that he would
execute his writ. As Smith stepped forward toward the house, a militiaman again raised his bayonet to the marshal's chest and General Bright
informed Smith that if he took another step it would be "at the peril
of your life." The marshal prudently withdrew, narrowly avoiding
violence. Contemporary commentators noted that the nation had stood
a bayonet's length away from a conflict that might have triggered a
major constitutional crisis and a civil war.[20]

Although the source of the conflict was "a paltry sum," the principle of states' rights was not a trifling matter to Governor Snyder, who
had put his own political reputation and the honor of his state on
the line. In framing their challenge to the federal court's decree,
Pennsylvania made ample use of the language of states' rights and the
fears of consolidation that had defined Anti-Federalist and Republican
thought for the previous decade. The survival of the "Federal system"

depended on the "State governments, with their inherent rights" which "must, at every hazard be preserved intire; otherwise the general government may assume a character, never contemplated by its framers." The governor's supporters in the legislature asserted that Pennsylvania had "a sacred duty" requiring it to "discard pusillanimity on the one hand, and rashness on the other." As had been true in the trial of Thomas Selfridge, the mixture of personal honor and partisan politics created a volatile situation.[21]

Snyder's critics lambasted "his imperil highness Ignoramus the First, governor of Pennsylvania and supreme commander of the defense of Fort Rittenhouse." His opponents took to the streets to protest his decision to risk war over such a trivial sum. On at least two occasions the confrontation between the militia and angry citizens erupted into a full-blown riot. Additional evidence of the controversial nature of Pennsylvania's policy can be gathered from the state's difficulty mustering its militia to support its policy. Once again, militiamen exercised an indirect veto over government policy, offering passive resistance to actions they viewed as rash and ill advised. General Bright complained on several occasions about the difficulty of finding troops to serve and worried that he might not be able to locate enough troops to mount an effective resistance against the federal marshal, who was summoning a federal posse to enforce the court's judgment. The looming conflict between Bright's militiamen and the federal marshal's posse cast a pall over a city already tense and deeply divided.[22]

While politicians debated how best to proceed, the federal marshal was engaged in a comic game of cat and mouse with the two elderly widows. On one occasion the resourceful marshal managed to evade the militia guard and enter the house, only to find that the ladies had absconded. The affair was finally resolved when the wily marshal scaled several fences and succeeded in crawling through a back window to deliver his writ. The tense situation in the streets of Philadelphia had dissolved into farce. With continued opposition now rendered moot,

Snyder withdrew the militia from the scene. The *Philadelphia Aurora* observed that the new nation had never experienced "any thing in which the serious and the ludicrous were so strangely intermixed."[23]

Pennsylvania's aggressive posture was particularly disturbing to the Madison administration, who were coping with the problem of maintaining Jefferson's embargo policy. At the very same moment that the nation was seeking to avoid hostile engagement with Britain and France, Pennsylvania appeared to be engaged in a deliberately provocative challenge to federal authority. The peaceful resolution of the siege of Fort Rittenhouse did not put an end to the affair. Angered by Pennsylvania's defiant behavior, the Madison administration brought charges against General Bright for "obstructing, resisting and opposing the execution of the writ of arrest issued out of the District Court." When the case went to trial, U.S. Attorney Alexander Dallas, who had defended James Reynolds, now represented the government. He reminded jury members of the serious nature of Bright's actions. "The whole power of the confederation, if necessary in arms, against the whole power of one of its members" was a "momentous crisis" that threatened the very foundation of the republic. Dallas compared Pennsylvania's efforts to the kind of lawless behavior of the Whiskey Rebels.[24]

One of the most remarkable exchanges in the trial dealt with the constitutional right of armed resistance. Bright's attorney, Jared Ingersoll, tried to force the U.S. attorney to concede that states retained a constitutional right of resistance. The prosecution disputed the logic of the states' rights position, arguing that such a view of the rights of the states and the obligations of citizenship would lead to anarchy and civil war. The prosecution even went so far as to concede that secession would be a more logical legal response to hypothetical federal tyranny than armed resistance to dully constituted authority. As long as she remained within the union, Pennsylvania was "bound to the authority of the union, expressed through the regular acts of government."

The resort to violence was tantamount to an act of rebellion or revolution. In short, while there might be a natural right of revolution, there was no constitutional right of armed resistance.[25]

The defense asserted a states' rights argument that had become a fixture of constitutional dissent since the Anti-Federalists first voiced it more than two decades before. "Pennsylvania is a free, sovereign and independent state, and has a right to call upon her citizens to protect her just rights and privileges." States retained a right of "self-preservation" and the defendants in this case "did no more than their duty in obeying the orders which they received." Bright's actions were hardly akin to those of the Whiskey Rebels. If anything, Bright's actions were closer in spirit to the American Revolutionaries'.[26]

The jury wrestled with the complex issues in the case and ultimately issued a special verdict, an unusual outcome that reflected their ambivalence about convicting Bright. The jury clearly was unhappy with the court's instruction on how the law was to be applied and came very close to exonerating Bright. Instead, they adopted a compromise, conceding that if the judge's rendering of the law was correct, then Bright had clearly broken the law. In the end Bright was sentenced to a fine and a three-month jail sentence. As one of Madison's supporters in Pennsylvania noted, "Altho nine tenth of the thinking men are of the opinion the sentence against General Bright and those under his command is perfectly correct yet notwithstanding nothing would give *us all* more pleasure and satisfaction than to see your Pardon extended to those men." Madison followed this sage advice and promptly issued a pardon to diffuse any lingering resentment. Although it had been a divisive issue, there was considerable popular sympathy for Bright, who after his release was paraded through the city. A celebration honoring Bright drew three hundred participants. The toasts offered on that occasion praised the principles of states' rights and the militia.[27]

The legacy of the Olmstead affair was mixed. While the federal government scored a modest victory, Bright's continuing popularity demonstrated that sympathy for the states' rights view of the militia had not been crushed. Indeed, the revolutionary potential of Pennsylvania's defense of states' rights was not lost on later proponents of this view who cited the "Pennsylvania Doctrine" as a vindication of their theory.[28]

CONTINUING CONTROVERSY OVER THE MILITIA

The conflict between Pennsylvania and the Madison administration over the Olmstead affair had been exacerbated by tensions arising from the embargo, a policy that was deeply resented in New England and seaport cities. Growing fears about the possibility of being dragged into European affairs in the Napoleonic era worried many in Congress and prompted a reconsideration of the problem of how to arm the militia. There was widespread agreement in Congress that the Militia Act of 1792, which required citizens to outfit themselves with a musket and ammunition, had been largely unsuccessful. A federal census of the militia's weaponry demonstrated that America's first line of defense against foreign and internal threats was woefully underarmed. To be sure, members of Congress bickered over how to interpret the numbers produced by the census, and a few voices in Congress even argued that the recent census might have underreported the number of guns. These quibbles aside, there was a broad consensus that America's militia was not yet properly armed. As one member lamented, "no discipline could make soldiers of men who mustered with canes and cornstalks." The idea that America needed a well-regulated militia composed of the trained and armed body of the people was beyond dispute. Widespread agreement on the importance of protecting this civic right did not mean that Americans were in agreement about how to achieve this venerable ideal. Should the government give muskets to citizens directly or provide the states with weapons? Some argued that guns given directly to citizens would be sold by individual militiamen for personal profit. Others argued the opposite case, noting that unless guns were owned by individuals there would be no incentive to maintain them in good working order.[29]

Even in the midst of a debate over how best to defend the nation against a potential threat from Europe, some within Congress worried about a danger closer to home from the "arbitrary exactions and unconstitutional oppressions" instigated by "the machinations of their own rulers." For those who carried forward this Anti-Federalist and Republican vision it was essential that the "States should be enabled effectually to assert those rights, or to resist those encroachments" by arming their own militias. This more radical states' rights conception of the militia did not garner much support in Congress, but the fact that it found any advocates in Congress at all in the midst of a military emergency is significant, and testifies to the enduring power of this ideology. When the issue about arming the militia was finally resolved, Congress adopted a compromise that gave the states tremendous latitude to determine the best manner for arming their populations.[30]

Despite the best efforts of Jefferson and Madison, America was drawn into war with Britain in 1812. Hostility to the war was especially keen in New England, which had taken up the banner of states' rights. Faced with a central government engaged in policies they viewed as inimical to their interests and potentially subversive of liberty, Federalists had adopted many of the ideas articulated by Republicans more than a decade earlier. In Massachusetts, petitions poured into the legislature demanding that the state "interpose" and protect the rights and well-being of its citizens. Some towns even suggested that it might be necessary to use force to oppose the embargo. Armed public safety committees were created in some towns. Some radical voices in New England advocated direct armed resistance and even went so far as to recommend creating a force of thirty thousand men to protect citizens from the unconstitutional violations of their liberty enacted by the Madison administration. The irony of Federalists invoking states' rights theory was not lost on contemporaries. The *Richmond Enquirer* proclaimed, "Things turned Topsy Turvy—Federalists turn Anti-Federalists—The Friends of Order turned Jacobin."[31]

The antiwar political campaign was led by an aggressive group of young Federalist newspaper editors. One of the most vociferous critics of the war was a young and impetuous Baltimore Federalist editor, Alexander Hanson, whose *Federal Republican* excoriated administration policy. Supporters of the war rioted and attacked the paper's offices, destroying Hanson's printing press. Rather than call out the militia, the mayor of Baltimore, Edward Johnson, intervened, calming down the crowd and ordering it to disperse. The mayor's reluctance to use force was not simply a reflection of his sympathy with the war effort, but an implicit recognition that mob action was a legitimate expression of the will of the people. Crowd action in both England and America had a long history. As long as the actions of the mob stayed within the limits established by custom, many magistrates and politicians were apt to overlook extralegal action. According to the traditional scenario that had been played out time and again in the Anglo-American world, the potential victims of mob violence had two options. Either they might flee, as British customs officials had done in the Liberty riot, or accept the ritual humiliation and physical harassment meted out by the community, as Federalists in Carlisle had suffered during ratification.[32]

While the Jeffersonian mob and the mayor of Baltimore followed the traditional script for this rough-and-tumble example of political street theater, Hanson and the young Federalists decided to adopt a different role. The Federalists prepared to defend their lives and their honor by arms if necessary. The mayor pleaded with the Federalists to abandon this defiant attitude, advising them that such action was not legally defensible and was likely to inflame the situation further. Johnson suggested that the Federalists return home and depend on his own authority to keep the peace.[33]

Rather than heed the mayor's advice, Hanson and his associates armed themselves and prepared to resume printing their antiadministration polemics. Hanson rented a solid, three-story brick building, a structure which he believed could be more easily defended from the mob. Republican supporters laid siege to his new residence, dubbed by some as "Fort Hanson." Resolved to defend "the house, which was his castle," Hanson and supporters were prepared to use deadly force if necessary. Some of his fellow Federalists doubted the wisdom of adopting such a defiant posture. Not everyone agreed with Hanson's view that armed resistance was fully justified. The group arrived at a compromise, deciding to fire a warning volley over the heads of the crowd in the hope that this would scatter them. The warning had the opposite of its intended effect. After dispersing, the enraged crowd returned to the scene with their own arms.[34]

When the armed crowd rushed the house, the occupants opened fire and killed one of the rioters. In the melee that followed, more shots were fired. Before the situation deteriorated into complete anarchy, a small contingent of militia finally arrived and intervened. The Federalists were escorted into protective custody and marched to the local jail. Rounding up enough militiamen to intervene had not been easy. Many citizens had refused the call to muster. As had been true during the Whiskey Insurrection and the Siege of Fort Rittenhouse, militiamen exercised a passive veto on government policy, reserving the right to judge for themselves whether or not the government's actions were legitimate. Believing the Federalists were traitors who did not deserve protection, many militiamen simply refused to turn out.[35]

The riot was widely covered in the press. One newspaper reported that the Baltimore Riot presented a "theater of the most distressing scenes this country has witnessed for many years." Another paper described the events as an example of "perfidy and cruelty" without parallel in American history. The devastation and destruction wrought by the rioters earned Baltimore the nickname "mob town" for years to come.[36]

Hanson's decision to use firearms to defend himself proved to be extremely controversial. Commentaries in the press broke down along partisan lines, with Federalists praising Hanson's actions and Republicans denouncing them. While Federalists praised Hanson's decision to resume publication as a vindication of "liberty of the press, guaranteed to him by the constitutional laws of his country," they did not see his use of firearms in similar terms. As had been true in both the Reynolds and Selfridge cases, the defensive use of firearms was not cast as an exercise of a right to bear arms but was defended under common law. Federalists defended the use of firearms by claiming that "a man's home is his castle." The Jeffersonian press disputed this claim, arguing that Hanson was not at home, but at a place of business. Moreover, they argued that his actions were not defensive, but that he had deliberately armed himself and intended to precipitate a bloody confrontation. Denouncing Federalists as Tories, the Jeffersonian press heaped scorn on them as a bunch of "desperados" intent on murder. Rather than accept the argument that Hanson had acted in accordance with well-established common-law principles of self-defense, Jeffersonians saw the events in a different light. As one paper noted, "They assembled in arms, to the terror of the people of Baltimore." If he feared violence, Hanson was obligated to seek lawful help, not take the law into his own hands.[37]

A special commission was held to investigate the cause of the riot. A number of witnesses viewed Hanson's belligerence as the root cause of the riot. In their view, his decision to arm himself had deliberately provoked a violent confrontation. Hanson's life was not in danger, only his sense of pride. If he refused to accept humiliation at the hands of the crowd, he should have fled the scene. Flight, not fight, was the only morally and legally acceptable course of action. Having rejected the option of flight, he was obliged to bear his humiliation and accept whatever punishment the crowd chose to deal him.[38]

The debate over who provoked the violence split the community along party lines. One Federalist testified that great effort had been expended to avoid "any display of arms." Another Federalist took great pains to prove that weapons had been smuggled into the building so that they would not attract attention. One person testified that Federalists had gone so far as to disguise a cask of gunpowder as a barrel of crackers. Republicans wove a different tale. According to their testimony, Federalists were brazen in their actions. The cache of weapons was not discretely brought into the printing offices but had been unloaded by a group of men with swords drawn, hardly an inconspicuous effort to avoid inflaming the situation.[39]

The commission investigating the riot explored a number of legal issues concerning the use of firearms, the legitimacy of mob action, and the use of the militia to maintain public order. The actions of the Baltimore mob harked back to an earlier time, when the use of crowd action as a means of enforcing communal norms was an accepted part of Anglo-American law. Indeed, one of the mayor's advisors testified that he was not even sure one could call out the militia to put down the mob. The militia, according to this view, could only be used in cases of invasion or insurrection. Since the mob was acting in support of government policy, it could hardly be described as insurrectionary. In this sense there was little commonality between this mob and the actions of the Whiskey Rebels or the farmers in Fries's Rebellion. The mob in Baltimore had directed its anger at private citizens who had criticized the government, going so far as to denounce them as Tories, an epithet that not only linked them to the British, but also clearly attempted to place them outside of the protection of American law. The mayor's reluctance to use the militia against citizens engaged in protest was entirely consistent with traditional republican approaches to crowd action. Until the violence escalated out of control and mob action moved beyond property damage and simple harassment of dissenters, Baltimore officials were prepared to tolerate the mob and its actions.[40]

The Baltimore Riot also demonstrates that ideas about the legitimate use of firearms for self-defense were far from settled in American law. The fact that the Federalists had chosen to arm themselves was read by Republicans as a sign of their nefarious designs, not as a legitimate exercise of the right of self-defense. Potential victims of crowd action were not entitled to defend themselves with force of arms. Federalists in Baltimore clearly refused to accept the role they had been assigned in this political street theater and believed that their decision to arm themselves was legal and perfectly moral.

The Baltimore Riot also provides another example of how ill defined American constitutional law was when it came to the subject of the militia. Once again, when faced with a crisis, the loyalty of the militia proved to be up for grabs. When ordered to defend the ideals of law and order and protect the Federalists, many militiamen simply refused the call to muster. This failure would have struck Federalists as yet another sign that this institution had failed to fulfill its proper legal function. Yet, for those who continued to adhere to a distinctly Anti-Federalist and Jeffersonian conception of states' rights, or even those who clung to a more populist and localist vision of American constitutionalism, the failure of the militia to turn out was a vindication of their ideals. Despite the efforts of the Constitution to nationalize aspects of this institution, the militia remained in many respects a creature of the states and in some cases of the local community.

Alexis de Tocqueville, author of *Democracy in America*, traveled to Baltimore more than two decades later and was regaled with stories about the "siege of Fort Hanson." Peter Hoffman Cruse, editor of the *Baltimore American*, explained to the young French nobleman that "the militia, itself, is the populace, and is of no use when it partakes or condones the passions of the majority." After summarizing the tumultuous events surrounding the siege of Fort Hanson, Cruse noted that "an attempt was made to call the militia; it refused to march against the rioters and did not respond to the call." The refusal of the militia to protect the protestors, Cruse noted, was a form of passive resistance and served as a popular check on government authority. In this sense the militia functioned in a fashion almost exactly analogous to the jury, which had refused to convict the leaders of the Republican mob. As Cruse noted, "An effort was made to prosecute in the courts, but the juries acquitted the guilty parties." Both the jury and the militia acted as faithful mirrors of popular belief, and when government overstepped its bounds, the jury and the militia could interpose themselves between citizens and the government to avert a miscarriage of justice.[41]

THE CONSTITUTIONAL QUARREL OVER THE MILITIA IN THE WAR OF 1812

The fate of Alexander Hanson and the destruction wrought by the mob in Baltimore were themselves a reflection of the intensity of feeling and the depth of the divisions generated by the War of 1812. Hostility to the Madison administration was felt most deeply in New England, where popular dissatisfaction bordered on rebellion. Even among the established elite in New England, opposition to the war led many to contemplate secession as a serious possibility. Given the depth of disagreement over the war, it is hardly surprising that governors in New England were reluctant to allow their state militias to support the war effort. The federal government even sought to use conscription to raise the necessary troops to meet the war effort. The challenges of raising troops for the war prompted another reexamination of the constitutional role of the militia.[42]

Federalists attacked conscription as unconstitutional, arguing that the Constitution authorized the use of militia or the creation of a volunteer professional army, not an army of conscripts. In yet another constitutional irony, the language of states' rights was again adopted by Federalists to challenge Madison's war plans. Perhaps the most eloquent attack on the administration's policies was framed by Daniel Webster, who argued that if necessary the states had a "solemn duty" to "interpose between their citizens and arbitrary power." To justify this stance, Webster turned to New Hampshire's own state constitution, which affirmed that "the doctrine of non-resistance against arbitrary power and oppression is absurd, slavish, and destructive of the good and happiness of mankind." Webster did not interpret this clause of his state constitution as authorizing individuals, or even local communities, to nullify unjust government policy, but he did believe that states might exercise such a check. The right of resistance was self-consciously framed in constitutional terms; Webster advocated legal measures, not extralegal armed violence. In the unlikely event that force was required, the only legitimate mode of action was through the state governments. Republican efforts to win approval for conscription ultimately foundered on the shoals of Federalist opposition.[43]

Conscription was not the only controversy arising from the ambiguous role of the militia under American constitutional law. New Englanders opposed the Madison administration's use of the militia to fight an offensive war against British Canada. Opponents of this policy insisted that state militias could only be used defensively to repel an imminent threat of invasion or put down domestic insurrection. The governor of Massachusetts took the extraordinary step of requesting an advisory opinion from his own state supreme court on the appropriate constitutional uses of the militia in time of war. The judges of the Massachusetts court held that the authority to decide when to call out the militia rested with the governors of each state. While the president might request that the militia be called out, he could only do so with approval of the governor of the state from which the troops were requested. The Massachusetts' court emphasized the limited nature of the Constitution's grant of authority over the militia and implicitly endorsed the idea that the states were constitutionally empowered to engage in a form of passive resistance to federal power by refusing to muster their militias when the summons came from the president.[44]

During the 1790s, when Federalists had been ascendant, Republican constitutional thought had embraced a strong states' rights agenda. Now that Republicans were in control of the central government,

Federalists found many of the same sorts of arguments congenial and used them to oppose Republican policy. James Monroe, Madison's secretary of war, reflected on this irony. He declared his own support for the "rights of the individual States" as indispensably necessary for the "existence of our Union, and of free government in these States." Acknowledging this point, however, did not mean that Monroe accepted the conclusions of the Massachusetts court's advisory opinion. Although the Massachusetts court had not sanctioned the most radical version of the states' rights theory of the militia employed during the electoral crisis of 1800, a view that would have authorized armed resistance to federal power, the court did lend its own considerable moral authority to the notion that states might exert a form of passive resistance to federal policy. Still, the fact that this more moderate variant of states' rights theory had been endorsed by the highest judicial body in Massachusetts alarmed Monroe. The judges, in Monroe's view, had carried "the doctrine of State rights further than I have ever known it to be carried in any other instance." Monroe was technically correct in his assessment. Although Jefferson had embraced a more radical view in 1800, he had not acted upon that theory. Moreover, Jefferson's views were not a formal legal pronouncement by a court. Even in the form of an advisory opinion, a judgment that had no legal force on its own, the Massachusetts high court had given the doctrine of states' rights an invaluable boost. The logic of the court's misguided interpretation of the Constitution, Monroe declared, would leave the nation exceedingly vulnerable to military attack. Monroe also used the occasion provided by his rebuke of the court to underscore the Madison administration's belief that there was no right of resistance against the "legitimate authority of the United States," a statement that took on added urgency in light of the unrest occasioned in New England by an unpopular war.[45]

The disagreement between Monroe and the Massachusetts Supreme Court judges arose because the exact boundaries between federal and state control of the militia outlined in the Constitution were open to widely different interpretations. In the case of *Houston v. Moore*, this problem came before the Supreme Court in another context. The case concerned the authority over courts-martial once the militia had been mustered, a seemingly less contentious issue than the one that divided Monroe and the Massachusetts State Supreme Court. While the incident at the root of *Houston v. Moore* appeared to be less momentous, the issues in the case forced the question of how authority over the militia would be divided between the states and the federal government. The case also marked the first time the Second Amendment was invoked in a Supreme Court decision.

The issue in *Houston* dealt with the court-martial of a Pennsylvania militiaman who failed to report to muster. Although Houston had violated a federal statute, he was tried by a state court-martial. The question before the court dealt with the right of the states to hold such tribunals. Had the state court trenched on a matter that was exclusively within the jurisdiction of the federal courts? The Supreme Court issued a divided ruling, a fact that further illustrated the unsettled nature of thinking about the militia's role in the federal system. Justice Bushrod Washington, George Washington's nephew, delivered the opinion of the court, declaring that Congress had not given the federal courts exclusive jurisdiction in these matters. Houston's conviction was upheld. The decision was hardly a model of clarity, and Justice Washington confessed that the Constitution's treatment of the division of authority over the militia had not been "formed with as much wisdom as, in the opinion of some, it might have been, or as time and experience may hereafter suggest." Justice Joseph Story, who appears to have consulted with Chief Justice Marshall, authored a dissent that asserted a more robust view of federal power over the militia. Story argued that Pennsylvania was precluded from exercising any authority once Congress had acted to legislate in this area. Story did not doubt the right of the states to "organize, arm, and discipline its own militia in the absence of, or subordinate to, the regulations of Congress." Once Congress acted, state authority was effectively preempted by federal supremacy.

In a brief aside, Story considered the Second Amendment and mistakenly described it as the Fifth. Story noted that there was disagreement over how to interpret the language of this provision of the Constitution. He captured this confusion when he noted that some would argue that it "may not, perhaps, be thought to have any important bearing" on the question before the Court. If it did have any relevance, Story thought it "confirms and illustrates, rather than impugns the reasoning already suggested." The Constitution clearly gave Congress ultimate authority over the militia.[46]

Story recognized that the Second Amendment had been adopted to assuage the exaggerated fears of Anti-Federalists. There had been many who had worried if "congress should refuse to provide for arming or organizing them, the result would be, that the states would be utterly without the means of defense, and prostrate at the feet of the national government." Story confessed it was difficult to understand why this concern had loomed so large in the minds of Americans at the time the Constitution was proposed. Although entirely unfounded, such fears had been "urged with much apparent sincerity and earnestness." Precisely because these apprehensions were "extensively felt, and sedulously cherished," Congress had included protection for a well-regulated militia and the right to bear arms had been included among the amendments proposed by Congress. The adoption of the Second Amendment did not, however, in Story's view, change the fact that the militia was ultimately controlled by Congress.[47]

A staunch nationalist, Story had little sympathy with the Anti-Federalist suspicions that lay at the core of the Second Amendment. Story's dissent in *Houston* made clear that the inclusion of the Second Amendment did not achieve what radical Anti-Federalists had sought, a restoration of state control of the militia. In Story's view the Second Amendment did not alter the allocation of control of the militia stated in Article I, Section 8, but merely reaffirmed concurrent jurisdiction. In essence, the Second Amendment stated a political truism:

the militia was a vital institution in America's republican system of government and law. The states would continue to play a vital role in nurturing this institution, but Congress would have the final say in all matters pertaining to the militia.[48]

Story's reiteration of the civic conception of the Second Amendment, a right of citizens to keep and bear arms in a well-regulated militia, captured the dominant view of this right in the period after the War of 1812. Challenges to this ideal would become more intense, not less, in the decades to follow. The notion that the Second Amendment embodied some type of states' rights check on tyranny continued to attract many who feared the federal government's growing power. The idea of a constitutional right of resistance grounded in the Second Amendment would find other sympathetic audiences as well. The constitutional ferment over this issue would even affect the well-established line dividing the constitutional right to bear arms from the common-law right of self-defense. Rather than mark a new period of consensus, the so-called Era of Good Feelings after the War of 1812 actually ushered in one of the most tumultuous periods of change in the history of the Second Amendment and comparable state constitutional provisions.

This depiction of a militia muster from 1841 illustrates the decline of the militia during the Jacksonian era. In contrast to the Founders' well-regulated militia, this muster is a burlesque scene that mocks this once-venerated institution. (Courtesy of the Pennsylvania Academy of the Fine Arts, Philadelphia. Bequest of Henry C. Carey [The Carey Collection])

CHAPTER FIVE

RIGHTS, REGULATIONS, REVOLUTION

THE ANTEBELLUM DEBATE OVER GUNS

During his travels in the United States, the young Charles Dickens noted Americans' penchant for arming themselves with a grisly assortment of guns and knives. The English novelist recounted one story that was emblematic of the growing problem of interpersonal violence in the early Republic. The bloody incident recounted by Dickens involved a verbal exchange that turned deadly. Angry words led to an exchange of blows, and when one of the disputants in this altercation attempted to cane the other, pistols were drawn by the two men and gunfire exchanged. The fatal wound, however, was not inflicted by either man's handgun. The mortal wound, Dickens recalled, was delivered with "one of those never failing weapons, a bowie-knife."[1]

A profound change in the nature of American gun culture occurred in the early decades of the new century. Americans began sporting weapons designed primarily for personal self-defense. The expanding economy of the new century made a staggering array of these personal weapons readily available to consumers. In addition to pistols, there was a gruesome assortment of edged weapons, which, as Dickens's sordid tale suggests, were more reliable and hence more deadly than handguns. Sword canes, small daggers such as the dirk, or the fearsome knife that came to define the rough-and-tumble world of frontier life, the bowie knife (sometimes described as an Arkansas toothpick) rounded out the options available to those who wished to arm themselves with a dependable edged weapon. While many citizens outfitted themselves with these weapons, others recoiled at their countrymen's penchant for traveling armed and demanded that their legislatures take strong measures to regulate, and in some cases prohibit, this practice. The enactment of these early gun control statutes prompted a backlash that produced the first systematic defense of an individual right to bear arms in self-defense. America's first gun violence problem not only occasioned the first efforts at gun control, it also helped crystallize a new gun rights ideology.[2]

GUNS AND THE NEW INDIVIDUALISM

American society in the decades after the War of 1812 was more democratic, more aggressive, and more fragmented than the eighteenth-century world the Founding generation had inhabited. American constitutionalism both reflected this profound change and sought to constrain it in ways consistent with the ideal of well-regulated liberty. One of the most astute observers of American society in this period was the French aristocrat Alexis de Tocqueville, who arrived in America in the spring of 1831 and set out on an extensive tour of the nation. Officially, his purpose was to inspect America's prisons and report on recent reforms. In the course of his travels and interviews, Tocqueville made detailed observations on American society, which he eventually published as *Democracy in America*. According to Tocqueville, a distinguishing characteristic of American society in the 1830s, the era of Jacksonian democracy, was a pervasive spirit of individualism. The French commentator confessed that individualism was a novel term coined to capture a new idea. The world

Tocqueville encountered was one in transition. The struggle between traditional republican values and a new culture of individualism had a profound impact on legal thinking about the right to bear arms, the militia, and the idea of self-defense.[3]

The practice of traveling armed with concealed weapons was one of the most dramatic examples of the new "individualism" described by Tocqueville. Some social commentators identified the origins of this practice with the more violent nature of southern culture. In an account of his travels in the South, landscape architect Frederick Law Olmstead, the designer of New York's Central Park, reported a conversation in Kentucky in which he was told, "Among young men a bowie-knife was a universal, and a pistol a not at all unusual, companion." Journalist and historian Richard Hildreth, another contemporary observer of southern culture, remarked that weapons were usually carried for two reasons: "as a protection against slaves" and for use "in quarrels between freemen."[4]

Although closely identified with southern culture, the problems posed by concealed weapons were hardly unique to the South. One Philadelphia clergyman lamented that "carrying deadly weapons, and avenging affronts, real or imaginary, with instant death" had become a common practice in the cities of the Northeast. Indeed, he complained that "the generation of young men now coming forward in our cities, seem to think it manly to wear dirks and pistols, and to use them on the slightest provocation." An account of life in San Francisco wryly reported that it "does furnish the best bad things that are obtainable in America," including "truer guns and pistols, larger dirks and bowie knives."[5]

A number of commentators viewed the problem of concealed weapons as a manifestation of deeper troubles in Jacksonian America. Whig journalist Joseph Gales editorialized on this problem, charging that these new developments in American society and law were a "perversion of our political doctrines." These new ideas were fueled by extravagant notions of "personal rights and personal independence." The aggressive theory of self-defense that had taken hold in America was the most dangerous expression of this ideology, turning "every man into an avenger, not only of wrongs actually committed against his personal peace and safety, but renders him swift to shed blood in the very apprehension of danger or insult." Gales blamed rising levels of interpersonal violence on the new, more aggressive theories of self-defense. He lambasted as "demagogical" those who opposed regulation as "an invasion of American rights" or "unwarrantable restriction of personal liberty."[6]

Other commentators looked to profound changes in American society, blaming the forces of the market revolution for fueling the rise of individualism. Seeking an explanation for the "low value of human life" in Jacksonian America, Reverend H. A. Boardmen blamed the values of the marketplace for corrupting America. Others followed Tocqueville's lead and blamed the violence of American society on democracy. The British traveler Charles Augustus Murray looked to an excess of democracy, a charge that prompted one reviewer of his book to denounce the suggestion that "the execrable custom of carrying about the person the bowie knife, or pistol, or other deadly weapon, are properly attributable to democratic habits."[7]

The proliferation of handguns and knives not only led to more deadly interpersonal violence, but also to an escalation in the number of mortalities resulting from collective violence. By the 1840s America had entered an intense period of political unrest. Rioting and mob action wreaked havoc on American towns and cities. The primary targets of this violence, African-Americans, abolitionists, Mormons, and Catholics, were considered outsiders in American society. Firearms played a central role in the carnage of this era.[8]

In response to the perception of increasing levels of interpersonal violence, states shifted their regulatory policies toward more comprehensive measures designed to limit the use or prohibit ownership of concealed weapons. Ironically, the first gun control movement helped give birth to the first self-conscious gun rights ideology built around a constitutional right of individual self-defense. The struggle between these two opposing ideologies would have profound consequences for the subsequent history of the right to bear arms in America.

AMERICA'S FIRST GUN CONTROL MOVEMENT

Kentucky passed the first law designed to curb the practice of carrying concealed weapons in 1813. Violation of the statute was punishable by a hefty fine of one hundred dollars. That same year, Louisiana passed an even more comprehensive act banning concealed weapons. The preamble of the act explained the urgent need for such a law to stem the "assassinations and attempts to commit the same," which the authors of the law complained "have of late been of such frequent occurrences as to become a subject of serious alarm to the peaceable and well disposed inhabitants of the state." In addition to imposing a fine for traveling armed, the Louisiana statute made it a capital offense "to stab, shoot, or in any way disable another person by such concealed weapons." Although the problem of concealed weapons was particularly acute in the South, the issue was hardly uniquely southern. Indiana adopted a ban on concealed weapons in 1820. Politicians and social commentators in other parts of the country also remarked on the social problem posed by this pernicious practice. Further east, New York's Governor De Witt Clinton warned the legislature that "our present criminal code does not sufficiently provide against the consequences which may result from carrying secret arms and weapons." This cowardly practice threatened "an essential right of every free citizen." Rather than treat the right to carry concealed weapons as a fundamental liberty or constitutional right, Clinton cast the practice as a threat to public liberty. The fundamental right government needed to protect, he argued, was the right of citizens to enjoy their liberty free from the fear created by concealed weapons. In the ensuing decades, Georgia, Virginia, Alabama, and Ohio enacted laws against concealed weapons.[9]

The first laws banning concealed weapons enacted in the period between 1813 and 1859 were essentially time, place, and manner restrictions. Acting under the authority of the individual states' police powers, regulations on weapons carried forward the logic of earlier exercises of the state's regulatory powers. Prohibitions on the practice of carrying concealed weapons were little different than laws that established rules about the storage of gunpowder, restricted hunting, or prohibited the discharge of weapons in certain areas. The second wave of regulations went even further, moving beyond time, place, and manner restrictions. These new, more robust laws criminalized the sale or possession of certain weapons, effectively moving from regulation to prohibition of certain classes of weapons. In 1837, Alabama increased the penalties for using bowie knives, one of the most fearsome edged weapons. The law also placed a heavy tax on the sale of such weapons. Georgia and Tennessee followed suit with more wide-ranging laws prohibiting the sale of pistols, dirks, and sword canes. These weapons were targeted as public nuisances that might legitimately be prohibited.[10]

At approximately the same time that some states were tightening gun regulations, others were writing into their constitutions more robust statements affirming the right of individuals to have weapons for self-defense. Rather than follow the eighteenth-century model that affirmed "the right of the people to bear arms in defense of themselves and the state," Mississippi (1819) paved the way with individualistic language that proclaimed that each citizen had a right "to bear arms in defense of himself and the state." A year later, Connecticut used Mississippi as the model for its new provision on the right to bear arms. Other states rejected the new language and reaffirmed the traditional civic model of the right to bear arms. Maine's constitution, adopted the same year as Connecticut's, declared that "every citizen has a right to keep and bear arms for the common defence." Perhaps the most interesting reformulation of the right to bear arms in the Jacksonian era occurred in the 1820 Missouri constitution, which asserted "that the people have the right peaceably to assemble for their common good, and to apply to those vested with the powers of government for redress of grievances by petition or remonstrance; and that their right to bear arms in defence of themselves and of the State cannot be questioned." Missouri not only chose the older civic language, but it also framed the right of assembly in a distinctly eighteenth-century fashion, affirming that it was a right to assemble to promote the common good. The right to assemble and the right to bear arms were each civic activities that engaged citizens in a collective effort. The linkage between the two in the Missouri Constitution made these connections even more pronounced.[11]

Detailed records of the debates within these early Jacksonian-era constitutional conventions do not exist. Some sense of the spectrum of contemporary opinion on the right to bear arms, however, can be obtained from the debates in the Michigan constitutional convention (1835), which were recorded. The convention's first formulation of this right echoed Mississippi's language, which provided that "every man shall have a right to bear arms in defense of himself and the state." A motion was made to strike this language and replace it with a more traditional civic formulation: "Every citizen shall have a right to keep and bear arms in the common defense." One delegate challenged this civic formulation, fearing that "the legislature might forbid a man to keep a musket." Proponents of a more expansive and individualistic conception of the right to bear arms eventually prevailed, and the convention restored the more individualistic language it had originally borrowed from Mississippi.[12]

The two opposing theories of the right to bear arms, civic and individual, collided in court when citizens challenged the new gun control laws enacted by state legislatures. As judges struggled to make sense of the meaning of the right to bear arms and weighed the new restrictions on the possession and use of firearms, they considered the scope and meaning of the right to bear arms under state constitutional law.

JUDGING THE RIGHT TO BEAR ARMS

Kentucky's law against wearing concealed weapons, including sword canes, produced the first serious court challenge to the new gun control laws. In *Bliss v. Commonwealth* (1822) the state supreme court reversed the lower court's decision that upheld this law. The Kentucky court not only interpreted bearing arms as an individual right, but it asserted that this right was not subject to reasonable regulation. "Whatever restrains the full and complete exercise of that right, though not an entire destruction of it, is forbidden by the explicit language of the Constitution." The notion that constitutional rights were "absolutes without any limits short of the moral power of the citizens to exercise it" stood well outside mainstream jurisprudence in both the Founding and antebellum eras.[13]

The *Bliss* court's extremism prompted outrage in Kentucky. A committee of the state's House of Representatives ridiculed the court's decision. To suppose that bearing arms referred to carrying weapons in a private capacity for self-defense was "perfectly ridiculous" since the state could not compel one to "wear dirks or knives for the purposes of self-defense." In its detailed critique of the logic and assumptions of the ruling, the Kentucky House not only delivered a stinging rebuke to the justices for their odd construction of the state constitution, but the legislature also presented one of the most lucid explications of the traditional civic meaning of bearing arms in the antebellum period.[14]

According to the Kentucky House, the *Bliss* court had misconstrued the historical origins of the right to bear arms, which had nothing to do with personal self-defense but was occasioned by the historical memory of specific "acts of tyranny and oppression" endured by the ancestors of those who had drafted the Constitution. The right to bear arms was intended to prevent the government from disarming the militia. The arms covered by this clause were clearly the "weapons of the soldier, such as could be advantageously used in opposition to government" not those "appropriate to individual contest in private broils." After faulting the court's shoddy understanding of history, the committee then turned to the language of the text, observing that "the term 'to bear arms,' is in common parlance, even at this day, most usually and most appropriately applied only to the distinctive arms of the soldier, such as the musket or rifle." Ordinary usage supported a military reading of this phrase, and to illustrate this point the committee pointed out that young boys, the old, and the infirm were still listed among those groups exempted from the obligation to bear arms.[15]

In addition to the historical evidence and textual arguments against the individualistic reading of the right to bear arms, the house committee offered one other argument based on the structure of the Kentucky Constitution. The phrase *bear arms* appeared in an earlier provision of the Constitution that exempted those with conscientious objections to military service from bearing arms. One of the "well established rules of construction" governing the interpretation of legal texts, they stated authoritatively, was that "the same phrase should receive one and the same construction, in every part of one and the same instrument; and where it is doubtful as used in one part, it shall be settled by its meaning as used in another part." The court should have interpreted the meaning of the phrase *bearing arms* in the same sense in which it was used in the clause protecting the rights of conscientious objectors. Since the legislature had no power to compel citizens to bear arms for personal defense, the only reasonable interpretation was that bearing arms did not refer to personal self-defense, but was an activity inextricably linked to common defense. Kentucky eventually changed the language of its state constitution to effectively overrule the *Bliss* court's holding, explicitly enacting an amendment allowing the legislature to ban concealed weapons.[16]

In the decades after *Bliss* a number of courts weighed in on the issue, and most rejected its individual rights reading of arms bearing. Two cases in particular would come to define the orthodox legal view of the matter. The first of these cases, *Aymette v. State* (1840), involved the constitutionality of a Tennessee law against bowie knives. The court's decision echoed many of the ideas advanced by the Kentucky House in its critique of *Bliss*. The meaning of the constitution's provision on arms bearing had to be deduced from the evil it had sought to alleviate. Tracing the roots of this principle to an ancient Anglo-American opposition to standing armies, the court concluded that the purpose of the right was to make it possible for the people to unite "for their common defense to vindicate their rights." Building on this premise, the court averred that the only weapons entitled to constitutional protection were those connected with the militia. Bearing arms, the court concluded, referred to an activity that was exclusively military in nature.

> A man in the pursuit of deer, elk, and buffaloes, might carry his rifle every day, for forty years, and yet, it would never be said of him, that had borne arms, much less could it be said, that a private citizen bears arms, because he has a dirk, or pistol concealed under his clothes, or a spear in a cane.

Although the court acknowledged that militia weapons were constitutionally protected, it accepted that the state could still regulate the manner in which these weapons might be kept or borne. Weapons that had little connection to military preparedness were not given any constitutional protection. In the view of the *Aymette* court, the legislature enjoyed the widest possible latitude to regulate pistols or other weapons that had negligible value in promoting the maintenance of a well-regulated militia.[17]

Two years later, in *State v. Buzzard*, the Arkansas Supreme Court refined the civic model advanced in *Aymette*. Invoking a concept central to Anglo-American jurisprudence since Blackstone, the court wrote that the goal of the Constitution was to protect those rights "essential to the enjoyment of well-regulated liberty." To conclude, as had the court in *Bliss*, that the right to bear arms was not subject to reasonable regulation was to encourage anarchy, not liberty. Regulation of weapons was a legitimate and necessary exercise of the state's police powers. The decision reiterated that the purpose of bearing arms was not to "enable each member of the community to protect and defend by individual force his private rights against every illegal invasion." Protection of this estimable right was intended to "enable the militia to discharge" their important public trust. One of the most interesting features of the decision was its frank recognition that two competing models of the right to bear arms had emerged under state constitutional law. Although some states had embraced a more expansive individual rights conception of arms bearing, the court took judicial notice of the fact that neither the Arkansas state constitution nor the federal Bill of Rights had employed this more individualistic formulation of the right.[18]

Additional evidence that American law was divided over the meaning and scope of the right to bear arms and its connection to the right of self-defense may be found in the notorious 1852 Kentucky murder trial of Mattews Ward. In contrast to *Reynolds* and *Selfridge*, which were both closely connected to bitter partisan conflicts of the Jeffersonian era, the Ward case was not linked to animosities stoked by party rage. Sadly, the events that triggered the fatal confrontation between Ward and his brother's teacher, William Butler, were almost trivial. The incident began over a bunch of chestnuts. The stern teacher had confronted the younger Ward boy about eating during class. When William Ward denied having consumed the chestnuts, Butler called him a liar and whipped him, a severe but not unusual form of school discipline in the mid-nineteenth century. The next day the boy's brother, Mattews Ward purchased two small pistols and returned to the school with William and another brother, Bob, to confront the teacher. Harsh words were exchanged, Matt calling the teacher a "Damned scoundrel" and a "coward." Mattews Ward and Butler scuffled, and in the course of the altercation, Ward pulled out his pistol and fatally wounded his opponent. Ward was arrested and charged with murder.[19]

The Ward family was among Louisville's most prominent. William Butler was also a pillar of the community. Given the high-profile nature of the killer and victim, the case attracted considerable attention and was widely covered in papers across the South, Midwest, and Northeast. Ward's father spared no expense defending his son. He hired a team of eighteen lawyers to defend Mattews, including John Crittenden, who had served as governor of Kentucky and attorney general of the United States.[20]

Ward's decision to arm himself was the central issue in the case. The same issue had been raised in both *Reynolds* and *Selfridge*. Two of the defense team mimicked the strategy employed in *Reynolds* and *Selfridge*, observing that the right of self-defense was a natural one that had been incorporated into common law. The right of self-defense, however, had been greatly expanded in America. While English common law required that individuals retreat, the defense reminded the court that the case of *Selfridge* had set a new standard that allowed a citizen to respond with deadly force if he had "reasonable grounds to apprehend that he is in such danger."[21]

The prosecution also adopted the same tactic used in both *Reynolds* and *Selfridge* and argued that Ward's decision to arm himself with a pistol prior to confronting Butler could be taken as evidence of his desire to provoke a conflict. This view was challenged by the defense, who asserted that

> a man has a right to carry arms; I am aware of nothing in the laws of God or man, prohibiting it. The Constitution of Kentucky and

our Bill of Rights guarantee it. The Legislature once passed an act forbidding it, but it was decided unconstitutional, and overruled by our highest tribunal, the Court of Appeals.

Crittenden made a similar appeal: "The Constitution guarantees to every man the right to bear arms. No law takes it away, and none ever could." Accordingly, Crittenden challenged the prosecution's argument that one could "impute unlawful motives" and "murderous intent" to a citizen exercising a basic constitutional right. In contrast to the two earlier cases, *Reynolds* and *Selfridge*, Ward's lawyers took advantage of the doctrine advanced in *Bliss* and wrapped their client's actions under the banner of a constitutional right to bear arms.[22]

Ward was acquitted. Although the jury may have been persuaded by the defense, particularly given the precedent established by *Bliss*, Louisville residents were outraged by the decision. Hundreds of angry citizens gathered to protest the verdict, and the crowd took the unusual step of hanging the jurors in effigy. Hostility to the decision was so great that money was raised to commission a statue to honor the slain teacher, Butler. A citizens' committee attacked the verdict as "contrary to our ideas of public justice, and subversive of the fundamental principles of personal security guaranteed to us by the Constitution of the state." Rather than embrace the expansive individual right to bear arms championed by Ward's lawyers, Lexington residents denounced this doctrine. For the people of Lexington, the right requiring protection was not an individual right of self-defense, but rather the right to be free from the danger posed by such aggressive behavior, a view similar to the one championed by Benjamin Austin in his appeal to the Massachusetts legislature written almost fifty years earlier. The people's right to be free from the threat of violence took precedence over the individual's right to arm himself. Ward's own fate may well be the most telling commentary on the whole trial. Although the jury exonerated him and he escaped legal punishment, he never recovered from the infamy and opprobrium attached to his reputation. His defense of personal honor cost him his place in polite society, and he remained a pariah for the rest of his life.[23]

Outside of Kentucky the case drew equally scathing condemnations. A lengthy article in the *Monthly Law Reporter* denounced the "atrocity of the deed for which the prisoner was indicted." The case was "a disgrace" that ultimately revealed more about "Kentucky justice" than it did about American law. Ward had clearly benefited from the anomalous holding in *Bliss*. Still, even outside of Kentucky the ideas advanced by Ward's lawyers had entered the legal mainstream. Although the civic model articulated in *Aymette* and *Buzzard* represented the dominant approach to this issue, the alternative individual rights conception presented by *Bliss* would only grow stronger over time.[24]

THE SECOND AMENDMENT IN ANTEBELLUM CONSTITUTIONAL COMMENTARIES

At the beginning of the nineteenth century, St. George Tucker had trouble finding a publisher for an edition of *Blackstone's Commentaries*. By the middle of the Jacksonian era there were at least a half a dozen learned constitutional treatises in print. In addition to scholarly discussions of the constitution, publishers also began printing popular guides intended for the average citizen. These popular texts soon outnumbered the more erudite works of learned jurists. A reader might learn constitutional ideas by following the lessons contained in a *Youth's Manual of the Constitution of the United States* or engage in *Familiar Conversations upon the Constitution*. To understand antebellum constitutional commentary one must consider these popular guides alongside the more familiar works by learned judges and celebrated lawyers.[25]

The most important legal figure to take up the meaning of the Second Amendment in the first half of the nineteenth century was the eminent jurist Joseph Story, who took a leading role in establishing Harvard Law School and was one of the most influential justices of the U.S. Supreme Court. Story also saw the purpose of the amendment in terms of the preamble's discussion of the need for a well-regulated militia, an institution essential to the survival of the American republic.

> One of the ordinary modes, by which tyrants accomplish their purposes without resistance, is, by disarming the people, and making it an offence to keep arms, and by substituting a regular army in the stead of a resort to the militia. The friends of a free government cannot be too watchful, to overcome the dangerous tendency of the public mind to sacrifice, for the sake of mere private convenience, this powerful check upon the designs of ambitious men.[26]

Echoing Tocqueville's critique of America's excessive individualism, Story worried that for the first time in American history, the institution of the militia was in danger of disappearing from American life. He bewailed citizens' growing tendency to abandon their public obligations for mere private convenience.

> And yet, though this truth would seem so clear, and the importance of a well regulated militia would seem so undeniable, it cannot be disguised, that among the American people there is a growing indifference to any system of militia discipline, and a strong disposition, from a sense of its burthens, to be rid of all regulations. How it is practicable to keep the people duly armed without some organization, it is difficult to see. There is certainly no small danger, that indifference may lead to disgust, and disgust to contempt; and thus gradually undermine all the protection intended by this clause of our national bill of rights.[27]

Story bemoaned this change and stated in unequivocal terms his fear that the decay in militia discipline would lead to something unthinkable during the Founding era: domestic disarmament and the rise of a standing army.[28]

Story was certainly not the only commentator to bemoan the decline of traditional republican values and the rise of a more individualistic ethos in America. Benjamin Oliver, another New Englander and a prolific author of popular law books, endorsed these judgments. In his influential guide to the *Rights of an American Citizen*, Oliver endorsed the traditional view that the Second Amendment's preamble provided the "true construction" for interpreting the meaning of the amendment. Indeed, Oliver declared that the original understanding of the right to bear arms was "intended to apply to the right of the people to bear arms for such purposes only." Oliver conceded that this original understanding was slowly being challenged by the new view that saw this right in more individualistic terms, a trend that he regarded as deeply disturbing. This new conception of the right to bear arms was reflected in the increasingly "common practice in some parts of the United States, for individuals to carry concealed weapons about their persons." In Oliver's view, this new behavior was "cowardly and disgraceful."[29]

THE ABOLITIONIST THEORY OF THE RIGHT TO BEAR ARMS

While support for an individual rights theory of arms bearing had slowly emerged under state constitutional law, another even more radical theory of the Second Amendment was being developed by abolitionists. According to this new theory, the Second Amendment not only protected a fundamental right of personal self-defense, it provided the constitutional foundation for an individual right of revolution. The abolitionists were not the first group in America to see the revolutionary potential of the Second Amendment. Their new theory, however, broke with earlier revolutionary views of the Second Amendment by severing this right from any connection to the militia. In the eighteenth century the most radical theories of the Second Amendment were all conceptualized in terms of a right of collective resistance. States' rights theorists such as St. George Tucker had argued that this awesome power resided in the states. Proponents of popular constitutionalism, including the Whiskey Rebels, had defended the right of local communities or popular conventions to assert this right. Radical abolitionists broke with both of these earlier militia-based views of resistance and fashioned a new individualistic conception of this right that not only included freemen, but also extended to slaves. The logic of this new theory would inexorably lead to John Brown's abortive raid on Harpers Ferry.[30]

Nineteenth-century abolitionists had been divided between proponents of gradual and immediate emancipation. Eventually support for incremental reform gave way to calls for an immediate end to slavery. Although their language was often inflammatory, most abolitionists continued to embrace nonviolence as the preferred method to achieve their goal. By the 1840s, however, the rifle usurped the Bible, as moral suasion gave way to armed resistance in the fight against the evil of slavery. By the middle of the century, a new revolutionary theory of the Second Amendment grounded in an individual right of armed resistance had become a cornerstone of abolitionist ideology.[31]

Abolitionist Joel Tiffany unabashedly defended an insurrectionary theory of the Second Amendment in his 1849 *Treatise on the Unconstitutionality of Slavery*. The expansive right Tiffany defended was about individual, not collective, self-defense: "The right to keep and bear arms, also implies the right to use them if necessary in self-defense." A similar view of the right to bear arms was defended by abolitionist Lysander Spooner, who averred that the U.S. Constitution recognized a right of armed resistance and noted that the "constitutional security for the right to keep and bear arms, implies the right to use them."

In keeping with his radical conceptualization of the right to bear arms, Spooner argued that the Second Amendment merely recognized "the natural right of all men to keep and bear arms for their personal defense." Such a right was "palpably inconsistent with the idea of his being a slave." There was no constitutional right, Spooner argued, to deny any individual, even a slave, the freedom to keep and bear arms for their own defense. Claiming such a right was one thing, but exercising it was another. In Spooner's constitutional vision, a reformulation of the Second Amendment could be achieved in practice by an equally bold reform of the jury. In essence, Spooner recommended a form of jury nullification. By refusing to convict those who exercised an individual right to bear arms, juries could help sustain a radical view of the Second Amendment. One need only, Spooner wrote, "show, to the satisfaction of a jury, *or even any one of a jury*, that the law he resisted was an unjust one."[32]

The radicalization of abolitionists intensified in the 1850s. A measure of this shift can be seen in the transformation of Henry C. Wright, an abolitionist who began as a pacifist but slowly adopted a more militant posture. Wright came to believe that the abolitionist credo—"resistance to tyrants is obedience to God"—no longer required peaceful resistance, but demanded that every individual "arm himself with a pistol, or a dirk, a bowie-knife, a rifle, or any deadly weapon" and kill any individual who would attempt to "re-capture and return to bondage fugitive slaves." Wright was not the only antislavery activist to make the intellectual journey from nonviolence to violence. This trend was greatly facilitated by the growing levels of violence in the western territory of Kansas. The passage of the Kansas-Nebraska Act in 1854 introduced the doctrine of popular sovereignty into American politics, effectively giving settlers the right to determine the issue of slavery in the Territory of Kansas. Proslavery forces and abolitionist supporters poured into Kansas, hoping to influence the outcome of the slavery question. Both sides came heavily armed and showed little reluctance in using violence to defend themselves. Some on both sides went even further, engaging in a campaign of terror against their political opponents. As a result of this escalation of bloodshed, Kansas was plunged into a miniature civil war in the mid 1850s.[33]

In response to the epidemic of violence in the Kansas territory, abolitionists mounted an effective campaign to arm antislavery settlers. In a widely quoted manifesto of the new, more militant abolitionist credo, Minister Henry Ward Beecher argued that in the battle against proslavery forces in Kansas "there was more moral power" in a Sharps rifle than "in a hundred bibles." Sharps rifles soon earned the nickname "Beecher's Bibles." Beecher took an active role raising money for weapons and rallying abolitionists to the cause of Kansas. On one occasion, Beecher pledged to pay half the cost of outfitting an expedition of recent Yale graduates with rifles. On their day of departure, Beecher presented each man with a Bible and a Sharps rifle. Aid committees formed to help abolitionist forces in Kansas raise money for the purchase of weapons. One group acknowledged donations by giving contributors a lithographed certificate with the language of the Second Amendment prominently emblazoned upon it. The Emigrant Aid Society, a New England–based abolitionist organization, shipped several hundred Sharps rifles in crates marked "books."[34]

The violence in Kansas prompted Senator A. P. Butler of South Carolina to suggest the government might indict and disarm those individuals who had chosen to use the cartridge box in place of the ballot box to achieve their political goals. Butler's suggestion prompted an angry response from the ardent abolitionist senator from Massachusetts, Charles Sumner. In an impassioned and widely reprinted speech, "The Crime against Kansas," Sumner reminded the Senate that "the rifle has ever been the companion of the pioneer, and under God, his tutelary protector against the red man and the beast of the forest." Having conjured up the mythic image of a lone pioneer, Sumner went on to lecture his fellow senators that "never was this efficient weapon more needed in just self-defense, than now in Kansas, and at least one article in our National Constitution must be blotted out, before the complete right to it can in any way be impeached."

The attack on Butler took a personal turn when Sumner compared the South Carolinian to Don Quixote and accused him of taking "the harlot, Slavery" as his mistress. Outrage over Sumner's inflammatory rhetoric was intense in the South. No one was more incensed by the attack on Southern honor than Congressman Preston Brooks, Butler's cousin. Attacking the "Crime against Kansas" speech as a "libel on South Carolina, and Mr. Butler," the impetuous congressman resolved to expunge the insult against his family and state by thrashing Sumner, whom he believed to be a man so bereft of honor that he was not even worthy of a duel. Brooks approached Sumner while he sat at his desk on the Senate floor, and before the Massachusetts senator could rise and meet his attacker, Brooks began beating him about the head with a cane. Trapped by his Senate desk, which was bolted in place, Sumner collapsed in a bloody heap on the floor of the Senate. Sumner's blood mingled with that of Kansas in the reports in the press. The pro-abolitionist *New York Tribune* bemoaned the fate of the nation when the decorum of the Senate could be shattered by the South's barbaric code of behavior, which glorified "the lash, the bowie-knife and the pistol." Southern responses were equally strong. To compensate him for the damage to his cane, proslavery sympathizers inundated the congressman with dozens of new canes.[35]

Sumner's speech captured the essence of the radical abolitionists' reformulation of the Second Amendment as an individual right enjoyed by everyone, including slaves. Abolitionists not only rejected the traditional linkage between the militia and the right to bear arms; they also believed that individuals, not states or communities, could legitimately claim a right of armed revolution. Radical abolitionist constitutional theory would come to play a crucial role in defining the ideology of an important segment of the Republican Party. The individual rights theory of the Second Amendment had now moved from the margins of American constitutional discourse to the center.

STATES' RIGHTS AND POPULAR CONSTITUTIONALISM: THE COLLECTIVE RIGHT OF RESISTANCE IN ANTEBELLUM CONSTITUTIONAL THEORY

The states' rights theory of armed resistance to federal authority took on a more immediate and potentially troubling character during the nullification crisis in the late 1820s. Triggered by opposition to federal tariff policy, which they believed posed an economic threat to the South's ability to export agricultural products, South Carolinians reasserted a radical version of the states' rights ideas. Although John C. Calhoun was the best-known advocate of states' rights, he was hardly the most radical voice within his state. Calhoun was outflanked by planter Robert J. Turnbull, whose "Brutus" essays addressed the issue of armed resistance directly. Brutus conceded that "the idea of resistance of any one State, or number of States, to the acts and measures of the government, is a measure that can never be contemplated but with pain." Still, such action was a necessary part of the checks and balances that protected liberty under the American constitutional system. "Resistance and *firm resistance* is the only course to preserve the Federal Constitution in its pristine purity." Turnbull took great pains to distinguish between acts of constitutional resistance and the anarchic actions of individuals or groups who acted against government authority. Although the theory Turnbull advanced came close to being tested in the late 1820s when South Carolina and the federal government nearly came to blows, an armed confrontation was averted by political compromise.[36]

South Carolina nullifiers and Northern abolitionists were hardly the only groups in America dissatisfied with the drift of American politics and constitutional development in the antebellum era, nor were they the only ones forced to ponder the limits of constitutional resistance within the framework established by the Constitution. The populist ideology that had impelled Shays and the Whiskey Rebels to take up arms had never been eradicated from American life. This revolutionary ideology bubbled to the surface of American politics during the Dorr Rebellion (1842).[37]

Rhode Island lagged behind many states in Jacksonian America in adopting universal white male suffrage. Frustrated by intransigence from powerful interests supporting the status quo in Rhode Island, Thomas W. Dorr and his supporters claimed a constitutional basis for overturning the existing government of the state of Rhode Island. When the Dorrites attempted to take control of the state government, the existing antireform government mobilized the state militia and requested help from the federal government to crush the rebellion.

The Dorrites themselves were divided over the appropriateness of using arms to force voting reform in Rhode Island. They called an extralegal constitutional convention in which they adopted a new frame of government that provided a more expansive right of suffrage for white men. Elections were then held under the new rules, and Dorr was elected governor. The existing government, however, refused to recognize the new regime. Committed to defending the new state constitution, Dorr and his supporters organized their own militia units and attempted to seize the public arms stored in the Providence arsenal. A combination of bad luck and even worse weather frustrated Dorr's plans. What might have become a deadly serious affair quickly descended into a comedy of errors. When the Dorrites demanded that the arsenal turn over its supply of weapons to the rebel forces, the officer in charge curtly responded that he had never heard of a Governor Dorr and refused to give up the weapons. The siege was a disaster. The Dorrites' artillery consisted of two rusted Revolutionary-era cannons that were so antiquated they were utterly useless. The existing state militia, loyal to the ruling anti-Dorr government, aided by the militias of neighboring states, easily put down the rebellion.

The issues the Dorr Rebellion raised came before the U.S. Supreme Court in a circuitous manner. One of Dorr's supporters, Martin Luther, sued a member of the state militia for trespass when the officer entered his home during the rebellion. Judge Story heard the case on circuit and delivered a blistering condemnation of the Dorrites' revolutionary aspirations. When the case eventually came before the Supreme Court as *Luther v. Borden*, the Supreme Court was asked to consider the meaning of the Constitution's provision guaranteeing each state a republican form of government. The Dorrites hoped to prove that a right of revolution was implicit in the concept of republican self rule.[38]

In his *Commentaries* Story had described the militia and the right to bear arms as "the palladium of the liberties of a republic." His response to the Dorrites demonstrated that his visions of the Second Amendment and the militia were hardly revolutionary. Construing the law of treason in broad terms, Story denounced the Dorrites in his jury charge. Indeed, Story's construction of treason seemed to hark back to the views of the Federalist judges during the Whiskey Rebellion. Story reminded the jury that if

> the assembly is arrayed in a military manner, if they are armed and march in a military form, for the express purpose of overawing or intimidating the public, and thus they attempt to carry into effect the treasonable design, that will, of itself amount to a levy of war, although no actual blow has been struck.

The Second Amendment was not the foundation for a constitutional right of revolution in Story's constitutional theory.[39]

Benjamin Hallet, the counsel for Martin Luther and a prominent Dorr supporter, defended the legitimacy of a constitutional right of revolution. To support this claim, Hallet noted that several constitutional provisions facilitated such a right. Among those he cited to substantiate this claim were those provisions of the Bill of Rights that "secured the right of the people peaceably to assemble, and to keep and bear arms." Hallet went further, declaring "that in changes in government, the people of the States hold the 'sacred right of revolution.'" The government's view was equally emphatic: "The Constitution of the United States has annihilated the right of revolution."[40]

Few Americans would have disputed Story's claim that the Second Amendment was the grand palladium of liberty. Finding any common ground on what this meant in practice proved increasingly difficult by midcentury. For Dorr's conservative opponents, an armed population organized as a militia was a bulwark against revolutionary upheaval. The Dorrites took the opposite view; in their minds the Second Amendment provided the foundation for a collective right of revolution. Although the Dorr Rebellion raised fundamental questions about the meaning of republican government and the right of revolution, the Supreme Court avoided ruling on these potentially explosive issues by developing the doctrine of political questions, a category of constitutional disputes that were best settled by the political branches, not the judiciary.[41]

THE WIDENING GULF OVER THE MEANING OF THE RIGHT TO BEAR ARMS

In the decade between 1845 and 1855 a half dozen states revised their constitutions. The debates within these conventions over the meaning of arms bearing reveal how deeply contested the right to bear arms was at midcentury. The two opposing theories that dominated state constitutional law, civic and individual, were pitted against one another in these debates.

The debate in the Texas Convention (1845) was particularly spirited. The issue before the convention focused on revising the language of the 1836 constitution that affirmed that "every citizen shall have the right to bear arms in defense of himself and the republic." One delegate proposed language closer to the eighteenth-century civic formulation, suggesting that the provision ought to read that "the free citizens of this state shall have a right to keep and bear arms for their common defense, provided the Legislature shall have the right to pass laws prohibiting the carrying of deadly weapons secretly." The author of this revision expressed his concern that under the 1836 constitution's more individualistic formulation of this right, the legislature might not be able to regulate concealed weapons. Another delegate endorsed this change by reminding the convention that "the object of inserting a declaration that the people shall have a right to bear arms" was for a specific purpose "that they may be well armed to the public defense." The distinction between the common-law right of self-defense and the constitutional right of bearing arms emerged in the course of debate when one member of the convention reminded his fellow delegates that "it is not a supposition which can arise in a country where the common law prevails, that it is necessary to bear arms for protection against a fellow citizen." The convention even considered explicitly borrowing the Second Amendment's formulation of the right to bear arms: "a well regulated militia being necessary to the security of a free state, the right of the people to keep and bear arms shall not be infringed." This motion passed but was later superceded by a subsequent proposal to restore the 1836 language affirming an individual right to bear arms. Ultimately the convention reaffirmed this language: "Every citizen shall have the right to bear arms in the lawful defense of himself and the state."[42]

Although the debating of the meaning of the right to bear arms was often done with an air of deadly seriousness, the subject occasionally provoked humor as well. When a delegate at the Indiana constitutional convention suggested that "no person shall be restricted in the right to carry visible arms," another delegate interjected that the words "or eyes" should be inserted after arms. The report of the proceedings wryly noted that "the convention was convulsed in laughter and thereafter returned to its business."[43]

The most astute observers of American society recognized that legal thinking on the meaning of the right to bear arms and self-defense was struggling to keep pace with changing mores and social norms. One measure of this change may be found in the profound shift in attitudes toward the use of firearms against mob violence. When confronting an angry crowd during the Baltimore Riot of 1812, the city's mayor counseled Federalists not to arm themselves, and he expressed considerable reluctance to call out the militia to preserve order. The deference to the will of the people expressed by Baltimore's mayor had largely eroded by the time of the Philadelphia Kensington Riots in 1844.[44]

Tensions in Philadelphia at this time combined elements of political and interethnic conflict. Protestants in the "City of Brotherly Love" were engaged in a protracted and bitter struggle with Catholics over the use of the Bible in public schools. They were also agitating for a series of anti-immigrant measures as a part of a larger nativist, anti-Catholic campaign. When the two groups encountered each other in the city's streets, the pitched battle that ensued escalated into a full-scale armed conflict that took the city more than a week to suppress.

Sidney George Fisher, a lawyer and political essayist, made a number of observations about the riot in his diary. He complained that American magistrates were hampered by the absence of a law comparable to England's Riot Act. In contrast to English law, public officials had to rest their authority on "a general common law authority to keep the peace & to make arrests & to use all necessary authority for this purpose." Common-law authority was, however, "very vague & the question always arises, what force was necessary." Fisher believed that the unprecedented level of violence occasioned by the riots changed American thinking about the legitimate use of force against the mob. One of the distinguishing features of the Kensington Riots was the prevalence of firearms.

These are strange things for Philadelphia. We have never had anything like it before, but now that firearms have been once used &

become familiar to the minds of the mob, we may expect to see them employed on all occasions, and our riots in future will assume a more dangerous character.

In Fisher's view, the widespread use of guns by the rioters was entirely unprecedented and had utterly transformed the way the law would have to address urban unrest in the future. After Kensington, "armed resistance was now a matter of common right & self defense."[45]

The transformation in legal thinking in the three decades that separated the Baltimore Riots and the Philadelphia riots was profound. While officials in Baltimore had been reluctant to use force to put down the mob, officials in Philadelphia not only brought the full force of the law down upon rioters, but they counseled individual citizens to arm themselves and assist the authorities. Francis Wharton, one of the most eminent legal authorities in the nation, devoted considerable space in his influential midcentury treatise on homicide to the legal obligations of citizens to assist authorities in suppressing mob violence. Wharton noted that "citizens have the right in extreme cases, when the municipal government is insufficient, to establish a preventive police, and, if it be necessary, take life in order to prevent crime." To illustrate this point, Wharton invoked the example of the Kensington Riots. He even included a jury charge delivered in one of the cases arising from the riots. The judge in that case instructed jurors that during times of public unrest and tumult, "citizens may, of their own authority, lawfully endeavor to suppress the riot, and for that purpose, may even arm themselves, and whatever is honestly done by them in the execution of that object will be supported and justified by the common law." Wharton's summary of the state of legal thinking after the Kensington Riots made it clear that the law now accepted the legitimacy of deadly force against mobs. Citizens had a legal obligation to come to the aid of magistrates.[46]

The breakdown of the traditional republican understanding of the legitimacy of the mob as a genuine expression of the will of the people is also evidenced in the decision of a number of cities to develop professional police forces in the late 1840s and early 1850s. The decision to abandon the more informal system of constables and urban watches and turn to uniformed police marked another important break with the traditional republican understanding of the mob as a legitimate expression of the popular will. Initially there was some reluctance to equip these new police forces with firearms, but this hesitancy soon gave way. Indeed, it seemed fitting that one of the last products introduced by Samuel Colt before his death in 1862 was the New Model Police Revolver.[47]

THE RIGHT TO BEAR ARMS AT MIDCENTURY

At midcentury American thinking about the right of self-defense, the right to bear arms, and the constitutional function of the militia was more unsettled than at any point in the previous hundred years. One measure of the depth of these divisions is provided by a popular mid-century debating manual, whose list of possible topics for discussion captured the unsettled nature of American thinking on many of these issues. The author of *American Debater* posed the following question: "Is resistance to the constituted authorities in the State ever justified?" Had one been able to gather Robert Turnbull, Thomas Dorr, Lysander Spooner, and Joseph Story together in a single room to debate this momentous issue, there would have been little common ground among any of the speakers. While there can be little doubt that each of these constitutional thinkers would have enthusiastically endorsed the idea that the Second Amendment was the palladium of liberty, there would be no consensus on the exact meaning of this provision of the Bill of Rights. Turnbull would have viewed a right of armed resistance as a legitimate constitutional option, one properly exercised by the individual states. Thomas Dorr also believed in a right of armed resistance, but his conception of this right looked to the authority of popular conventions. Lysander Spooner's radical abolitionist vision rejected both of these collective understandings of the Second Amendment's revolutionary character. For Spooner the existence of a constitutional right of armed resistance was indisputable. The agent of this revolutionary theory was not the states or popular conventions, but individuals. For conservative nationalists such as Joseph Story there simply was no constitutional right of resistance. Unfortunately for those embracing a right of armed resistance, it was the conservative Story who sat on the U.S. Supreme Court.[48]

The issue of self-defense also provided the *American Debater* with material suitable for spirited academic disputation. Despite the fact that American law had moved toward a more aggressive view of the right of self-defense, it was still possible at midcentury to frame a debate around the question: "Has a man a right to kill another in self-defense?" Even the seemingly sacrosanct notion that the militia was superior to a standing army had come to be a subject worthy of forensic discussion. While it would have been hard to imagine any eighteenth-century debating manual asking "Would a large standing army be conducive to our country's prosperity?" by the middle of the nineteenth century it was at least possible to offer up this proposition for consideration.[49]

Nineteenth-century Americans were forced to grapple with a host of problems that the framers of the Second Amendment had never anticipated. For many, the Second Amendment continued to represent the ultimate check on tyranny. How this vital checking function might be implemented continued to be a source of division. The revolutionary potential of the militia and the Second Amendment would be sorely tested in the decades to come.

The Negro militias in the South were an important part of Reconstruction. The disarmament of these militias by the Ku Klux Klan became a test case for the incorporation of the Second Amendment through the Fourteenth Amendment. (*Harper's Weekly*, Library of Congress)

CHAPTER 6

_____

INDIVIDUAL OR COLLECTIVE RIGHT

THE FOURTEENTH AMENDMENT AND THE ORIGINS
OF THE MODERN GUN DEBATE

On April 12, 1861, soldiers from the Palmetto Guard, an elite volunteer unit of South Carolina's militia, fired on the Union forces garrisoned in Fort Sumter. The Confederacy's attack on the fort plunged the nation into the bloodiest conflict in American history. The Civil War proved to be a watershed moment in the contentious history of the Second Amendment. The actions of the South Carolina militia took the antebellum states' rights interpretation of the Second Amendment to its logical conclusion. The idea that a state might use its militia against the federal government, an idea vaguely theorized during the original debate over the Constitution in 1788 and that had been elaborated by Jeffersonians in the decade after ratification, was finally put into practice with tragic results. The Union's triumph over the South discredited this insurrectionary theory of states' rights, much as John Brown's prewar raid on Harpers Ferry had discredited the radical abolitionist idea that individuals might take up arms against their government. After the defeat of the Confederacy the notion that a state or an individual might exercise such a right was simply no longer tenable.

While the Civil War drained the Second Amendment of its most radical revolutionary potential, it left a host of other questions about the meaning of the right to bear arms unsettled. For Republicans and their Democratic opponents, the Second Amendment would become a valuable tool for asserting their radically different constitutional agendas. Democrats recast the states' rights reading of the amendment, stripping it of its revolutionary character and harnessing it as an engine to challenge their Republican opponents' effort to expand federal power. Republicans hoped to use the amendment as a means of testing their new theory of incorporation, giving the federal government the power to force states to respect the rights enumerated in the Bill of Rights, particularly the rights of newly freed slaves in the South.

The difficult question for Republicans was not whether to defend the Second Amendment rights of all citizens, but how these rights would be construed. Would the Second Amendment become an individual right of self-defense or would it remain wed to participation in a well-regulated militia, one that was now firmly under the control of the federal government?[1]

THE RIGHT TO BEAR ARMS IN THE RECONSTRUCTION SOUTH

The Thirteenth Amendment (1865) abolished slavery but did nothing to settle the nettlesome question of former slaves' legal status. While Northern Republicans insisted that basic rights be extended to the African-American population, many Southerners resisted this effort. In late 1865, Mississippi and South Carolina became the first states in the postwar South to adopt "black codes," laws designed to severely limit freedmen's rights. The codes limited Freedmen's access to the courts, prevented blacks from entering many trades, and forced blacks to sign labor contracts to avoid being charged with vagrancy. Among the many restrictions placed on blacks were limits on the ownership and use of firearms and other weapons. Mississippi's law forbade any "freedmen, free negro, or mulatto, not in the military service of the United States Government, and not licensed to do so by the board of police of his or her county" from keeping or carrying firearms, dirks, or bowie knives. The law also prohibited whites from selling arms to blacks. Interestingly, the code acknowledged that blacks in military service enjoyed special protection, an implicit acknowledgment of the civic conception of bearing arms. South Carolina's black codes took a different approach, deliberately excluding blacks from the militia and prohibiting them from keeping firearms, swords, and other military weapons. In contrast to Mississippi, which sought wholesale disarmament of freedmen, South Carolina's law acknowledged a right to keep nonmilitary weapons in one's home. The law made an exception for "owners of a farm," who were allowed to "keep a shot gun or rifle such as ordinarily used in hunting," but not weapons "appropriate for purposes of war." In South Carolina blacks were excluded from the militia and prevented from owning military weapons.[2]

Outrage over the Southern black codes spread throughout Northern Republican circles. In early January 1866, *Harper's Weekly* reported that the militia in Mississippi, controlled by ex-Confederates, "have seized every gun and pistol found in the hands of the (so called) freedmen of this section of the county. They claim that the statute laws of Mississippi do not recognize the negro as having any right to carry arms." The effort to disarm blacks prompted a swift response from American military forces charged with keeping order in the Reconstruction South. General Daniel E. Sickles was so outraged by South Carolina's exclusion of blacks from the militia and general disarmament that he issued a military order suspending the statute. Sickles decreed "all laws shall be applicable alike to all the inhabitants" and proclaimed "the constitutional rights of all loyal and well-disposed inhabitants to bear arms will not be infringed." Sickles's response focused on the law's racism, stating unequivocally that the state might

regulate firearms use in a nondiscriminatory fashion, including prohibitions on carrying concealed weapons. Sickles conceded that the
state might be justified in excluding a variety of dangerous persons
from owning firearms, including vagrants, disturbers of the peace, and
the disorderly. Sickles's response to the black code reflected orthodox
antebellum ideas about the scope of state firearms regulation. Although
Sickles's order prohibited race-based disarmament, he acknowledged
that the state might legitimately exclude certain categories of persons
from owning guns and impose time, place, and manner restrictions
on the use of firearms. As long as these prohibitions were not based
on invidious racial categories, had a rational basis, and were intended
to promote public safety, they were entirely legal.[3]

Congress responded to the Southern black codes by expanding the
authority of the Freedmen's Bureau and passing the Civil Rights Act of
1866. President Andrew Johnson, an opponent of congressional Republicans' more radical vision of Reconstruction, vetoed the two bills, but
the Republican-dominated Congress overrode the veto. The Civil Rights
Act affirmed that "all persons in the United States, and not subject to
any foreign power, excluding Indians not taxed, are hereby declared
to be citizens of the United States" and were entitled to "equal benefit
of all laws and proceedings for the security of person and property."[4]

In the congressional debate over the new Civil Rights Act,
Republican Senator Lyman Trumbull of Illinois pointed to the discriminatory character of the Mississippi black codes, singling out their
effort to disarm blacks as one particularly odious practice. He
approached the issue in much the same way abolitionists had before
the war. Others in Congress offered a different interpretation of the
Civil Rights Act, viewing it as articulating nothing more than a general principle of equality. For these Republicans the primary focus was
protecting freedmen's economic rights such as the right to make and
enforce contracts, sue, inherit, sell, lease, and hold property.[5]

The Freedmen's Bureau was an important institution created
within the War Department to help African-Americans cope with the

transition to freedom. Congress expanded the scope of the bureau and explicitly noted the need to protect the rights of "personal liberty" and "personal security," including "the constitutional right to bear arms," which was to be "enjoyed by all the citizens of such State or district without respect to race or color." Some in Congress clearly thought that bearing arms encompassed both the use of firearms for personal self-defense and the more traditional civic notion that tied arms bearing to participation in the militia.[6]

Several speakers in the debate over the extension of the Freedmen's Bill and the Civil Rights Act referred to reports of the outrages being committed in the South. Representative Sidney Clarke, a Republican from Kansas, referenced the many letters that poured into Congress detailing a campaign of violence against freedmen. To buttress his argument, Clarke quoted extensively from the Alabama black codes, which prohibited "any freedmen, mulatto, or free person of color in this State, to own fire-arms, or carry about his person a pistol, or other deadly weapon." Clarke found it particularly galling that in Mississippi the militia had adopted Confederate uniforms and confiscated weapons owned by black veterans of the Union Army.[7]

THE FOURTEENTH AMENDMENT

The most important protection of freedmen's rights passed by the 39th Congress was the Fourteenth Amendment. Section 1, focusing on federal protection for the privileges and immunities of citizenship asserted that:

> All persons born or naturalized in the United States, and subject to the jurisdiction thereof, are citizens of the United States and of the state wherein they reside. No state shall make or enforce any law which shall abridge the privileges or immunities of citizens of the United States; nor shall any state deprive any person of life,

liberty, or property, without due process of law; nor deny to any person within its jurisdiction the equal protection of the laws.

While there was widespread enthusiasm for the amendment among Republicans, there were some important disagreements among supporters over key terms such as "privileges and immunities." Some within Congress viewed the amendment as specifically protecting the rights affirmed in the first eight amendments to the Constitution while others viewed it as guaranteeing a narrow range of economic rights, most notably the right to own property, make contracts, and sue in court. Others viewed the amendment as doing little more than forcing states to apply their own laws equally.[8]

Republican Senator Jacob Howard of Michigan argued explicitly that the Fourteenth Amendment would incorporate the first eight amendments under federal protection and thus apply them against the states. Republican Senator Samuel Pomeroy of Kansas affirmed that among these inestimable rights were the right to "bear arms for the defense of himself and family and his homestead." A different view was articulated by Senator Luke Poland, a Vermont Republican, who suggested that the language of the amendment merely extended a principle articulated in the comity clause of the Constitution, which asserted, "The Citizens of each State shall be entitled to all Privileges and Immunities of Citizens in the several States." Poland's model of the privileges and immunities clause was less sweeping than either Pomeroy's or Howard's and appeared to point toward a principle of legal equality, rather than full incorporation of the Bill of Rights. Although it stopped short of fully incorporating the Second Amendment, the application of this equality principle would have prevented southern states from enacting discriminatory legislation aimed at disarming blacks.[9]

The chief architect of Section 1 of the Fourteenth Amendment was Republican Congressman John A. Bingham of Ohio, an abolitionist lawyer who had been won over to the antislavery crusade at an early age. To understand Bingham's views of the Fourteenth Amendment, one must root his thinking within the context of abolitionist theory and antebellum constitutional law. Schooled in an abolitionist interpretation of the Constitution, he believed that the states had no right to violate any provision of the Bill of Rights. The problem Bingham and abolitionists of a legalistic cast of mind encountered was that the original understanding of federalism placed state violations of individual rights in the purview of state constitutional law, not federal law. In practice this meant blacks and abolitionists had no real remedy in southern courts or legislatures prior to the Civil War. The structure of federalism had created a refuge for opponents of liberty and equality. Even if one believed that state violations of the federal Bill of Rights were unconstitutional, the Constitution provided no basis for appeals to the federal courts, and Congress lacked any direct authority to alleviate these injustices. Indeed, Bingham had argued that the abolitionist-inspired Civil Rights Act enacted by Congress was unconstitutional precisely because the Constitution had not bestowed this type of sweeping authority on Congress or the courts. The Fourteenth Amendment solved this problem by giving Congress the legal mandate to deal with state deprivations of basic rights.[10]

While the debates in Congress provide solid evidence of what many of the Fourteenth Amendment's framers thought about the meaning of Section 1, sorting out what the state legislatures and the vast majority of Americans thought about the meaning of the Fourteenth Amendment is more difficult. The debates in the press provide some scattered evidence of how the Fourteenth Amendment was presented to the public. There was some discussion of the amendment during the bitter election of 1866, and a few of the stump speeches made by candidates during that campaign have survived.

Once debate shifted from the halls of Congress to the nation's rostrums and town squares, Republican supporters of the Fourteenth Amendment, including Bingham, were forced to confront a determined Democratic opposition who conjured up a host of horrors that would follow from the principle of racial equality, including black suffrage and miscegenation. To counter these savage racist arguments, Republicans had to reframe their support for the Fourteenth Amendment in terms better calculated to win popular support. Republicans, even those sympathetic to the plight of African-Americans, had to play down the issues of empowering African-Americans and highlight the innocuous nature of the Fourteenth Amendment. Republicans fell back on the argument that the Fourteenth Amendment did nothing more than require the states to treat their citizens equally. While inspirational appeals invoking the struggles of heroic freedmen defending their homesteads with rifle in hand might resonate in the halls of Congress, the image of armed African-Americans was more likely to have frightened many voters. The dynamic of the public debate meant that Republicans, even those most sympathetic to the individual rights conception of arms bearing, were forced to downplay this principle in order to sell the amendment to the American people.[11]

The problems Republicans faced in trying to persuade Americans to embrace the Fourteenth Amendment are evident in Bingham's appeals to the citizens of his own state. Rather than highlight ideas drawn from antebellum abolitionist rhetoric and defend gun-toting freedmen as some in Congress had chosen to do, Bingham stressed the much less threatening notion that the amendment simply forced the states to abide by the principle of equality before the law. In an August 1866 speech reported in the *Cincinnati Commercial*, Bingham explained that Section 1 of the Fourteenth Amendment did little more than embody "in the Constitution the golden rule, learned at the mother's knee, 'to do as we would be done by.'" A couple of days later he offered another summary of the import of Section 1: "It is a simple, strong, plain declaration that equal laws and equal and exact justice shall hereafter be secured within every State of this Union." He dismissed the charge that the amendment would destroy the federal system, effectively reducing individual states and their laws to mere ciphers in an all-powerful centralized system of government. "It takes from no State any right which hitherto pertained to the several States of the United States."[12]

Whether Bingham was consciously responding to the vicious black-baiting tactics of his opponents is unclear. Bingham may have believed that these subtle shifts in emphasis and tone were entirely consistent with his earlier congressional speeches. His listeners, however, likely took a very different message away from these speeches. For the average man or woman on the street listening to one of Bingham's addresses, the Fourteenth Amendment probably seemed to do little more than require states to treat citizens equally.

THE RISE AND FALL OF THE NEGRO MILITIAS

The problem of southern violence, particularly the activities of state militias dominated by former Confederate soldiers, prompted congressional Republicans to propose temporarily disbanding all militias in the South. The measure was introduced by Senator Henry Wilson from Massachusetts, who also admitted into the Congressional record detailed reports of the horrors being committed by these rebel-dominated militias. He cited evidence provided by the head of the Freedmen's Bureau, General Oliver O. Howard, who reported that "officers and agents of the bureau as well as military authorities and the newspapers" confirmed that militias were "engaged in disarming the negroes." Howard suggested abolishing the militias and temporarily replacing them with a federal police force. Congressional Democrats protested that the proposal to disband Southern militias clearly violated the Second Amendment. Senator Willard Saulsbury from Delaware declared emphatically that Congress could not "disarm the militia of a State, or [to] destroy the militia of a State." He explicitly evoked the Second Amendment and then quoted its text verbatim. Wilson responded to Saulsbury's critique by reiterating that these so-called militias were little more than roving bands of Confederate bandits terrorizing southern citizens. Others in the debate sought middle ground, conceding that Congress might regulate the militia, effectively disarming rebel units without abolishing the institution itself. Despite efforts to find a middle ground, Republican voices prevailed, and the bill disbanding the militia passed.[13]

Eliminating the neo-Confederate state militias did little to lessen the chaos and violence in the South. Republicans soon realized that some type of military force was necessary to restore order, and they turned to a newly constituted militia as the best solution. Democrats charged them with playing politics with the Constitution. Pennsylvania Senator Charles Buckalew observed that Republicans had done away with the militia "in order to weaken the then existing political governments in the South." Now, he added, they wish to reconstitute them "because the political power which now exists is politically friendly to them." Buckalew believed that the Republicans clearly aimed to use the militia as a political tool.[14]

The formation of a new militia, one that included African-Americans, became a high priority for southern Republicans. The decision to allow blacks to serve alongside whites meant that most southerners refused to join the new militia. Dubbed the "Negro militia" by contemporaries, it became an indispensable political and military institution, providing a means of protecting and organizing freedmen. Blacks eagerly joined these units, which were outfitted with the latest weaponry. The social role of the militias within the African-American community was at least as important as its military function. Drilling and parading served an important symbolic function, inspiring and rallying the African-American community. For Republicans, participation in the new militia became one of the most important privileges and immunities of citizenship, a foundation for the exercise of other rights such as voting or participation in juries.[15]

The arming of the Negro militias met with especially fierce resistance in South Carolina. Violent clashes between the Ku Klux Klan

(KKK) and the Negro militia in 1869 prompted congressional investigation. Democrats denounced the militia as a tool of Republican tyranny. Republicans argued that the militia was the only means to protect the black population from Klan terror.[16]

Republican South Carolina Governor Robert Scott, a former Union officer from Ohio, was denounced by his enemies as a carpetbagger. Scott believed that arming the militia was essential to fighting Klan violence. His actions clearly struck a sensitive nerve in his opponents, who viewed Scott's decision to arm the Negro militia as the greatest Republican outrage perpetrated on the state of South Carolina. The sight of organized, armed freedmen incensed opponents of Reconstruction and led to an intensified campaign of Klan terror. Leading members of the Negro militia were beaten or lynched and their weapons stolen. The destruction of the Negro militia became a top priority for the Klan and its supporters.[17]

Congressional investigation of Klan violence was so intensely partisan that the hearings became little more than an exchange of accusations. Democrats and Republicans blamed each others' policies for the escalation of violence. Not surprisingly, the committee could not agree on a report, and a minority account emerged from the hearings. The minority Democratic report was highly critical of the Negro militias for provoking violence. The majority Republican report blamed violence on Klan provocations.[18]

Democrats charged that Governor Scott had deliberately politicized the militia by arming freedmen. Adopting a highly inflammatory tone, the Democrats investigating Klan activity charged that Scott had "corruptly and *secretly* sent his emissaries through the State to enroll and organize the negro population." The governor's policy of arming "the negro militia, in the summer of 1870, and during the progress of the political campaign, was done for the purpose, and for none other than to carry the election by force and intimidation." Democrats echoed charges Klan members had made to justify their terrorist actions. Scott, they maintained, had refused to allow whites to enroll in the militia and had even confiscated arms from white militia units and redistributed them to blacks. In his memoir of Reconstruction, South Carolina Democrat Henry T. Thompson reported that Scott had boasted that "the only law for these people [South Carolinians] was the Winchester Rifle." Democrats introduced into evidence the records of the state adjutant general, which showed that South Carolina had purchased and distributed more than seven thousand weapons and issued ninety thousand rounds of ammunition to the Negro militias. Finally, with characteristic racist derision, the Democrats remarked, "Even the miserable testimony of the negroes themselves shows that the principle object of the visitation of their disguised assailants was the search for the very guns distributed among them by the governor." The Klan's chief objective according to contemporary testimony was the disarmament of the Negro militia.[19]

Republicans painted a different picture. Klan violence, not the arming of the Negro militias, had produced civil unrest in South Carolina. "Whatever other causes were assigned for disorders in the late insurrectionary States, the execution of the laws and the security of life and property" were "seriously threatened by" the Klan, who acted as "organized bands of armed and disguised men." Republicans did not dispute that there may have been isolated examples of corruption and that individual militiamen may have acted inappropriately on occasion, but they resolutely denied that the militia was functioning as an extension of the state Republican Party. Republicans also disputed the charge that arming state militias had spurred Klan violence, which they argued had long preceded this decision.[20]

U.S. Attorney Daniel Corbin, a Republican sympathetic to the plight of freedmen, admitted that "although a friend of the administration," he nevertheless "disapproved entirely of the matter of organizing the colored people and arming them, without doing it generally in regard to all people." Neither Democrats nor Republicans on the committee disputed the fact that arming of the militias intensified the violence in South Carolina.[21]

THE SECOND AMENDMENT
BEFORE THE COURTS

In response to heightened violence in the South, Congress enacted a series of Enforcement Acts beginning in 1870. The third act, dubbed the Ku Klux Klan Act, criminalized conspiracies against the civil rights of citizens and empowered the president to use military force to suppress violence. Under the act, the federal government was given broad new powers to arrest and detain suspects. The newly organized Department of Justice headed by Attorney General Amos Akerman was given the task of prosecuting the large number of cases the Enforcement Acts generated. South Carolina became a testing ground for Akerman's aggressive strategy of civil rights enforcement. Akerman, a southerner who had fought for the Confederacy but then embraced the Republican cause after the war, toured South Carolina and consulted extensively with U.S. Attorney Daniel Corbin. To assist them, Major Lewis Merrill of the U.S. Army prepared a detailed report that documented the outrages that the Klan had committed in South Carolina. Based on the recommendations of Merrill and Akerman, President Ulysses S. Grant issued an executive order empowering federal officials to arrest and detain large numbers of Klansmen.[22]

In preparation for what became known as the Klan trials, Corbin deposed at least three hundred Klansmen and at least as many freedmen. After reviewing these statements, Corbin concluded they revealed "a state of things quite as bad, if not worse, than any of us then anticipated." Indeed, he noted plaintively, "these confessions and statements exhibit a catalogue of crimes probably never surpassed, if equaled, in the history of any country. No person can have an adequate idea of their enormity without carefully perusing these statements."[23]

In consultation with Attorney General Akerman, Corbin recommended that the prosecution explore violations of Second Amendment rights when framing their case against the Klan. "It happens that in connection with all the whippings and murders, in this county, nearly, the arms of the negroes were seized and appropriated by" the Klan. Corbin intended to bring indictments "charging a conspiracy to injure, oppress, etc., a citizen of the United States, with intent to prevent and hinder his free exercise and enjoyment of a right and privilege secured to him by the Constitution of the United States," namely, "the right to keep and bear arms." Using the Second Amendment as the basis for a federal prosecution was a novel strategy, and Corbin actively sought out Akerman's advice on how best to proceed. In his response to Corbin's query, Akerman pondered the constitutional questions that the Klan's campaigns of terror and attempts to disarm blacks posed. Akerman confessed doubts about the ability to sustain a claim about a general right of personal security under the Constitution: "I do not feel quite certain that the right to be secure in one's person et cet., as that language is used in the Constitution, is violated by an irregular and unofficial seizure." On the Second Amendment issue, Akerman was far more confident, declaring, "Upon the right to bear arms, I think you are impregnable." The Klan had seized guns given to the Negro militia by the state of South Carolina, and the two Republican lawyers concluded that this gave them an unassailable Second Amendment claim to take before the courts.[24]

Rather than seek indictments against all of those arrested under the Enforcement Act, Corbin and Akerman resolved to prosecute a select number of leading Klan members. The first of these Second Amendment cases, *U.S. v. Avery*, became embroiled in technical questions about the authority of the federal courts to prosecute murder, a crime which the defense argued was only punishable under the laws of South Carolina and hence ought to be tried in state, not federal, court. Hugh Lennox Bond, a moderate Republican from Maryland, and George S. Bryan, a conservative Democrat, former slaveholder, and secessionist appointed by Andrew Johnson, heard the case. The judges divided over the complicated issues of federal jurisdiction. This disagreement triggered a review by the Supreme Court.[25]

With the disposition of the federalism issue in *Avery* awaiting resolution by the Supreme Court, Corbin and Akerman proceeded with their plan to use the Klan prosecutions to push their belief that the Fourteenth Amendment had incorporated the Second Amendment as a civic right. The next Klan case, *U.S. v. Mitchell*, focused on the intimidation and brutal murder of Negro militia Captain Jim Williams. The government charged that the Klan had been engaged in a conspiracy to deprive Williams of his constitutional right to bear arms and to intimidate him and thereby prevent his exercise of his constitutional right to vote.[26]

During the trial, Corbin faithfully followed the strategy he had worked out with Akerman. A key element in the case was the Klan's violation of the right to bear arms. Corbin highlighted this issue in his opening address, when he declared that "if there is any right that is dear to the citizen, it is the right to keep and bear arms," a protection "secured to the citizen of the United States on the adoption of the Amendments to the Constitution." The issue of incorporation was dealt with explicitly by Corbin. He noted the U.S. Supreme Court had settled the issue of whether the federal Bill of Rights was binding on the states in the antebellum case of *Barron v. Baltimore*. Having conceded that *Barron*'s ruling denied federal authority to protect the rights of citizens against state action, Corbin went on to assert that the Fourteenth Amendment "changes all that theory, and lays the same restrictions upon the States that before lay upon the Congress of the United States." Corbin then explained how members of the Klan had attempted to disarm members of the Negro militia.

> Imagine, if you like—but we have not to draw upon the imagination for the facts—a militia company, organized in York County, and a combination and conspiracy to rob the people of their arms, and to prevent them from keeping and bearing arms furnished to them by the State Government. Is not that a conspiracy to defeat the right of the citizens, secured by the Constitution of the United States, and guaranteed by the Fourteenth amendment?[27]

Corbin's opening address logically and succinctly stated the government's theory of the Second Amendment as a militia-based, civic right.

The defense objected to Corbin's effort to make the Second Amendment central to the case. Henry Stanbery, one of the distinguished team of constitutional lawyers Democrats procured to defend the Klan and champion the cause of states' rights, presented a different view of the meaning of the Fourteenth Amendment. Stanbery's résumé was impressive; he had served as Andrew Johnson's attorney general and defended the president during his impeachment trial. Stanbery denied that the right to bear arms was one of the privileges and immunities of citizenship protected by the Fourteenth Amendment. Echoing what had become a mantra among postwar Democrats, he argued that the Fourteenth Amendment had minimal impact on the legal meaning of the Second Amendment; he argued that the amendment was merely "a restriction upon Congress" and that "it is one of the rights of the State."[28]

Reverdy Johnson, cocounsel for the defense, had an equally impressive career before the bar and in politics. Johnson had been a U.S. senator and had argued the Dred Scott case before the Supreme Court. Johnson was even more aggressive in challenging the prosecution's Second Amendment claims. Not only was the right to bear arms subject to a wide variety of restraints by the state when public safety demanded such limitations, but he claimed that it was also entirely within the state's police power to determine "whether any particular class should be permitted to bear arms, and every other class denied the privilege." In his view there was no universal right to bear arms as part of the militia.[29]

The Democrats defending the Klan took advantage of an earlier ruling by the two judges in *Avery*, the case pending before Supreme Court. In that earlier Klan case, the judges had ruled exactly as Akerman had predicted they would; the court concluded that "the right to be secure in one's house is not a right derived from the Constitution, but it existed long before the adoption of the Constitution, at common law, and cannot be said to come within the meaning of the words of the act, 'right, privilege, or immunity.' " The judges' ruling did not directly address the meaning of the right of individual self-defense, but it appeared to adopt the orthodox legal view of the matter, treating the common-law right of self-defense as legally distinct from the constitutional right to bear arms in a well-regulated militia. Building on the judges' ruling in *Avery* and his own cocounsel's argument that bearing arms was distinct from the right of self-defense, Johnson developed a bold argument. It was the Klansmen, not the Negro militia, who had acted in self-defense. The Negro militia were intent on visiting death and destruction on southern whites. The actions of the Klan, Johnson claimed, were not only rational, but also entirely legal. In essence, Johnson's strategy invoked the common-law right of self-defense to challenge Corbin's assertion of a Second Amendment claim. The Klan's right of self-defense trumped the constitutional right of citizens to bear arms as part of the militia.[30]

Asserting a self-defense argument on behalf of the Klan required Stanbery and Johnson to prove that it was the Negro militia who were the aggressors. Williams, the murder victim, was portrayed by the defense as "a dangerous character, and a violent man." Whites felt threatened by Williams, who "commanded this company, and had a formidable force under him, armed with the best arms of the day." According to Stanbery's account of events, Williams "threatened again, and again, injuries to whites," including an ominous boast to kill "from the cradle to the grave." Rather than mount an aggressive campaign against the Negro militias, Stanbery claimed the Klan acted defensively. Until the arming of these militias, he argued, there had been no Klan in this region of South Carolina.[31]

Corbin's frustration with the judge's refusal to address his Second Amendment claims was palpable. The lack of a definitive judgment on this key point of law left him deeply irritated. He declared that the "conspiracy to deprive citizens of the right to have and bear arms" was key to the government's case, and he vowed, "We will never abandon it until we are obliged to." Corbin pressed the issue, reminding the court, "We are waiting the decision of the Court on the count as to the right of bearing arms; I might as well say here, that we regard it as one of the vital grounds of the prosecution." Judge Bond replied curtly: "The Court is not ready to give you an opinion on that subject now."[32]

The court's refusal to decide on the Second Amendment issue left the prosecution in a difficult situation. They would have to expend considerable time and energy laying out their theory of a clear Second Amendment violation knowing that the judges might declare this part of their case inadmissible. Although the status of the Second Amendment claim remained in constitutional limbo, pending the court's final determination, the issue of the right to bear arms figured as a major theme in both the defense's and prosecution's accounts of the events leading up to Williams's murder. Corbin did his best to portray Williams as a sober citizen and a fearless soldier, whose only mistake was his unwillingness to bow to the Klan's campaign of terror. The Klan's lawyers cast Williams as a ruthless desperado who had been well armed by corrupt Republican politicians who let him terrorize whites in the countryside.[33]

Corbin hoped that the details of the Klan's murderous rampage that evening would discredit the defense's strategy. The brutal murder of Williams was a ghastly tale. The image of Williams' fate at the hand of the Klan clearly left a profound impression on Corbin's young assistant, Louis Post. More than fifty years later, Post had little trouble recalling this incident; the details remained vividly etched in his mind.[34]

A cavalcade of sixty cowardly white men, completely disguised with face masks and body gowns, rode up one night in March 1871, to the house of Captain Williams, roughly and coarsely awoke him and his wife from their sleep, marched him to a little wood near by, forced his wife to remain behind when she had piteously but vainly pleaded for her husband's life and then begged to go with him, and in the wood hanged him to the limb of a tree and poured bullets from their rifles into his dying body. On the dangling corpse, those despicable savages then pinned a slip of paper inscribed, as I remember it, with these grim words "Jim Williams gone to his last muster."[35]

The Klan's defense team dismissed the prosecution's novel theory of Second Amendment incorporation through the Fourteenth Amendment. The Second Amendment, they confidently asserted, was a states' right. Giving citizens the right to bear arms had been intended to prevent Congress from disarming the state militias. The notion that the Fourteenth Amendment had any relevance to the right to bear arms was absurd; there was absolutely nothing in its text to support such a view. The defense attacked Governor Scott's efforts to arm the militia, claiming that they were tools of a corrupt Republican regime so intoxicated with power that they posed a serious threat to whites. The defense was so confident that the prosecution's Second Amendment argument would fail that they engaged in a bold legal gamble, conceding that a conspiracy had existed to disarm the Negro militia but insisting that nothing had been done to interfere with blacks' right to vote. Such a strategy would have been foolhardy if they expected Corbin's incorporation argument to find a sympathetic audience among the judges in the case or in the Supreme Court.[36]

The results of the case were a partial victory for supporters of incorporation. Corbin obtained a conviction against Robert Hayes Mitchell (a Klansman who had participated in the murder) for engaging in a conspiracy to intimidate and obstruct Williams's right to exercise his right of suffrage. The federal government clearly could protect the right to vote. The Second Amendment incorporation argument, however, had utterly failed. The notion that one might incorporate the Second Amendment as a privilege and immunity of national citizenship had been rejected by the court in favor of the rival states' rights theory of the Democrats, which cast this principle in the narrowest possible terms.

According to this view the Second Amendment did no more than restrain Congress from disarming the militia.[37]

The one theory of the Second Amendment that did not have any discernible impact on the disposition of the case was the radical abolitionist theory of the Second Amendment that had inspired some of the amendment's framers in Congress. Neither the government nor the defense argued that the Second Amendment was an individual right of private citizens to bear arms for personal self-defense. Indeed, the defense argued that individual right of self-defense was in conflict with the Second Amendment.[38]

CONSTITUTIONAL COMMENTARY ON THE SECOND AMENDMENT DURING RECONSTRUCTION

The meaning of the Second Amendment and the related questions about the possible impact of the Fourteenth Amendment on the scope of this constitutional right prompted a number of comments by judges and legal scholars during Reconstruction. Although mainstream Republicans defended the idea of incorporating the Second Amendment as a civic right, the rival states' rights theory espoused by Democrats continued to gain ground during this period. By the time the Supreme Court finally weighed in on the issue, the constitutional center of gravity had shifted away from the civic conception and toward the states' rights conception of the Second Amendment.[39]

The dean of the New York University Law School, John Norton Pomeroy, captured mainstream Republican legal thinking about the interconnected meanings of the Second Amendment and the Fourteenth Amendment. He began his consideration of the issue by reiterating the view that the scope of the amendment's protections were shaped by the preamble. The "object of this clause is to secure a well-armed militia." Pomeroy reminded readers that "government is forbidden by any law or proceeding to invade or destroy the right to keep and bear arms." Conceding this point, however, did not mean that government could not extensively regulate firearms. As he explained, "This constitutional inhibition is certainly not violated by laws forbidding persons to carry dangerous or concealed weapons, or laws forbidding the accumulation of quantities of arms," which were entirely consistent with the notion of a well-regulated society.[40]

Pomeroy explicitly took up the issue that had troubled so many Republicans before the adoption of the Fourteenth Amendment, the absence of any constitutional mechanism to force states to respect the rights of their citizens. His example to illustrate this point could have been lifted from any of the notorious southern black codes. "Let it be supposed," he mused, that a particular state had an explicit provision in its constitution affirming a right to bear arms and then passed "statutes by which certain classes of inhabitants—say negroes—are required to surrender their arms, and are forbidden to keep and bear them under certain penalties." While a person ought to be able to appeal such a manifestly unjust law to their own state's courts, in the event the court failed to act there would be no option for appeal. The Fourteenth Amendment, Pomeroy noted, provided just such a remedy, and he urged the American people to adopt the Fourteenth Amendment to the Constitution, which he viewed as "more important than any which has been adopted since the organization of the government, except alone the one abolishing the institution of slavery."[41]

While there was some disagreement among Republicans over the nature of the Second Amendment incorporated by the Fourteenth, there was little disagreement that the states retained broad powers to regulate firearms, including a right to ban certain classes of weapons with little utility for the preservation of a well-regulated militia. Rather than mark a sharp break with antebellum case law, most legal commentators emphasized continuity with prewar jurisprudence. The most important postwar effort to synthesize all of the diverse strains of antebellum legal thinking about the right to bear arms under both state and federal constitutional law occurred in Joel Prentiss Bishop's influential *Commentaries on the Law of Statutory Crimes* (1873).

Although Bishop noted that a few courts had embraced a more expansive conception of bearing arms under state constitutional law, the dominant view was the more limited civic, militia-based right articulated in *Buzzard*, an interpretation Bishop characterized as the "Arkansas doctrine." Only a small class of weapons suitable for the goal of preserving a well-regulated militia enjoyed full constitutional protection. Weapons "employed in quarrels, brawls, and fights between maddened individuals" were excluded from constitutional protection and fell entirely within the scope of individual states' police powers.[42]

One measure of Bishop's influence may be seen in the authority accorded his interpretation by one of the most influential jurists and legal scholars of the Reconstruction era, John Forrest Dillon. A former Iowa Supreme Court judge, Dillon was elevated to the U.S. Circuit for the Eighth District by President Grant. By the end of the 1870s, Dillon had assumed a prestigious professorship at Columbia Law School. In a series of articles published in the *Central Law Journal* in 1874, Dillon explored the state of American legal thinking on the right to bear arms. Recognizing that the U.S. Supreme Court had not yet entered the fray and offered a definitive judgment, Dillon concluded that lawyers and judges ought to look to the small body of state case law for guidance. The spectrum of antebellum jurisprudence was wide, running from the expansive individual rights view enunciated in *Bliss* to the narrow civic conception elaborated in *Buzzard*. Dillon endorsed Bishop's view that *Buzzard*'s "Arkansas doctrine," not the libertarian views exhibited in *Bliss*, captured the dominant strain of American legal thinking on this question.[43]

There was a strong judicial consensus, Dillon explained, that time, place, and manner restriction, including bans on carrying concealed weapons, "did not deprive citizens of his *natural* right of self-defense, or his constitutional right to bear arms." Although the line demarcating the constitutional right to bear arms and the common-law right of self-defense had become murkier over the course of the century in some places, Dillon continued to treat the two concepts as though they were legally distinct. According to the "Arkansas doctrine" the only weapons entitled to constitutional protection were those associated with the goal of preserving a well-regulated militia.[44]

Dillon recognized that the thorniest legal issue was posed by the inevitable conflict between the common-law right of self-defense and the state's prerogatives to use police power to promote public safety. Rather than argue that the right of self-defense rendered robust regulation unconstitutional, as the *Bliss* court had done, Dillon turned to the common law for guidance. There would always be unusual "circumstances under which to disarm a citizen would be to leave his life at the mercy of treacherous and plotting enemy." When such circumstances arose, "such a case might clearly be said to fall within that class of cases in which the previously existing common law interpolates exceptions upon subsequently enacted statutes." Individuals who violated a statute under extraordinary circumstances were, he believed, entitled to leniency in court.[45]

Dillon ably encapsulated the larger problem courts faced when attempting to balance the right of individual self-defense against the right of public safety. Society could not "require the individual to surrender and lay aside the means of self-protection." Nonetheless, "the peace of society and the safety of peaceable citizens plead loudly for protection against the evils which result from permitting other citizens to go armed with dangerous weapons." The right to be protected and the right to protect oneself might come into conflict on occasion. Faced with such an intractable situation, the best the law could achieve was to "strike some sort of balance between these apparently conflicting rights."[46]

Rather than embrace Pomeroy and Akerman's incorporation theory, Dillon concluded that the Fourteenth Amendment had not radically transformed the meaning of arms bearing. According to Dillon, "there would seem to remain no doubt that if the question should ever arise in that court it would be held that the Second Amendment of the federal constitution is restrictive upon the general government merely and not upon the states." Furthermore, he argued, "every state has the power to regulate the bearing of arms in such a manner as it may see fit, or to restrain it altogether." In choosing to side with the limited states' rights view of the Fourteenth Amendment advanced by Democrats and opposing the strong incorporation doctrine championed by many Republicans, including theorists such as John Pomeroy, Dillon anticipated the future direction of federal jurisprudence on this issue. Within a year of publishing these prescient words, the Supreme Court followed the same logic outlined by Dillon in the *Central Law Journal.*[47]

THE END OF RECONSTRUCTION AND THE TRIUMPH OF STATES' RIGHTS: *U.S. V. CRUIKSHANK*

In 1875, the meaning of the Second Amendment finally came before the Supreme Court in *U.S. v. Cruikshank*, a Louisiana case arising from one of the bloodiest and most brutal episodes in the Reconstruction era, the Colfax Massacre. In contrast to the South Carolina KKK trials, where the Second Amendment issue was raised but never actually resolved by the Supreme Court on appeal, *Cruikshank* considered this issue directly. The Court decisively rejected both the individual and civic interpretations of the right to bear arms. Instead, the Court placed its full weight behind the Democrats' more narrow states' rights view.[48]

The Colfax Massacre was the culmination of a long and bitter conflict between Republicans and Democrats for control of Louisiana. The site of this heinous crime, Grant Parish, was about 245 miles north of New Orleans and had only recently been created by legislative gerrymandering, a partisan move designed to give blacks a numerical majority in this district. Republicans named this new district after President Grant and the seat of its government after Grant's vice president, Schuyler Colfax. The region had a troubled history and boasted a Klan-like paramilitary organization and a well-organized unit of the Negro militia.[49]

The immediate trigger for violence in Grant Parish was the contested election of 1872. Both sides claimed to have triumphed in the election, and the inconclusive outcome in the governor's race meant that local offices, including that of the sheriff, were also in dispute. The Democratic choice for sheriff gave notice to the incumbent Republican sheriff that he would take possession of the courthouse in Colfax. Upon learning that a large posse sympathetic to the Democrats was gathering to seize the courthouse, the Republican sheriff summoned his own *posse comitatus* composed largely of men from the local Negro militia, who prepared to defend the building from attack. Fearing for their lives, additional members of the African-American community, many of whom had served in the Union Army, sought refuge in the courthouse. The men organized themselves in a military fashion: drawing up a muster roll, electing officers, and erecting an earthen works barrier around the courthouse. Armed with Enfield rifles and shotguns, the veterans had also cleverly fashioned a cannon out of a metal pipe to defend the courthouse.[50]

Efforts to negotiate a truce between the two sides failed. After allowing women and children to leave the building, the whites opened fire. A standoff continued until the better armed and more numerous white forces stormed the fortifications and forced the black defenders back into the courthouse. After they torched the building, whites gunned down those fleeing the inferno. The carnage only ended when federal troops arrived the next day. Although an exact death toll was never confirmed, conservative reports estimated more than one hundred blacks had been murdered.[51]

The task of prosecuting the perpetrators of the Colfax Massacre fell to Attorney General Amos Akerman's successor, George H.

Williams. Although much less zealous than Akerman in his support of Reconstruction, the magnitude of the Colfax incident forced Williams to push the local federal prosecutor, James R. Beckwith, to prosecute aggressively those responsible for the deaths in Grant Parish. In an indictment running to 150 pages, 98 defendants were brought before a grand jury. Although William Cruikshank lent his name to this case, achieving a dubious sort of legal notoriety, he was not a leading player in the massacre, but had been one of the white mob that brutally attacked the courthouse in Colfax. The 32 charges brought against the defendants alleged violations of the Enforcement Acts, including a conspiracy to deprive citizens of "the free exercise and enjoyment" of a "right or privilege granted or secured" by the Constitution, including the right to bear arms.[52]

Although the prosecution had named more than ninety cocon-spirators in its lengthy indictment, only nine were brought to trial. One of the nine was acquitted and a hung jury necessitated a retrial for the remaining eight. Three of the eight were found guilty. Lawyers for the defense appealed the verdict and challenged the constitutionality of Section 6 of the Enforcement Acts, which made it a felony to conspire to "injure, oppress, threaten, or intimidate any citizen with intent to prevent or hinder his free exercise and enjoyment of any right or privi-lege granted or secured to him by the Constitution or laws of the United States."[53] The defense maintained that the crimes committed were not judicially enforceable under federal law, but were entirely within the legal sphere of the states. The case was heard by Judge William Woods and Associate Supreme Court Justice Joseph Bradley. While Woods believed the charges were indictable under federal law, Bradley disagreed, arguing that the Fourteenth Amendment prohib-ited state action, not the actions of private citizens. To concede that the federal government could prosecute private individuals would in effect create a general federal police power, something Bradley believed was not warranted by the Fourteenth Amendment. This division between the two judges on the constitutionality of the

Enforcement Act ultimately brought the case before the Supreme Court. *U.S. v. Cruikshank* would become a test case, not only for rival theories of the Second Amendment, but also for the theory of incorporation itself.[54]

Judge Woods not only believed that the federal government had the authority to prosecute the case, but he also embraced a fairly broad individual rights reading of the Second Amendment. Woods framed the right to bear arms in a distinctly individualist idiom, observing "a man who carries arms openly, and for his own protection, or for any other lawful purpose, has as clear a right to do so, as to carry his own watch or wear his own hat." The right to carry arms openly, Woods concluded, was clearly one enjoyed by all citizens. Curiously, the government's Supreme Court brief abandoned the Second Amendment issue entirely. It abjured the civic line of argument that had been developed by the previous attorney general, Amos Akerman, and also rejected the individual rights argument that Judge Woods developed in his circuit court ruling. The briefs filed for the defense took up the meaning of the right to bear arms explicitly and both affirmed the states' rights view and attacked the individual rights view endorsed by Woods. Against this more expansive individual rights conception, the defense countered, "The right to bear arms, if it be a right, is a matter to be regulated and controlled by the State, as each State may deem best for itself." In the view of one of the briefs filed on behalf of the perpetrators of the massacre,

> the power to regulate and control the bearing of arms on the part of the people, and their assembling together in great numbers, belongs to the police authority of the State, and it is a necessary power to be exercised by the State for peace of society and the safety of life and property.

Another brief filed on behalf of Cruikshank and his coconspirators reminded the Court that the Second Amendment's preamble, which declared the necessity of a well-regulated militia, established the clear military focus of the right, which had nothing to do with individual self-defense.

> The right which the people intended to have secured beyond the power of infringement by Congress, is the right to keep and bear arms for the purposes of maintaining, in the States, a well regulated militia, acknowledged in the article to be necessary for the security of a free State.

One of the defense briefs acknowledged that there had been some slippage in ordinary usage of the term *bear arms* between the eighteenth century and the nineteenth century. Having conceded this linguistic point, the defense vigorously disputed the notion that shifts in colloquial usage since the adoption of the amendment could transform the original understanding of the text's meaning. The right protected by the Second Amendment was not, as Woods's opinion had suggested, intended to protect an individual right of self-defense, but had been exclusively concerned with the problem of arming the militia.[55]

Regarding the Fourteenth Amendment incorporation of the Second Amendment, the defense maintained that states retained exclusive authority over the right to bear arms, "with the single qualification that these must not discriminate between different races of men." Rather than incorporate an individual right to bear arms, the defense argued, the Fourteenth Amendment only required the states to apply their laws about arms bearing in "a non-discriminatory fashion."[56]

The Supreme Court dismissed Woods's expansive reading of the right to bear arms as an individual right of private self-defense. While the Court appeared to implicitly acknowledge that the meaning of the term *bear arms* had evolved to encompass more than arms used for military purposes, this linguistic observation did not alter the meaning of the original constitutional text. Indeed, the Court went on to assert in unambiguous terms that "bearing arms for lawful purposes" was not identical to the right protected by the Second Amendment that linked bearing arms to participation in a well-regulated militia. In essence, the Court argued that the common-law right to keep and carry arms and the right to bear arms protected by the Second Amendment were legally distinct. The Second Amendment in their view was "one of the amendments that has no other effect than to restrict the powers of the national government." The purpose of the amendment was to guard the state militias against the danger of federal disarmament. According to this view, states were free to enact whatever measures they deemed appropriate regarding the militia or firearms, as long as these laws were nondiscriminatory. The ruling not only consigned the individual rights view of the right to bear arms to the margins of federal jurisprudence for more than a hundred years, but also effectively displaced the original civic conception of the amendment with this narrow states' rights conception of the Second Amendment.[57]

Cruikshank was a decisive moment in the history of an evolving Second Amendment jurisprudence. The government's decision to abandon its Second Amendment argument marked a retreat from the more aggressive policy of enforcing civil rights through the Fourteenth Amendment. *Cruikshank* hastened the demise of incorporation theory. The government also rejected the opportunity to make an individual rights claim, eschewing the arguments articulated by Judge Woods in his circuit court opinion. The Supreme Court's ruling endorsed a limited states' rights conception of the Second Amendment and pushed aside the civic conception of the Second Amendment that had dominated mainstream constitutional theory since the adoption of the Bill of Rights. *Cruikshank* not only marked the end of a hundred years of constitutional thinking about the right to bear arms, but it also inaugurated a new phase in the history of this provision of the Bill of Rights. After *Cruikshank*, the Second Amendment would be understood to be a limit on federal power to disarm the state militias.[58]

Cruikshank recast the Second Amendment's scope, reframing it in narrow states' rights terms. This legal narrowing of the ambit of the right to bear arms by the courts was followed by an equally profound change in the definition of the militia under federal law. As the century drew to a close, the issue of how to reform the militia and make it an effective fighting force for the modern age was vigorously debated. At the dawn of the new century, Congress took up the task of militia reform with renewed energy. Dissatisfied with the organization and effectiveness of the militia, Congress set about to reshape the nature of this venerable institution. The two key pieces of federal legislation were the Dick Act of 1903 and the National Defense Act of 1916. The Dick Act created an organized Militia, the National Guard, and the Reserve Militia. This new system was subsequently redefined by the National Defense Act as the National Guard and the Unorganized Militia. Taken together these two statutes effectively nationalized the function and control of the militia. By wresting control of the militia from the states, these acts had the practical effect of draining the Second Amendment of much of its remaining force. Although the Second Amendment was understood to be a restraint on the power of Congress to disarm the militia, the new National Guard was clearly a creature of the federal government.

The changes in the militia were part of a broader shift in American attitudes toward the ideal of an armed citizenry. In colonial America the law required that most white male citizens bear arms in the militia. The reorganization of militia into the modern National Guard prompted a more wide-ranging debate over the value of military training for civilians. One critic not only proclaimed his opposition to "making military training compulsory," but also went on to argue that "it is entirely adverse to the spirit and principles of the Constitution." This view seemed to turn the traditional conception of the militia on its head. The idea of the citizen solider was no longer the minuteman, but the National Guardsman. Mandatory military training for the civilian population was no longer cast as the necessary means of instilling virtue in the citizenry, but a means of corrupting individuals. Requiring citizens to obtain military training was deemed too Prussian and militaristic. This was nearly the opposite of the view championed during the Founding era. The most astute observers of this profound shift in American attitudes recognized that it represented a break with the past but accepted that times had simply changed. As one legal scholar noted, "The day is past when a group of hardy pioneer citizens could defend their rights by a few muskets or homemade pikes."[59]

THE MODERN GUN CONTROL DEBATE AND THE EMERGENCE OF THE COLLECTIVE RIGHTS THEORY

On a pleasant August day in 1910, William J. Gaynor, mayor of New York, waved good-bye to friends and supporters aboard a cruise ship docked along the Hudson River. A noted reformer who had vowed to clean up city hall politics, Gaynor was looking forward to a much-deserved vacation. The calm of the moment was shattered when a disgruntled city employee wielding a pistol rushed out of the crowd of well-wishers and shot Gaynor. Although he had been seriously injured, the mayor survived the failed assassination attempt, which shocked the city and gave additional impetus for those eager to enact more stringent firearms regulations. Within a year's time another noted city politician, Timothy "Big Tim" Sullivan, had persuaded the New York State legislature to enact the most wide-ranging gun control statute in American history. The Sullivan law not only regulated the right to carry firearms, but also severely restricted the possession of firearms in one's home and business. The law also instituted a license requirement for the ownership of handguns. Gun owners protested the law. Although a few challenges invoked the authority of the Second Amendment, these were easily dismissed in light of the holding in *Cruikshank*. The *New York Times* editorialized on this theme, confidently declaring that the Second Amendment "does not restrict the right of the states, in the exercise of their police power, to regulate the manner in which arms shall be kept or borne." Although the *Cruikshank* precedent appeared to effectively rule out future Second Amendment claims against gun control law, supporters of gun rights clung to the hope that their alternative view of the Second Amendment might someday gain ascendancy.[60]

Another barrier against making the Second Amendment the foundation for opposition to gun control was the emergence of the collective rights reading of *Cruikshank*. This theory was developed in a short but influential article in the *Harvard Law Review* (1914) authored by Lucillus A. Emery, chief justice of the Maine Supreme Court. Profound changes in American society, Emery warned, necessitated the articulation of a theory to justify more robust regulation of firearms. Among the pressing reasons that prompted a new approach to gun regulation, Emery listed the following: the "greater deadliness of small arms," the "alarming frequency of homicides," and the rise of a distinctive criminal class "known as 'gunmen' from their ready use of such weapons for criminal purpose." These developments inspired Emery to ponder "the question of the reason, scope, and limitation of the constitutional guaranty of a right to keep and bear arms,—of the extent of its restraint upon the legislative power." He concluded that the Second Amendment posed minimal restraints on the power to regulate firearms.[61]

Emery began his consideration of the amendment's meaning with the preamble's affirmation of the need for a well-regulated militia. Reading the text of the amendment through the lens of the preamble was hardly a novel legal strategy; most constitutional commentators since the adoption of the amendment had done so. Profound changes in the legal definition of the militia had transformed the meaning of the preamble's words. Writing after the emergence of the modern National Guard, Emery viewed the militia in fairly narrow terms. The words of the preamble no longer referred to the universal militia of the Founding era, but now described the modern National Guard. The Second Amendment's guarantee only applied to persons who "bear arms in military organizations." Perhaps the most significant aspect of Emery's argument was his explicit reformulation of the Second Amendment as a collective right. "The right guaranteed is not so much to the individual for his private quarrels or feuds as to the people collectively for the common defense against a common enemy, foreign or domestic." After Emery, the debate over the meaning of the Second Amendment was cast in terms of a simple dichotomy: collective versus individual right. By reframing arms bearing as a collective right, not a right of the states, Emery's model implicitly absorbed the new modern understanding of the militia encoded in the Dick Act. The collectivity that exercised this right was no longer the militias of the individual states, but rather the National Guard.[62]

According to Emery's collective rights theory, the Second Amendment posed absolutely no barrier to gun regulation. Asserting such a claim did not mean citizens had no rights to keep and use firearms. The common law continued to provide some protections for gun owners. In the absence of any explicit legislation, citizens were, of course, free to own whatever guns they desired. For citizens living in states that had embraced the more individualistic Jacksonian model of arms bearing in their state constitutions, there was even more protection for gun rights. In the absence of such explicit state constitutional provisions, however, legislatures were free to follow New York's example and enact highly restrictive gun control legislation.[63]

The collective rights paradigm developed by Emery effectively recast the late nineteenth-century debate about the meaning of the right to bear arms that had arisen during Reconstruction in terms that better suited the demands of the twentieth century's equally acrimonious debate over gun control. In its original Anti-Federalist form, the states' rights theory of the Second Amendment was intended to give the states the potential to challenge federal authority. The post-Civil War version of the states' rights theory jettisoned these revolutionary aspirations. Democrats used the Second Amendment as a convenient constitutional hook upon which to hang their challenge to the Republican theory of incorporation. By recasting the states' rights theory as a collective right, Emery further diluted the amendment's connection to federalism. In a sense, Emery's argument was more concerned with demonstrating that the Second Amendment was not an individual right than with probing its positive contribution to American constitutionalism. Henceforth, the debate over the Second Amendment would be framed around the requirements of the modern debate over gun control.

Demand for more effective gun control was closely tied to public perception of crime. The growth of organized crime during the Prohibition era made gangster weapons such as the machine gun powerful symbols of the danger posed by firearms. The most notorious episode of machine gun violence occurred on St. Valentine's Day in 1929 when a group of gunmen from Al Capone's gang executed members of a rival gang. Outrage over the St. Valentine's Day Massacre helped focus public attention on the need for more effective gun regulation. The demands for some type of federal involvement finally bore fruit in 1934 when Congress enacted the first comprehensive federal firearms law. The National Firearms Act regulated firearms dealers and imposed a series of taxes on particular classes of weapons, including machine guns. The law took advantage of congressional authority to levy taxes and used this power to target the types of weapons associated with gangsters and bootleggers. The National Firearms Act of 1934 taxed the manufacture, sale, and transfer of sawed-off shotguns, machine guns, and silencers. The act sought to limit access to this class of weapons, which was closely identified with criminal behavior.[64]

The constitutionality of this law was challenged on Second Amendment grounds in *U.S. v. Miller*. The defendants in the case, Jack Miller and Frank Layton, had allegedly transported an unregistered, sawed-off shotgun across state lines. The district court in Arkansas quashed the indictment on Second Amendment grounds, and the government appealed directly to the Supreme Court, which agreed to hear the case. Miller and Layton took flight rather then stick around to defend their Second Amendment rights. The only brief filed in the case was the one prepared by Franklin Roosevelt's solicitor general, Robert Jackson, who eventually went on to become a prosecutor at the Nuremberg trials and a Supreme Court justice.[65]

The government's brief advanced a set of familiar arguments. Solicitor General Jackson drew on Emery's collective rights formulation. The government described the scope of the Second Amendment's protection as "generally restricted to the keeping and bearing of arms by the people collectively for their common defense and security." Furthermore, the brief asserted that "the Second discloses that this right has reference only to the keeping and bearing of arms by the people as members of the state militia or other similar military organizations provided by law." The government also quoted extensively from *State v. Buzzard*, the case that enunciated what Bishop had called the "Arkansas doctrine." In addition to a long list of state cases, the brief cited many of the major nineteenth-century commentators, including Bishop, Joseph Story, and Francis Wharton, to support its collective rights reading. According to the government's theory, the right to bear arms had been intended to preserve a citizen's right to defend public liberty as part of a well-regulated militia and did not extend to weapons owned for individual self-defense. Thus, while the brief employed the newer language of Emery's collective rights argument, the substance of its claims drew on the "Arkansas doctrine," a well-established body of antebellum jurisprudence that Bishop and others had identified as the orthodox view of bearing arms in American law. Indeed, apart from Emery's novel collective rights terminology there was nothing in the government's brief that would not have been available in Bishop's important treatise.[66]

The Supreme Court did not expressly adopt Emery's collective rights language. Instead, the court seemed to reach back further in history, quoting colonial militia practices and antebellum case law. The theory the Court embraced was clearly militia based, fusing elements of the traditional civic conception and the states' rights view that had emerged at the end of the nineteenth century. The emphasis in *Miller* was on bearing arms in the militia, not on the right of the states to maintain their militias. One thing was clear, the Court rejected the lower court's anomalous individual rights reading of the amendment. To dispel any possible doubt on this issue, Justice James C. McReynolds offered his own gloss on the case in the introductory remarks he made before the decision was announced in court. The *New York Times* reporter covering the case wrote, "Justice McReynolds drawled from the bench: 'We construe the amendment as having relation to the military service and we are unable to say that a sawed-off shotgun has relation to the militia.' "[67]

Although the Court cited the antebellum case of *Aymette*, it tightened the principle articulated in that case by requiring that the weapon not only be of a type associated with militia duty, but that it also be used in conjunction with some type of militia-related activity. The only weapons entitled to Second Amendment protection were those that met both criteria. As for the first point, the Court concluded that

> in the absence of any evidence tending to show that the possession or use of "a shotgun having a barrel of less than eighteen inches in length" at this time has some reasonable relationship to the preservation or efficiency of a well regulated militia, we cannot say that the Second Amendment guarantees the right to keep and bear such an instrument.

Miller's weapon was not "part of the ordinary military equipment" of the militia, nor did the occasion of its use "contribute to the common defense." The Court had decisively rejected the notion that one had an individual right under the Second Amendment to own firearms for reasons unconnected with militia activity.[68]

Miller and Layton, the defendants in the case, had no connection to the militia and thus were technically without standing to bring a Second Amendment claim. Rather than address this issue, the Court wisely recognized that the definition of the militia could change. If Congress decided to recreate the universal militia of the Founding era, a plausible scenario in an era when Europe was at war, the defendants might well have been able to raise such a claim. It was therefore important for the Court to reach a determination on the scope of congressional power over firearms quite apart from the issue of who might claim to be a member of the militia. Had the Court dismissed the case on the standing issue it never would have reached a decision on the type of weapon at the root of the case. The Court took the opportunity to settle this issue, which was a pressing public policy concern, the right to ban certain types of weapons closely associated with criminal behavior. The Court prudently developed a two-prong test to evaluate a Second Amendment claim: weapons had to be of a type related to militia activity and had to be used in conjunction with participation in a well-regulated militia. This test avoided the potentially absurd result of giving criminals the opportunity to claim that if their guns were used by the National Guard and part of the ordinary equipment of the soldier they were entitled to Second Amendment protection. If the court had focused exclusively on the type of weapon and ignored the context in which the weapon was used, it would have given Second Amendment protection to criminals bearing bazookas and flamethrowers.[69]

While the language of the decision appeared to be closer in spirit to the antebellum civic rights view than Emery's collective rights theory, these legal subtleties were lost on most contemporary commentators, who read the decision as a straightforward endorsement of the collective rights view. Emery's interpretation had achieved something like a hegemonic dominance among legal commentators and scholars, and this view was reflected in contemporary reports of the case. Reactions among legal scholars were uniformly supportive of some variant of the collective rights reading of the decision. In its "Case Notes," the *California Law Review* noted that the Court "held that the right refers to the people as a collective body."[70]

The case attracted relatively little attention in the mainstream press. Reports of the case did not treat it as a momentous ruling in the history of the Second Amendment. As one might expect for a case decided during the New Deal, the issue that sparked the greatest interest was the Court's vindication of the federal government's broad powers to regulate economic conduct, in this case the sale and transfer of firearms. In particular, the press seized on the government's ability to deal with weapons closely associated with criminal behavior, in this case a sawed-off shotgun. This issue seemed more resonant than any Second Amendment claims that had arisen in the lower court decision. A brief notice about the case in the *Chicago Tribune* bore the headline "U.S. High Court Bars Sawed Off Shotgun Sales."[71]

Subsequent federal court decisions interpreted *Miller* through the same lens as contemporary law reviews used to understand the case. The Second Amendment protected a collective right tied to participation in the militia. Four years later in *U.S. v. Tot*, the Third Circuit Court of Appeals held that

> it is abundantly clear both from the discussions of this amendment contemporaneous with its proposal and adoption and those of learned writers since that this amendment, unlike those providing for protection of free speech and freedom of religion, was not adopted with individual rights in mind, but as a protection for the States in the maintenance of their militia organizations against possible encroachments by the federal power.

Employing the language used by Emery, the Court concluded that the Second Amendment protected a collective right. *Tot*'s collective reading of *Miller* soon became the orthodox interpretation of the meaning of the Second Amendment by the federal courts.

While federal courts and mainstream legal academics continued to accept the orthodox reading of *Miller* as affirming a collective right, proponents of gun rights steadfastly adhered to their own individual rights reading of the Second Amendment. The most important organization lobbying for this individual rights view was the National Rifle Association (NRA), which began as an organization devoted to improving marksmanship after the Civil War era. The rise of modern gun control, beginning with the enactment of the Sullivan law at the dawn of the twentieth century, pushed the NRA toward greater political activism. The final evolution of the NRA into its current form, a militant gun rights organization built around an aggressive Second Amendment ideology, occurred largely in response to the passage of the Gun Control Act of 1968. This law was enacted after the assassinations of Robert F. Kennedy and Martin Luther King, Jr. The most comprehensive federal gun regulation in American history, it added new prohibitions on interstate sale of weapons, prohibited sales to certain classes of dangerous persons, and tightened regulation of firearms dealers. Much as the first gun control laws passed in Jacksonian America only intensified the ideology of gun rights, so, too, the passage of more restrictive federal gun control laws during the turbulent era of the 1960s led to a more aggressive commitment to gun rights.[72]

Gun rights ideology has continued to flourish in America, particularly in many parts of America where firearms remain deeply embedded in popular culture. Efforts to challenge federal gun control laws on Second Amendment grounds, however, gained little ground in the courts. The legal campaign of gun rights advocates has proven far less effective than grassroots organizing and lobbying by the NRA and other pro-gun organizations. Although the NRA has mounted many legal challenges to federal and local gun laws on Second Amendment grounds, these cases invariably ran up against the orthodox collective rights reading of *Miller*. Undaunted by this fact, a small but industrious group of legal academics committed to gun rights, aided by gun rights activists outside of the academy, began churning out at an astonishing rate law review articles that supported the individual rights view of the Second Amendment. This revisionist body of scholarship was eventually dubbed the "new Standard Model" of the Second Amendment by its supporters. This view prompted others within the legal academy, particularly those with a contrarian bent, to embrace this new individual rights theory. While legal scholarship had been firmly supportive of the collective rights reading for most of the twentieth century, the pendulum began to shift toward the individual rights reading in the last decade of the century.[73]

While the so-called "Standard Model" was dismissed by most federal courts, proponents of gun rights finally scored a modest victory in *U.S. v. Emerson* (2001). Building on this revisionist body of academic scholarship associated with the Standard Model, the Fifth Circuit held that the Second Amendment did protect an individual right that had no connection with participation in an organized militia. The victory in *Emerson* proved somewhat hollow. While the court declared that the Second Amendment was an individual right, it upheld the federal gun control law at issue in the case. The court did not apply strict scrutiny, the most rigorous form of judicial review of federal laws. Rather, the court deferred to Congress, giving it the broadest possible latitude in crafting gun regulations. The gun regulation in question in *Emerson* involved a prohibition on firearms ownership by persons under a domestic violence restraining order. The court concluded that the law clearly had a rational basis, the most lax standard of judicial review, and so it easily passed constitutional muster. If the right to bear arms was an individual right, the court seemed to say, it was not like other fundamental liberties such as freedom of speech. Apparently guns were not like words. Perhaps even more disappointing to supporters of gun rights was the fact that no other federal courts rushed to follow the example of the *Emerson* ruling. Rather than mark a departure from orthodox readings of *Miller*, *Emerson* appears to have been an anomalous ruling that has exerted little influence on firearms law.[74]

Ultimately, legal challenges to gun control on Second Amendment grounds have proven to be less significant than the impressive political strength and organization of grassroots gun rights activists, who have not only blocked the passage of any new federal gun control laws, but also have won an impressive string of victories in Congress furthering their cause. Gun rights advocates successfully blocked the renewal of a ban on assault weapons and crafted legislation preventing lawsuits against the gun industry. At the state level, gun rights supporters have been equally effective securing laws favorable to gun rights, including the passage of scores of laws allowing citizens to carry concealed weapons. The only arena in which gun rights supporters have failed to win is in the courts.

While the orthodox reading of *Miller* remains the law of the land, it is impossible to predict the future of Second Amendment jurisprudence. Given the inevitable changes in the composition of the Supreme Court, it is likely that a new test might well come before the high court and revisit *Miller*. Indeed, the future of Second Amendment jurisprudence remains very much up for grabs.[75]

Although the Second Amendment can hardly be blamed for creating the impasse that has prevented Americans from developing a rational and effective policy for dealing with firearms, the simplistic individual/collective rights dichotomy that continues to structure public discourse over this issue certainly has not helped matters much. At the dawn of the twenty-first century it is worth pausing to consider whether or not the individual/collective rights dichotomy model bequeathed to us by Emery and elaborated by subsequent commentators may have outlived its usefulness. This simplistic framework not only distorts the complex history of the struggle to define the meaning of the right to bear arms, but it also has made it difficult to frame a calm and rational public debate over this issue. The time may be ripe for a new paradigm for the Second Amendment, one that is more faithful to its rich history and better suited to the task of helping Americans move forward on this divisive issue.

FOR DEFENSE

BUY
UNITED
STATES
SAVINGS
BONDS
AND STAMPS

ASK ABOUT OUR PAY ROLL ALLOTMENT PLAN

During the Second World War the image of the Concord minuteman was frequently used by the government to encourage civic participation and collective sacrifice. In the contemporary gun debate, the minuteman image has been appropriated by gun rights groups committed to a more individualistic and antigovernment ethos. (World War Poster Collection, Manuscripts Division, University of Minnesota Libraries, Minneapolis, Minn.)

CONCLUSION

A NEW PARADIGM FOR THE SECOND AMENDMENT

Given the profound transformations that have altered the political, social, and constitutional landscape in the two hundred years since the Second Amendment was adopted one might reasonably ask whether or not there is still anything practical to be gleaned from its history. The collective and individual rights theories that have long dominated public debate over this contentious topic were not bequeathed to us by the Founding generation, but were the products of a struggle at the end of the nineteenth century. Can the constitutional framework established more than a hundred years ago provide a workable jurisprudence for dealing with the complex problems posed by guns in contemporary America? Historians, of course, need not worry about such matters. For historians, simply uncovering the unexpected twists and turns in this convoluted history and relishing the many ironies in this story are reward enough. Yet, while historians may revel in the richness of the history and marvel at the ironies that permeate it, lawyers, judges, and policy makers are faced with the difficult task of learning from the past and shaping the future. Moving from history to constitutional theory is always tricky. One must approach such a task with a good deal of constitutional humility, a far cry from the constitutional hubris that characterizes so much constitutional scholarship in an originalist vein.[1]

The most important consequence of recovering the original understanding is that it demonstrates that both of the modern interpretations of the Second Amendment do great violence to the text, effectively erasing half of its meaning. Modern collective rights theorists believe that the meaning of the amendment can be encapsulated by its first clause, which affirms the need for a well-regulated militia. According to this view the Second Amendment protects the right of states, not individuals, to maintain a well-regulated militia. For most modern collective rights theorists the amendment is an artifact of the eighteenth century, a time when the fear of standing armies and faith in a militia exercised a powerful hold on American culture. In essence, this states' rights approach asserts that the Second Amendment is a constitutional anachronism, a historical relic with little contemporary relevance. In place of the well-regulated militias venerated by the Founders, Americans now depend on organized police forces and highly trained professional armies. This view is an anathema to gun rights advocates, who focus on the final clause of the amendment that affirms the right of the people to keep and bear arms. Partisans of this individual rights interpretation do not believe that the right to bear arms is a relic of lost revolutionary heritage. They read the amendment as protecting a right of individuals to keep arms and when necessary to bear them for individual self-defense, or recreation, or to wage revolution when government threatens liberty.

The one interpretation that has been lost, buried at the end of the nineteenth century, is the civic view of arms bearing. Rather than give greater weight to only part of the amendment's text, as both modern interpretations do, the original civic rights interpretation of the Second Amendment demands that the text be read holistically. The Second Amendment serves as a reminder that the right to bear arms is as much an obligation owed to government as it is a claim against government interference. Moreover, the original civic conception of the Second Amendment emphasizes that there can be no right to bear arms without extensive regulation.[2]

Some scholars have argued that whatever the history of the Second Amendment might have been, the reality is that most Americans believe it protects an individual right. While the notion may have started out as a minority view in the Founding era, it gradually evolved into the majority view in America. The National Rifle Association (NRA) and other gun rights organizations have not only helped bring about this transformation, but they also have exploited it, attacking any who disagree with their interpretation of this provision of the Constitution as somehow anti-Second Amendment. There is no doubt that the Second Amendment has been swept up in the modern rights revolution. Accepting this fact graciously, some argue, might even make gun control laws more palatable to many gun rights supporters. While such a view makes for good sociology, it makes for bad law. One can certainly make a plausible argument that under a living constitution the Second Amendment ought to be treated as an individual right. Still, there is a big difference between treating the text of the Constitution as a living document and turning the Bill of Rights into an Etch-a-Sketch in which some clauses can be simply erased by judicial or legislative fiat.

If we really wish to amend the Constitution and get rid of the preamble of the Second Amendment, we ought to be honest and do so. As a practical matter there is no reason to believe that the most ardent gun rights advocates would ever accept robust gun regulation even if the courts suddenly reversed themselves and declared that the Second Amendment was an individual right. The only people clamoring for recognition of an individual right before the courts are adamantly opposed to the most modest types of gun regulation. The idea that the courts ought to engage in judicial activism to protect one of the most powerful lobbies in America seems odd to say the least. Given that the federal courts, with one notable exception, have rejected the individual rights view and given the obvious fact that America is awash in guns, recognition of an individual right hardly seems necessary to protect gun owners. Despite an effective rhetorical campaign by gun rights advocates, gun rights are not under siege in America, which has the most lax gun laws of any industrial democracy. The individual rights theory of the Second Amendment is not only unnecessary, but it also feeds the mistaken notion that the only way to protect our rights is to amend the Constitution, a dubious proposition at best. As long as guns are deeply woven in the fabric of American life, there is little danger of gun prohibition and no need to tinker with the Second Amendment.[3]

The greatest failing of both the modern collective rights and individual rights paradigms is that they have obscured the link between citizenship and bearing arms in the Founding era. In this regard, each of these modern interpretations of the Second Amendment reflects the precipitous decline in the ideal of civic participation in American culture, an idea that was central to the Founding era's conception of arms bearing. The original vision of a well-regulated militia was premised on the notion that rights and obligations were inseparable. Arms bearing was a public activity, a way of nurturing and demonstrating one's capacity for virtue. The militia was viewed by the Founders as a vital political and social institution, part of a seamless web that knit the locality, the state, and the national government together into a cohesive political community.[4]

While the ideal of the Founders' militia functioned as a means of producing a common civic culture, modern gun rights ideology has largely worked to undermine this goal. Gun rights ideology has fostered an anticivic vision, not a vision of civic-mindedness. In this ideology guns are primarily viewed as a means of repulsing government or other citizens, not a means for creating a common civic culture. Modern gun control ideology has also failed to create a positive constitutional vision in which the Second Amendment is more than a vestigial part of our legal culture. Indeed, to achieve the goal of sensible gun regulation, proponents of gun control have abandoned the language of constitutionalism entirely and adopted an epidemiological discourse, warning Americans of the very real dangers guns pose to American society. Supporters of the collective rights theory have failed to articulate a compelling theory of the role of the Second Amendment in contemporary American constitutionalism. Instead, confident that precedent supports their policy objectives, partisans of gun control have devoted scant energy to creating a theory of the Second Amendment that could inspire public support. This is a grave political mistake that only contributes to the impoverishment of constitutional discourse in America. Neither side in the contemporary debate has risen to the challenge of finding a way to imbue the Second Amendment with a positive vision that enriches American constitutional life. Currently, the Second Amendment is a source of division, not a means for uniting Americans.[5]

Ultimately, the only way to revitalize the civic conception of the Second Amendment is to transform public culture. While reinstating the draft seems ill advised given the increasingly complicated nature of modern warfare, some form of required public service for young Americans might help restore part of this lost world of civic obligation and community. One might imagine some sort of government-sponsored program for high school students in which students were given a civilian or military option. Young citizens could work on rebuilding our cities, reclaiming some of the environmentally ravaged countryside, or mastering some of the skills routinely instilled in basic training in the military, including the safe use of firearms. Recreating a vital civic culture will not be easy, but the alternative is far worse.

The other important lesson to be gleaned from understanding the history of the Second Amendment is the centrality of regulation to the Founders' vision of the right to bear arms. The idea of well-regulated liberty is alien to modern Americans. Regulation has come to be seen as the antithesis of liberty, not the necessary precondition for the exercise of liberty. The most pressing task facing Americans is

how to create a body of firearms law and develop a firearms jurisprudence that fit within the scheme of well-regulated liberty. Whatever
the Second Amendment might have meant historically, or whatever it
now means, the reality is that many Americans believe they have some
sort of right to own firearms. Fashioning a regulatory system for guns
that honors the Second Amendment and recognizes the complex and
deeply contested role of guns in contemporary America must do several things. First, it must not demonize gun owners or proponents of
gun regulation. Both sides have a long history that needs to be recognized as legitimate. Registration, safe storage laws, and limited
bans on certain types of weapons with no connection to the goal of
supporting a well-regulated militia are all consistent with this original
vision; wholesale gun prohibition or domestic disarmament is not. The
common-law right of self-defense is no less valid today than it was in
the era of the Second Amendment. Yet, the problems of balancing the
individual right of self-defense with the requirements of public safety
are no less complicated than they were in Jacksonian America.[6]

At various moments in America's long argument over the role of
guns in our society there have been those who have claimed that there
exists a right to be free of the fear of gun violence. Although this type
of constitutional argument has dropped out of American public
debate, it is at least as old as the individual rights ideology that fuels
the gun rights movement. Supporters of gun rights need to recognize
that this concern also has a long history. Formulating an effective regulatory scheme that can promote public safety and that recognizes the
radically different roles guns play in different American subcultures will
not be easy. We currently have a national market in which guns sold
in Virginia easily find their way to the Bronx. The gun cultures of Virginia
and the Bronx, however, are radically different, and restrictions that
might be prudent in one region might seem intrusive in the other. The
nature of the American federal system and incredible diversity of
American regional subcultures continue to complicate the task for
formulating an effective set of policies to deal with the gun issue.

The simplest way to regulate firearms would be to return to the original model used by the Founders. Originally, militia laws served as a form of taxation, requiring citizens to pay the costs of public defense and providing a regulatory framework to monitor compliance with this system of taxation. Creating some type of national firearms tax would allow society to shift part of the cost of gun violence back to those gun owners who do not act responsibly. Taxation would also provide a simple, relatively nonintrusive means of registering firearms. To dispel the notion that such a policy would be anti-gun or part of some nefarious plan to confiscate firearms, Congress could provide a series of generous tax incentives for those who take gun safety courses and encourage sensible gun storage by giving a tax break to those who lock up their guns, giving new incentives to those who don't.[7]

Another approach to gun regulation that might achieve some results is mandatory gun insurance. The federal government might tie state and local medical and police funding to requirements that states enact their own schemes for gun insurance. Such an approach would acknowledge that owning a hunting rifle in Alaska poses a far lower risk to society than owning a handgun in Philadelphia. This approach would shift part of the social cost of gun violence, something borne by responsible gun owners and non-gun owners alike, back to irresponsible gun owners, those who stockpile arms or who keep their guns loaded and unlocked. Sensible gun owners, the vast majority of gun owners, already lock up their weapons and would pay negligible amounts for such insurance. Another advantage of using insurance markets to achieve reasonable gun regulation would be that information about gun ownership would remain in private hands, not the government's. Given the profoundly antigovernment ideology associated with modern gun rights theory, such a system is probably more plausible. A firewall could exist separating insurance company records from government prying. Obtaining such information would require a court order. Given the vast amount of information already in the hands of insurance companies, it is hard to argue that additional information about gun ownership would pose any greater threat to individual rights.

The intellectual poverty of the current debate over the Second Amendment ought to serve as a wake-up call to Americans. It is unrealistic to imagine a gun-free America. Nor is it realistic to expect Americans simply to accept that inordinately high levels of gun violence are simply the price of freedom. Both sides in this debate need to back away from extremist rhetoric. The notion that the Second Amendment somehow belongs to a small number of gun rights advocates is simply wrong. The Second Amendment belongs to all Americans. Defining and implementing a new paradigm for the Second Amendment is something all Americans have a stake in.

NOTES

Introduction

1. "Heston Fight to Death," *London Times*, May 22, 2000. When historian Michael Bellesiles suggested that Americans of the Founding generation were generally less well armed than had previously been thought, his work was subjected to a torrent of criticism and eventually discredited. On the Bellesiles scandal, see James Lindgren, "Fall from Grace: Arming America and the Bellesiles Scandal," *Yale Law Journal* 111 (2002): 2195–2249. For a discussion of the scandal, see Peter Charles Hoffer, *Past Imperfect: Facts, Fictions, Fraud—American History from Bancroft and Parkman to Ambrose, Bellesiles, Ellis, and Goodwin* (New York, 2004). For a summary of the way the individual and collective rights paradigms play in the modern gun control debate, see Jesse Mathew Ruhl, Arthur L. Rizer, III, and Mikel J. Wier, "Gun Control: Targeting Rationality in a Loaded Debate," *Kansas Journal of Law and Public Policy* 13 (2003): 13–83.

2. Robert A. Gross, *The Minutemen and Their World* (New York, 1976); David Hackett Fischer, *Paul Revere's Ride* (New York, 1994). In recent years a number of scholars have challenged the idea that the Second Amendment can be fit into either the individual rights or collective rights model; see Richard Primus, *The American Language of Rights* (Cambridge, U.K., 1999); David Yassky, "The Second Amendment: Structure, History, and Constitutional Change," *University of Michigan Law Review* 99 (2000): 588–688; H. Richard Uviller and William Merkel, *The Militia and the Right to Arms, or, How the Second Amendment Fell Silent* (Durham, N.C., 2002); and David Konig, "The Second Amendment: A Missing Transatlantic Context for the Historical Meaning of 'the Right of the People to Keep and Bear Arms,'" *Law and History Review* 22 (2004): 119–59. For a good effort to chart the current state of the debate, see

Stuart Banner, "The Second Amendment, So Far," *Harvard Law Review* 117 (2004): 898–917. The debate on originalism, the belief that the constitution ought to be interpreted according to the original understanding of the text at the time that it was adopted, remains a controversial method of constitutional interpretation. The literature on originalism is immense; see the essays collected in Jack N. Rakove, *Interpreting the Constitution: The Debate over Original Intent* (Boston, 1990). A detailed philosophical discussion of originalism may be found in Keith E. Whittington, *Constitutional Interpretation: Textual Meaning, Original Intent, and Judicial Review* (Lawrence, Kans., 1999). For the most recent attempt to defend this methodology, see Randy E. Barnett, "An Originalism for Nonoriginalists," *Loyola Law Review* 45 (1999): 611–54. On the notion of standards for originalists, see H. Jefferson Powell, "Rules for Originalists," *Virginia Law Review* 73 (1987): 659. On originalism as a form of forensic history, see John P. Reid, "Law and History," *Loyola Law Review* 27 (1993): 193–223. For trenchant critiques of this method and its lack of historical sophistication, see Mark Tushnet, "Inter-Disciplinary Legal Scholarship: The Case of History-in-Law," *Chicago Kent Law Review* 71 (1996): 914; Martin S. Flaherty, "History Lite in Modern American Constitutionalism," *Columbia Law Review* 95 (1995): 523–90; Larry D. Kramer, "When Lawyers Do History," *George Washington Law Review* 72 (2003): 387–423. For discussions of the problems with Second Amendment originalism, see Michael C. Dorf, "What Does the Second Amendment Mean Today?" *Chicago Kent Law Review* 76 (2000): 291–347, and Daniel A. Farber, "Disarmed by Time: The Second Amendment and the Failure of Originalism," *Chicago Kent Law Review* 76 (2000): 167–94. Historian Jack Rakove has likened much recent scholarship to a scholarly "twilight zone," on this point, see Jack N. Rakove, "Confessions of an Ambivalent Originalist," *New York University Law Review* 78 (2003): 1346–56.

3. Saul Cornell and Nathan Dedino, "A Well Regulated Right: The Early American Origins of Gun Control," *Fordham Law Review* 73 (2004): 487–529.

4. On the early American regulatory state, see William J. Novak, *The People's Welfare: Law and Regulation in Nineteenth-Century America* (Chapel Hill, N.C., 1996).

5. On the role of the militia in colonial and revolutionary society, see Edmund S. Morgan, *Inventing the People: The Rise of Popular Sovereignty in England and America* (New York, 1988), and John W. Shy, *A People Numerous and Armed: Reflections on the Military Struggle for American Independence*, rev. ed. (Ann Arbor, Mich., 1990).

6. Glenn Harlan Reynolds, "A Critical Guide to the Second Amendment," *Tennessee Law Review* 62 (1995): 461; Clayton E. Cramer, "The Racist Roots of Gun Control," *Kansas Journal of Law and Public Policy* 4 (1995): 17. Both of these accounts ignore the antebellum efforts at gun regulation that were aimed at reducing violence, not social control. While colonial laws disarmed racial minorities, these laws were not efforts at gun control but were aimed primarily at preventing armed rebellion. An alternative view of the early history of gun regulation may be found in Saul Cornell, "The Early American Origins of the Modern Gun Debate," *Stanford Law and Policy Review* 17 (2006): 101–26. For a

general overview of the history of gun regulation, see Alexander Deconde, *Gun Violence in America: The Struggle for Control* (Boston, 2001).

7. Saul Cornell, *The Other Founders: Anti-Federalism and the Dissenting Tradition in America, 1788–1828* (Chapel Hill, N.C., 1999).

8. Eric Foner, *Reconstruction: America's Unfinished Revolution, 1863–1877* (New York, 1988). There is a large body of scholarship on incorporation. Opponents of incorporation include Charles Fairman, "Does the Fourteenth Amendment Incorporate the Bill of Rights? The Original Understanding," *Stanford Law Review* 2 (1949): 5–139, and Raoul Berger, *Government by Judiciary: The Transformation of the Fourteenth Amendment* (Cambridge, Mass., 1977). More recent scholarship has generally endorsed the incorporation thesis; see Michael Kent Curtis, *No State Shall Abridge: The Fourteenth Amendment and the Bill of Rights* (Durham, N.C., 1986), and Akhil Amar, *The Bill of Rights: Creation and Reconstruction* (New Haven, Conn., 1998). For a critique of the recent incorporation literature for its tendency to posit too broad consensus over this issue, see Bret Boyce, "Originalism and the Fourteenth Amendment," *Wake Forest Law Review* 33 (1998): 909–1034, and Lambert Gingras, "Congressional Misunderstandings and the Ratifiers' Understanding: The Case of the Fourteenth Amendment," *The American Journal of Legal History* 40 (1996): 41–71. For a sensible effort to find middle ground, see William E. Nelson, *The Fourteenth Amendment: From Political Principle to Judicial Doctrine* (Cambridge, Mass., 1995). For discussions of the connection between the Fourteenth Amendment and the Second, see Stephen P. Halbrook, *That Every Man Be Armed: The Evolution of a Constitutional Right* (Albuquerque, N.Mex., 1984) and Halbrook, *Freedmen, the Fourteenth Amendment, and the Right to Bear Arms, 1866–1876* (Westport, Conn., 1998); Sanford Levinson, "The Historians Counterattack: Some Reflections on the Historiography of the Second Amendment," in *Guns, Crime, and Punishment in America*, Bernard Harcourt, ed. (New York, 2003). There is considerable disagreement over how to interpret the test case for Second Amendment incorporation, the South Carolina KKK trials. Some scholars see the trials as a defeat for incorporation; see Kermit L. Hall, "Political Power and Constitutional Legitimacy: The South Carolina Ku Klux Klan Trials, 1871–1872," *Emory Law Journal* 33 (1984): 921–51, and Lou Falkner Williams, *The Great South Carolina Ku Klux Klan Trials, 1871–1872* (Athens, Ga., 1996). For an alternative view stressing the outcomes as a vindication of incorporation, see Robert J. Kaczorowski, *The Nationalization of Civil Rights: Constitutional Theory and Practice in a Racist Society, 1866–1883* (New York, 1987), and *The Politics of Judicial Interpretation: The Federal Courts, Department of Justice and Civil Rights, 1866–1876* (Dobbs Ferry, N.Y., 1985). The issue came before the Supreme Court in *U.S. v. Cruikshank*, 92 U.S. 568 (1875); on the context of this case, see Robert M. Goldman, *Reconstruction and Black Suffrage: Losing the Vote in Reese and Cruikshank* (Lawrence, Kans., 2001).

9. Lucillus A. Emery, "The Constitutional Right to Keep and Bear Arms," *Harvard Law Review* 28 (1914–15): 473–77; Daniel J. McKenna, "The Right to Keep and Bear Arms," *Marquette Law Review* 12 (1927–28): 138–49; Zechariah Chafee, Jr., "Right to Bear Arms," *Encyclopedia of the Social Sciences* (New York, 1930),

2: 209–10. S. T. Ansell, "Legal and Historical Aspects of the Militia," *Yale Law Journal* 26 (1916–17): 471–80. The principles of modern Second Amendment jurisprudence were articulated in *United States v. Miller*, 307 U.S. 174 (1939).

10. For two thoughtful summaries of the current state of the debate over guns in America that are also well attuned to the historical issues hanging over this controversy, see Robert Weisberg, "The Utilitarian and Deontological Entanglement of Debating Guns, Crime, and Punishment in America," *University of Chicago Law Review* 71 (2004): 333–59, and Weisberg, "Values, Violence, and the Second Amendment: American Character, Constitutionalism, and Crime," *Houston Law Review* 39 (2002): 1–51. For a good sampling of the range of views on guns in contemporary America, see Jan E. Dizard, Robert Merrill Muth, and Stephen P. Andrews, eds., *Guns in America: A Reader* (New York, 1999). For an argument stating that positions in the gun debate are rooted in deeply entrenched cultural values, see Dan M. Kahan, "The Gun Control Debate: A Culture-Theory Manifesto," *Washington and Lee Law Review* 60 (2003): 3–12.

Chapter One

1. For a discussion of the Liberty Riot, see Robert Middlekauff, *The Glorious Cause: The American Revolution, 1763–1789* (New York, 1982), 162–73, and Merrill Jensen, *The Founding of a New Nation: A History of the American Revolution, 1763–1776* (New York, 1968), 288–300. William M. Fowler, Jr., *Samuel Adams: Radical Puritan* (New York, 1997), 85–91; John Phillip Reid, *In a Rebellious Spirit: The Argument of Facts, the Liberty Riot, and the Coming of the American Revolution* (University Park, Pa., 1979). For a general discussion of Adams's political thought, see Pauline Maier, *The Old Revolutionaries: Political Lives in the Age of Samuel Adams* (New York, 1982), 3–50.

2. Jensen, *Founding of a Nation*, 292; *Letters to the Ministry from Governor Bernard, General Gage, and Commodore Hood* (Boston, 1769), 21.

3. "Sidney," *Boston Gazette*, August 29, 1768. For a good statement of Adams's view of the danger posed by standing armies, see "Vindex" in *Boston Gazette*, December 12, 19, 26, 1768; Alonzo Cushing, ed., *The Writings of Samuel Adams*, vol. 1 (1904; repr., New York, 1968), 264–68, 272–78; Algernon Sidney, *Discourses Concerning Government*, ed. Thomas G. West (Indianapolis, Ind., 1990), 199. For a general discussion of the importance of Sidney's thought to the Revolutionary era, see Caroline Robbins, "Algernon Sidney's *Discourses Concerning Government*: Textbook of Revolution," *William and Mary Quarterly* 4 (1947): 267–96. For a general discussion of the role of classical and Whig theory in shaping the political and constitutional ideas of the Founding generation, see Forrest McDonald, *Novus Ordo Seclorum: The Intellectual Origins of the Constitution* (Lawrence, Kans., 1985), and Bernard Bailyn, *The Ideological Origins of the American Revolution*, enl. ed. (Cambridge, Mass., 1992); J. G. A. Pocock, *The Machiavellian Moment: Florentine Political Thought and the Atlantic Republican Tradition* (Princeton, N.J., 1975). On the historical figure of Vindex, see N. G. L. Hammond and H. H. Scullard, *The Oxford Classical Dictionary* (Oxford,

1970), 1122. Elaine Scarry, "War and the Social Contract: Nuclear Policy, Distribution, and the Right to Bear Arms," *University of Pennsylvania Law Review* 139 (1991): 1257–1316, argues that the Second Amendment evolved from a desire to rest the power of war in the population as a whole. Scarry's argument relies heavily on the work of Akhil Amar, who tends to overstate the democratic character of eighteenth-century thought; for an elaboration of Amar's thesis, see *The Bill of Rights: Creation and Reconstruction* (New Haven, Conn., 1998). While it is true that a citizens' militia was seen as a counterweight to a standing army, only a small minority within the Founding generation would have embraced the democratic values that Scarry and Amar ascribe to them.

4. *At a Meeting of Freeholders and Other Inhabitants of the Town of Boston . . .* [broadside] (Boston, 1786). For an account from the British point of view, see *Letters to the Ministry*, 54. The American account of events may be found in Samuel Adams, *An Appeal to the World, or, a Vindication of the Town of Boston* (Boston, 1769); Oliver Morton Dickerson, ed., *Boston under Military Rule, 1768–1769* (Westport, Conn., 1971), 61; Jensen, *Founding of a Nation*, 294; Fowler, *Radical Puritan*, 87. For an analysis of these events from the perspective of modern gun rights ideology, see Stephen P. Halbrook, "Encroachment of the Crown on the Liberty of the Subject: Pre-Revolutionary Origins of the Second Amendment," *University of Dayton Law Review* 15 (1989): 91–124.

5. *Boston Gazette*, September 19, 1786.

6. For summary of militia's role in colonial society, see Allan R. Millet, "The Constitution and the Citizen-Soldier" in *The United States Military under the Constitution of the United States, 1789–1989*, Richard H. Kohn, ed. (New York, 1991). For other discussions of the centrality of the militia ideal to American culture, see Lawrence Delbert Cress, *Citizens in Arms: The Army and the Militia in American Society to the War of 1812* (Chapel Hill, N.C., 1982); Edmund S. Morgan, *Inventing the People: The Rise of Popular Sovereignty in England and America* (New York, 1988).

7. *Boston Gazette*, September 26, 1768.

8. "E.A." [Samuel Adams], in Cushing, *Writings of Adams*, 317.

9. Samuel Adams, "Shippen," in Cushing, *Writings of Adams*, 299.

10. Sir William Blackstone, *Commentaries on the Laws of England* (1765; repr., Chicago, 1979), 1: 136–40.

11. Blackstone, *Commentaries*, 4: 184. On the changing duty to retreat and the law of homicide, see Richard Maxwell Brown, *No Duty to Retreat: Violence and Values in American History and Society* (New York, 1991). On English views of the right of self-defense, see William Hawkins, *A Treatise of the Pleas of the Crown* (London, 1716), and Michael Foster, *A Report of Some Proceedings . . .* (Oxford, 1762). In his defense of the soldiers accused of murder in the Boston Massacre cases, John Adams recognized the existence of two competing views of the nature of self-defense and cited Blackstone, Hawkins, and Foster; see L. Kevin Worth and Hiller B. Zobel, *The Legal Papers of John Adams* (Cambridge, Mass., 1965) 3: 84, 236–48. *Conductor Generalis, or, The Office, Duty and Authority of Justices of the Peace, High-Sheriffs, Under-Sheriffs, Coroners, Constables . . .* (New York, 1788),

216–17. In his annotated edition of Blackstone, the Virginia jurist echoed Blackstone's distinction between the political right to have arms and the common-law right of self-defense; for a more detailed treatment of this issue, see Saul Cornell, "St. George Tucker and the Second Amendment: Original Understandings and Modern Misunderstandings," *William and Mary Law Review* 47 (2006), 1123–1155.

12. The Virginia model was adopted by Delaware and Maryland. The Pennsylvania model was emulated by Vermont. North Carolina adopted language similar to but somewhat more restrictive than Pennsylvania's; see *The Constitutions of the Several Independent States . . .* (Philadelphia, 1781), 88–89, 104–51, 19, 147. Many of these texts have been collected in Neil H. Cogan, *The Complete Bill of Rights: The Drafts, Debates, Sources, and Origins* (New York, 1997), 183–85. On state constitutional development in the Founding era, see Gordon S. Wood, *Creation of the American Republic, 1776–1787* (Chapel Hill, N.C., 1969); Willi Paul Adams, *The First American Constitutions: Republican Ideology and the Making of the State Constitutions in the Revolutionary Era*, Rita Kimber and Robert Kimber, trans. (Chapel Hill, N.C., 1980).

13. Blackstone, *Commentaries*, 1: 119; Philip Pettit, *Republicanism: A Theory of Freedom and Government* (Oxford, Eng., 1997), and Quentin Skinner, *Liberty before Liberalism* (New York, 1998); Ronald Dworkin, "Rights as Trumps," in *Theories of Rights*, Jeremy Waldron, ed. (New York, 1984). On the distinction between negative and positive liberty, see Isaiah Berlin, *Four Essays on Liberty* (New York, 1969). On liberty in the Anglo-American world of the Founders, see John Phillip Reid, *The Concept of Liberty in the Age of the American Revolution* (Chicago, 1988). David Hackett Fischer, *Liberty and Freedom: A Visual History of America's Founding Idea* (New York, 2005), 19–151.

14. For further discussion of the pre-Revolutionary struggles in Pennsylvania between Quakers and those in favor of creating a militia, see Saul Cornell, "The Early American Origins of the Modern Gun Control Debate: The Right to Bear Arms, Firearms Regulation, and the Lessons of History," *Stanford Law and Policy Review* 17 (2006), 101–26.

15. Traditional Whig views of the militia may be found in the writings of the Commonwealth tradition: John Trenchard, *An Argument Shewing that a Standing Army is Inconsistent with a Free Government . . .* (London, 1697), 7; Andrew Fletcher, *A Discourse of Government with Relation to Militias* (Edinburgh, 1698), 44–47, 39–40; John Toland, *The Militia Reformed . . .* (London, 1695), 16; James Burgh, *Political Disquistions . . .* (Philadelphia, 1775), 3: 400, 402, 404–5; Sidney, *Discourses Concerning Government*, chap. 2.

16. George Mason, "Fairfax County Militia Association," in *The Papers of George Mason*, Robert Rutland, ed. (Chapel Hill, N.C., 1970), 1: 210–11; Mason, "Fairfax County Militia Plan, For Embodying the People," *Papers of George Mason*, 1: 212. Faced with the threat posed by British tyranny, Mason and other Americans quite naturally turned their attention to organizing their militias. Although it invoked the idea of a "well regulated" militia and was framed in legalistic terminology, Mason's volunteer militia was not, strictly speaking, an agent of government. In 1775 Americans were still legally a part of the British

Empire, and the militia was ultimately at the service of the Crown. Mason's plan was a temporary measure necessitated by the unusual crisis faced by Americans. The volunteer companies, Mason noted, were an expedient until "a regular and proper Militia law for the Defense of the Country shall be enacted by the Legislature of this Colony"; George Mason to George Washington, October 14, 1775, *Papers of George Mason*, 1: 255–56.

17. "Virginia Declaration of Rights," *Papers of George Mason*, 1: 274–76.

18. "First Draft of the Declaration of Rights," *Papers of George Mason*, 1: 284.

19. Julian P. Boyd, ed., *The Papers of Thomas Jefferson* (Princeton, N.J., 1950) 1: 344. Jefferson's biographers all agree that his constitutional thinking was somewhat out of step with his contemporaries; see Noble E. Cunningham, Jr., *In Pursuit of Reason: The Life of Thomas Jefferson* (New York, 1987), 44, and Dumas Malone, *Jefferson and His Time: Jefferson the Virginian* (New York, 1948). Cesare Beccaria, *Of Crimes and Punishments*, Edward D. Ingraham, trans., 2nd ed. (Philadelphia, 1778); Gilbert Chinard, *The Commonplace Book of Thomas Jefferson* (Baltimore, 1926), 314. On the influence of Beccaria more generally, see David Lundberg and Henry May, "The Enlightened Reader in America," *American Quarterly* 28 (1976): 262–93, and Donald S. Lutz, "The Relative Influence of European Writers on late Eighteenth-Century American Political Thought," *American Political Science Review* 78 (1984). According to May only slightly more than a third of all libraries in the period 1777–90 contained a copy of the essay by Beccaria favored by Jefferson. In his study of the patterns of citation to various thinkers in published writing in the Founding era, Donald Lutz found that Beccaria accounted for about 1 percent of citations in the 1770s, 3 percent in the 1780s, and 0 percent in the 1790s. For a critique of modern uses of Jefferson's fondness for Beccaria, see David Konig, "Influence and Emulation in the Constitutional Republic of Letters," *Law and History Review* 22 (2004): 179–82. For illustrations of the problematic use of Beccaria in modern Second Amendment scholarship, see Stephen Halbrook, *That Every Man Be Armed* (Albuquerque, N.Mex., 1984); Halbrook makes much of John Adams's decision to quote another passage from Beccaria in the context of his defense of the Boston Massacre. L. Kinvin Wroth and Hille B. Zobel, eds., *Legal Papers of John Adams* (Cambridge, Mass., 1965), 3: 242. Parliament had rejected the suggestion that such a provision be included in the English Game Act; Lois G. Schwoerer, "To Hold and Bear Arms: The English Perspective," in *The Second Amendment in Law and History: Historians and Constitutional Scholars on the Right to Bear Arms*, Carl Bogus, ed. (New York, 2000), 220–21. Slowly over the course of the next century, English courts came to recognize such a right, essentially rewriting the history; see *Wingfield v. Stratford*, 95 *English Reports* 637 (King's Bench, 1752).

20. "The Apology of the Paxton Volunteers" (1764), in *The Paxton Papers*, John R. Dunbar, ed. (The Hague, 1957), 187.

21. Nathan Kozuskanich, "For the Security and Protection of the Community: The Frontier and the Makings of Pennsylvanian Constitutionalism, 1750–1776," Ph.D. dissertation, Ohio State University, 2005.

22. "Declaration of Rights" and "Plan or Frame of Government," *Constitutions of the Several Independent States* 87–89; Douglas M. Arnold, *A Republican*

Revolution: Ideology and Politics in Pennsylvania, 1776–1790 (New York, 1989), and Robert L. Brunhouse, *The Counter-Revolution in Pennsylvania, 1776–1790* (Harrisburg, Pa., 1942).

23. "Declaration of Rights" and "Plan or Frame of Government," 87–89.

24. "Plan or Frame of Government," 90, 100–101. For unpersuasive efforts to read this provision from a modern individual rights perspective, see Joyce Lee Malcolm, *To Keep and Bear Arms: The Origins of an Anglo-American Right* (Cambridge, Mass., 1994), 148; Halbrook, *That Every Man Be Armed*, 64; David Kopel, "The Second Amendment in the Nineteenth Century," *BYU Law Review* (1998): 1406–7. For a more persuasive argument that a right of the people could have either a collective or individual connotation, see Richard A. Primus, *The American Language of Rights* (Cambridge, U.K., 1999).

25. "Article XVII Constitution of 1780," in Oscar Handlin and Mary Handlin, eds., *The Popular Sources of Political Authority* (Cambridge, Mass., 1966), 446.

26. Gary Wills, "To Keep and Bear Arms," in *Whose Right to Bear Arms Did the Second Amendment Protect?*, Saul Cornell, ed. (Boston, 2000). Wills argues that introduction of the word *keep* in conjunction with the right to bear arms did not alter the military focus of the text of the Second Amendment. Robert E. Shalhope, "To Keep and Bear Arms in the Early Republic," *Constitutional Commentary* 16 (1999): 269–81, takes the contrary view and argues that the inclusion of this term gave the text a more individualistic meaning. Such a view fits neither the strong collective nor the strong individual rights view that has dominated modern debates but comes closer to the notion of a civic right described earlier, on this point see Saul Cornell, "Don't Know Much about History: The Current Crisis in Second Amendment Scholarship," *Northern Kentucky Law Review* 29 (2002): 657–81.

27. "Town of Northhampton Returns to the Convention on the Constitution (1780)," in Handlin and Handlin, *Popular Sources of Political Authority*, 574.

28. "Town of Williamsburgh Alternations in the Constitution (1780)," in Handlin and Handlin, *Popular Sources of Political Authority*, 624.

29. The classic statement of this element of New England culture is Michael Zuckerman, *Peaceable Kingdoms: New England Towns in the Eighteenth Century* (New York, 1970).

30. A similar concern was voiced by the town of Mendon in response to the absence of any provision on the right to bear arms or the militia in the rejected 1778 constitution; "Return of the Towns: Mendon (1778)," in Handlin and Handlin, *Popular Sources of Political Authority*, 267. On the political culture of Worcester County, see John L. Brooke, *The Heart of the Commonwealth: Society and Political Culture in Worcester County, Massachusetts, 1713–1861* (Cambridge, U.K., 1989).

31. "Senex," *Cumberland Gazette*, January 12, 1787; "Scribble-Scrabble," *Cumberland Gazette*, December 8, 1786, and January 26, 1787.

32. John Joachim Zubly, *The Law of Liberty* (Philadelphia, 1775). On the importance of the idea of a well-regulated society, see William J. Novak, *The People's Welfare: Law and Regulation in Nineteenth-Century America* (Chapel Hill, N.C., 1996). The Founding generation's concept of well-regulated liberty shares many features

with modern legal theory's notion of ordered liberty; *Palko v. Connecticut*, 302 U.S. 319 (1937).

33. For a good example of the scope of early American militia laws, see "An Act for Forming, Regulating, and Conducting the Military Force of this State," *Acts and Laws, Made and Passed by the General Assembly* . . . (New London, Conn., 1782), 585–99. For a good sampling of colonial laws regulating firearms use, see *A Collection of All the Laws of the Province of Pennsylvania: Now in Force* (Philadelphia, 1742), 85, 197–99, 315–16, 318. Laws regulating the storage of gunpowder were common; for one of the most sweeping examples of such a law see *The Perpetual Laws of the Commonwealth of Massachusetts* (Boston, 1789), 240. On the evolution of race-based prohibitions on firearms in Virginia, see Kathleen M. Brown, *Good Wives, Nasty Wenches, and Anxious Patriarchs: Gender, Race, and Power in Colonial Virginia* (Chapel Hill, N.C., 1996), 177–79, 219.

34. "An Act for Repealing Part of an Act . . ." (1779), *The Acts of the General Assembly of the Commonwealth of Pennsylvania* (Philadelphia, 1782), 192–93.

35. For a good example of a race-based prohibition, see *Collection of All the Laws of the Province of Pennsylvania*, 85.

36. James Madison, "A Bill for the Preservation of Deer" (1785), in Boyd, *Papers of Thomas Jefferson*, 2: 443–444. The bill was introduced twice but the House took no action on it. Virginia had enacted two earlier game laws, a 1738 law and another in 1772.

37. On the common law as a protection for liberty, see Martin Howard, Jr., *A Letter from a Gentleman at Halifax* . . . (Newport, R.I., 1765), 7–8. On the law of self-defense, see Blackstone, *Commentaries*, 1: 121, 125, 139; 4: 185. Much of the confusion in modern scholarship on the Second Amendment stems from the tendency to conflate Blackstone's fifth auxiliary right with his discussion of the right of personal self-defense. For anachronistic and presentist readings of Blackstone that conflate these two ideas, see Don Kates, "The Second Amendment and the Ideology of Self-Protection," *Constitutional Commentary* 9 (1992): 87–104, and Nelson Lund, "The Second Amendment, Political Liberty, and the Right to Self-Preservation," *Alabama Law Review* 39 (1987): 103–30. A much more historically sophisticated reading of Blackstone may be found in Steven J. Heyman, "Natural Rights and the Second Amendment," *Chicago Kent Law Review* 76 (2000): 237–90.

38. Henry Care, *English Liberties, or the Free-born Subject's Inheritance* . . . , 5th ed. (Boston, 1721), 248. The best study of the complex process by which English common law evolved into a distinctively American common law is William E. Nelson, *The Americanization of the Common Law: The Impact of Legal Change on Massachusetts Society, 1760–1830* (Cambridge, Mass., 1975). "Statute of Northampton" (1328), in Philip B. Kurland and Ralph Lerner, eds., *The Founders' Constitution*, (Chicago, 1987), 5: 209; *Conductor Generalis, or, The Office, Duty and Authority of Justices of the Peace, High-Sheriffs, Under-Sheriffs* . . . (Philadelphia, 1722), 10–12. The text went through many editions in the colonies and was later reprinted in three separate editions in the Second Amendment era (1788, 1792, 1794). The most comprehensive study of gun ownership in America puts the figure at about half the households probated;

on this point see James Lindgren and Justin Lee Heather, "Counting Guns in Early America," *William and Mary Law Review* 43 (2002): 1777–1842.

39. David Ramsay, *The History of the American Revolution* (Philadelphia, 1789), 1: 253.

40. "Copy of a Letter from Luke Day," *New Haven Gazette and Connecticut Magazine*, February 1, 1787; Daniel Shays letter, Oct 16, 1786, published in the *Middelsex Gazette*, November 6, 1786, and *Worcester Magazine*, February 1, 1787, p. 535.

41. William Pencak, "The Fine Theoretic Government of Massachusetts is Prostrated to the Earth: The Response to Shays's Rebellion Reconsidered," in *In Debt to Shays: The Bicentennial of an Agrarian Rebellion*, Robert A. Gross, ed. (Charlottesville, Va., 1993). For additional examples, see Leonard L. Richards, *Shays's Rebellion: The American Revolution's Final Battle* (Philadelphia, 2002), 63; Brooke, *Heart of the Commonwealth*, 222–23.

42. James Bowdoin, *A Proclamation* [broadside] (Boston, 1786).

43. For a useful narrative overview of the events in Shays's Rebellion, see Richards, *Shays's Rebellion*.

44. Ibid.

45. For a more detailed extended discussion of the corporate character of Regulator ideology, see Brooke, *Heart of the Commonwealth*, 223.

46. "A Congregational Pastor Counsels Moderation," in Richard Brown, ed., *Major Problems in the Era of the American Revolution, 1760–1791*, 1st ed. (Lexington, Mass., 1992); on Samuel Adams's reaction to Shays's Rebellion, see William Pencak, "Samuel Adams and Shays's Rebellion," *New England Quarterly* 62 (1989): 63–74.

47. On the difficulties faced by the government in recruiting troops and the government's turn to Boston merchants for support, see Richards, *Shays's Rebellion*, 10–25.

48. The Disqualification Act is discussed in Richards, *Shays's Rebellion*, 36.

49. Mercy Otis Warren, *History of the Rise, Progress, and Termination of the American Revolution* (1805; repr., Indianapolis, 1988), 2: 656; Stephen Higginson to [Henry Knox], November 25, 1786, quoted in Stephen E. Patterson, "The Federalist Reaction to Shays's Rebellion," in Gross, *In Debt to Shays*, 116; George Washington to David Humphreys, October 22, 1786, Washington Papers, Series 2, Letter book 13, Library of Congress, also available at http://memory.loc.gov/ammem/gwhtml/gwhome.html; George Washington to Henry Knox, December 26, 1786, Series 2, Letter book 13, also available at http://memory.loc.gov/ammem/gwhtml/gwhome.html.

50. Thomas Jefferson to James Madison, January 30, 1787, in Merrill Peterson, ed., *The Portable Thomas Jefferson* (New York, 1975), 416–17.

Chapter Two

1. Gordon S. Wood, *Creation of the American Republic, 1776–1787* (Chapel Hill, N.C., 1969); Forrest McDonald, *Novus Ordo Seclorum: The Intellectual Origins of the Constitution* (Lawrence, Kans., 1985); Jack N. Rakove, *Original Meanings: Politics and Ideas in the Making of the Constitution* (New York, 1996).

2. Carol Berkin, *A Brilliant Solution: Inventing the American Constitution* (New York, 2002); Richard H. Kohn, "The Constitution and National Security," in *The United States Military under the Constitution of the United States, 1789–1989*, Richard H. Kohn, ed. (New York, 1991); James Madison, *Notes of Debates in the Federal Convention of 1787*, bicentennial ed. (New York, 1987), 478.

3. *Madison's Notes*, 484, 515.

4. Ibid., 482.

5. Ibid., 389, 512.

6. Richard Henry Lee, "Proposed Amendments," *Documentary History of the Ratification of the Constitution* (Madison, Wis., 1976–), 1: 337 (hereafter *DHRC*).

7. David Redick to William Irvine, September 24, 1787, ibid., 135; George Lee Tuberville to Arthur Lee, October 28, 1787, ibid., 8: 127; Saul Cornell, *The Other Founders: Anti-Federalism and the Dissenting Tradition in America, 1788–1828* (Chapel Hill, N.C., 1999).

8. "Blessings of the New Government," *Philadelphia Independent Gazetteer*, October 6, 1787, *DHRC* 13: 345; "Old Whig I," October 12, 1787, *Philadelphia Independent Gazetteer*, *DHRC* 13: 378–79; James Wilson, "Speech at a Public Meeting in Philadelphia," October 6, 1787, *Pennsylvania Herald and General Advertiser*, *DHRC* 13: 339.

9. "A Democratic Federalist," *DHRC* 2: 196–97; [Samuel Bryan], "Centinel, II" Oct. 24, 1787, *Philadelphia Independent Gazetteer*, *DHRC* 13: 457–67. For another attack on Wilson's defense of the necessity of a standing army see "Old Whig, V," *Philadelphia Independent Gazetteer*, November, 1, 1787, *DHRC* 13: 540.

10. [Luther Martin], "Genuine Information," in *The Complete Anti-Federalist*, Herbert J. Storing, ed. (Chicago, 1981), 2: 58–59, 71–72, 44.

11. Noah Webster, *A Citizen of America* (Philadelphia, 1787), reprinted in Gary McDowell and Colleen Sheehan, eds., *Friends of the Constitution: Writings of the "Other Federalists," 1787–1788* (Indianapolis, 1998), 393, 398.

12. Ibid.

13. The literature on *The Federalist* is massive; a good starting point is Larry Kramer, "Madison's Audience," *Harvard Law Review* 112 (1999): 611–79. A useful collection of essays may be found in Charles R. Kessler, *Saving the Revolution: The Federalist Papers and the American Founding* (New York, 1987). On the literary dimensions of *The Federalist*, see Albert Furtwangler, *The Authority of Publius: A Reading of the Federalist Papers* (Ithaca, N.Y., 1984). For a systematic effort to understand the philosophy of *The Federalist*, see David F. Epstein, *The Political Theory of* The Federalist (Chicago, 1984).

14. "Publius" [Hamilton], "Federalist No. 29," *DHRC* 15: 320.

15. "Publius" [Hamilton], "Federalist No. 25," *DHRC* 15: 62–63.

16. "Publius" [Hamilton], "Federalist No. 28," *DHRC* 15: 104.

17. Ibid.; [Madison], "Federalist No. 46," ibid., 492.

18. "Robert Whitehill Speech, Pennsylvania Convention," *DHRC* 2: 597–98; [Samuel Bryan], "Dissent of the Minority," in Storing, *Complete Anti-Federalist*, 3: 151–52. Modern scholars eager to prove that the Second Amendment protects an individual right have placed enormous emphasis on this single phrase in the Dissent; see Don Kates, "Handgun Prohibition and the Original

Meaning of the Second Amendment," *Michigan Law Review* 82 (1983): 204–73; Nelson Lund, "The Ends of Second Amendment Jurisprudence: Firearms Disabilities and Domestic Violence Restraining Orders," *Texas Review of Law and Politics* 4 (1999): 158–91. For a more detailed discussion of the spectrum of sentiments on this issue, see Saul Cornell, "Beyond the Myth of Consensus: The Struggle to Define the Right to Bear Arms in the Early Republic," in *Beyond the Founders: New Approaches to the Political History of the Early Republic*, Jeffery L. Pasley, Andrew W. Robertson, and David Waldstreicher, eds. (Chapel Hill, N.C., 2004), 251–73.

19. [Tench Coxe], "A Pennsylvanian III," *DHRC*, 2: microfiche 1779. For an anachronistic effort to fit Coxe's thought into the modern individual rights view of the Second Amendment, see David Kopel and Stephen Halbrook, "Tench Coxe and the Right to Keep and Bear Arms, 1787–1823," *William and Mary Bill of Rights Journal* 7 (1999): 347–99. The circulation of and response to the Dissent are discussed in a long editorial note by the editors of the *DHRC*, 15: 7–13. The most persistent critic of the Dissent was Tench Coxe, who authored eight separate essays attacking its argument; see also "Philanthropos," *Philadelphia Independent Gazetteer*, January 16, 1788; "A Freeman," I–III, *Pennsylvania Gazette*, January 23 and 30, 1788, and February 6, 1788. Alexander White, *Winchester Virginia Gazette*, February 22 and 29, 1788; [Noah Webster], "America," in McDowell and Sheehan, *Friends of the Constitution*, 175–76.

20. George Mason, "Objections," in Storing, *Complete Anti-Federalist*, 2: 13; George Mason to Thomas Jefferson, May 26, 1788, *DHRC* 9: 883. The impact of Dunmore's efforts to seize the powder is discussed in Woody Holton, *Forced Founders: Indians, Debtors, Slaves, and the Making of the American Revolution in Virginia* (Chapel Hill, N.C., 1999), and John E. Selby, *The Revolution in Virginia, 1775–1783* (Williamsburg, Va., 1988).

21. Patrick Henry, "Speech in the Virginia Convention, June 14," *DHRC* 10: 1276. The most detailed study of firearms ownership in this period is James Lindgren and Justin Lee Heather, "Counting Guns in Early America," *William and Mary Law Review* 43 (2002): 1777–1842, which notes considerable regional and class variations in patterns of gun ownership. Lindgren and Heather analyzed gun ownership in Mason's own community and discovered pronounced variations by class. Gun ownership was much more common among elites than those at the bottom of Virginia society. This more nuanced and methodologically sophisticated approach to guns has effectively superceded Michael Bellesiles's discredited thesis about the absence of guns in early America: Michael Bellesiles, *Arming America: The Origins of a National Gun Culture* (New York, 2000). On the *Arming America* scandal, see Peter Charles Hoffer, *Past Imperfect: Facts, Fictions, and Fraud in the Writing of American History* (New York, 2004). Although the thesis of *Arming America* has been effectively challenged, there is ample evidence to support the notion that Americans believed that they had not yet attained the level of armament necessary to meet the militia ideal; on this point, see Jack Rakove, "Words, Deeds, and Guns: Arming America and the Second Amendment," *William and Mary Quarterly* 59 (2002): 210.

22. James Madison, "Speech Virginia Ratification Debates," June 14, 1788, *DHRC* 10: 1273; James Madison, "Speech Virginia Ratification Debates," June 6, 1788, *DHRC* 9: 992; James Madison, "Speech Virginia Ratification Debates," June 16, 1788, *DHRC* 10: 1304.

23. Patrick Henry, "Speech Virginia Ratification Debates," June 16, 1788, ibid., 1304–5, 1309. See also the speech supporting Madison by George Nicholas, "Virginia Ratification Debates," June 16, 1788, ibid., 1313.

24. The Virginia proposal for a declaration of rights and amendments to the body of the Constitution was eventually presented by Madison in Congress; see Helen E. Veit, Kenneth R. Bowling, and Charlene Bangs Bickford, eds., *Creating the Bill of Rights* (Baltimore, 1991), 17–21 (hereafter, *CBR*).

25. On Anti-Federalist protest, see Saul Cornell, *Other Founders*; for a more general discussion of parades and other forms of symbolic expression used by Federalists, see David Waldstreicher, *In the Midst of Perpetual Fetes* (Chapel Hill, N.C., 1997).

26. Cornell, *Other Founders*, 109–120; Waldstreicher, *In the Midst of Perpetual Fetes*, 93–103.

27. "Aristocrotis" [William Petrikin], "The Government of Nature Delineated," in Storing, *Compete Anti-Federalist*, 3: 202–3. Additional evidence that plebeian populists placed little faith in their state governments is shown by their suspicion regarding Pennsylvania's effort to recall public arms distributed to the militia for cleaning and repair. For additional documentation, see *DHRC* 2: microfiche 1361–73.

28. "Extract of a Letter from Franklin County 24th April 1788," *DHRC* 17: 252; Theodore Sedgwick to Henry Van Schaak, November 28, 1787, *DHRC* 5: 1035.

29. Cornell, *Other Founders*, 115, 136–40; *Documentary History of the First Federal Elections* (Madison, Wis., 1976–89), 1: 258–64.

30. Madison explains his reasons for embracing the idea of amendments in a letter describing the "nauseous project of Amendments"; James Madison to Richard Peters, August 19, 1789, *CBR*, 281–82. Paul Finkelman, "James Madison and the Bill of Rights: A Reluctant Paternity," *Supreme Court Review* (1990): 301–47; Jack N. Rakove, "The Madisonian Moment," *University of Chicago Law Review* 55 (1988): 473–505, and "The Madisonian Theory of Rights," *William and Mary Law Review* 31 (1990): 245–66.

31. For a discussion of the rights associated with amendments proposed by the individual states, see Donald S. Lutz, *A Preface to American Political Theory* (Lawrence, Kans., 1992), 55–68. Lutz's tally of individual provisions includes the list of proposed amendments prepared by the Maryland Anti-Federalist minority, which was not formally approved by the state convention; for the text of these proposals, see *DHRC* 17: 236–46. Much like the list of amendments produced by Pennsylvania's Anti-Federalist minority, the Maryland amendments were not actually introduced by Madison for consideration in Congress; for copies of the amendments that were considered, see *CBR*, 14–28.

32. The text of the New Hampshire amendment is available in *CBR*, 17. On New Hampshire political culture in this period, see Jere Daniell, *Experiment in*

Republicanism: New Hampshire Politics and the American Revolution, 1741–1794 (Cambridge, Mass., 1970).

33. "Proposal by Madison," Neil H. Cogan, ed., *The Complete Bill of Rights: The Drafts, Debates, Sources, and Origins* (New York, 1997), 169; James Madison, "Notes June 1789," in *The Papers of James Madison*, William T. Hutchinson and William M. E. Rachal, eds. (Chicago, 1962–), 12: 193–94; Charles F. Hobson, "The Negative on State Laws: James Madison, the Constitution, and the Crisis of Republican Government," *William and Mary Quarterly* 36 (1979): 215–35; James Madison to Thomas Jefferson, October 17, 1788, in Marvin Meyers, ed., *The Mind of the F ounder: Sources of the Political Thought of James Madison*, rev. ed. (Hanover, N.H., 1981), 157. Modern supporters of the individual rights view of the Second Amendment have focused on Madison's suggestion that the primary purpose of the bill of rights was individual rights; see Kates, "Handgun Prohibition," and Stephen P. Halbrook, "To Keep and Bear Their Private Arms: The Adoption of the Second Amendment, 1787–1791," *Northern Kentucky Law Review* 10 (1982): 13–39. Madison did not, however, argue that the list of amendments was exclusively about individual rights, but primarily about the rights of individuals. For further discussion, see Cornell, "Don't Know Much about History: The Current Crisis in Second Amendment Scholarship," *Northern Kentucky Law Review* 29 (2002): 657–81.

34. Fisher Ames to Thomas Dwight, June 11, 1789, *CBR*, 247; "Speech of Aedanus Burke," *CBR*, 175. Burke's metaphor was adopted by Federalist Noah Webster in a newspaper essay critical of Madison's proposed amendments: "Pacificus," August 14, 1789, ibid., 276. For other sarcastic comments dismissing the content of the Bill of Rights, see George Clymer to Tench Coxe, June 28, 1789, ibid., 255. For a discussion of the politics of the framing of the Bill of Rights, see Ken Bowling, "'A Tub to the Whale': The Founding Fathers and Adoption of the Federal Bill of Rights," *Journal of the Early Republic* 8 (1988): 223–51, and Leonard Levy, *The Origins of the Bill of Rights* (New Haven, Conn., 1999).

35. The changes in the language of the proposed amendment can be most easily tracked in Cogan, *Complete Bill of Rights*, 169–80. For an account of this process, see Rakove, "The Second Amendment: The Highest Stage of Originalism," *Chicago Kent Law Review* 76 (2000): 103–66. Roger Sherman also sought to limit federal control of the militia, but his proposal was rejected; see *CBR*, 267. Individual rights theorists have mistakenly seen this placement as evidence of Madison's belief that the right to bear arms was an individual right. If Madison viewed the right as tied to the militia then, so the argument goes, why didn't he propose to place the right next to the militia clause in Article I, Section 8? For examples of scholars who have adopted such an anachronistic interpretation, see L. A. Powe, Jr., "Guns, Words, and Constitutional Interpretation," *William and Mary Law Review* 38 (1997): 1311–1403, and William W. Van Alstyne, "The Second Amendment and the Personal Right to Arms," *Duke Law Journal* 43 (1994): 1236–55. Madison followed the model used in most state constitutions that separated the statement of the right to bear arms from discussions of the organization of the militia. The placement merely tells us it was a right, not what kind of right. Indeed, Virginia proposed two amendments

dealing with the militia and the right to bear arms, one of which would have been more appropriate to place in Article I, Section 8. Correctives to these anachronistic approaches are suggested by Jack Rakove, who argues the original placement suggests a restraint on Congress, not an assertion of an individual right; see "Highest Stage of Originalism," 103–66.

36. Elbridge Gerry, "Speech," CBR, 182.

37. Cogan, Complete Bill of Rights, 174. On the fear of slave insurrection as a major factor in shaping southern views of what became the Second Amendment, see Carl T. Bogus, "The Hidden History of the Second Amendment," U.C. Davis Law Review 31 (1998): 309–408.

38. John Randolph to St. George Tucker, September 11, 1789, CBR, 293.

39. Modern debate over the Second Amendment has devoted considerable attention to the role of the preamble, which asserted the need for a well-regulated militia. Eugene Volokh, "The Commonplace Second Amendment," NYU Law Review 73 (1998): 793–821, erroneously claims that lawyers in the eighteenth century treated preambles and proems as mere justification clauses rather than as explanations of the purpose of a particular statute or constitutional provision; on this point, see David T. Konig, "The Second Amendment: A Missing Transatlantic Context for the Historical Meaning of the Right to Bear Arms," Law and History Review 22 (2004): 119–59. On the evolution of the amendment's language, see Cogan, Complete Bill of Rights, 169–80. Cogan notes that some transcriptions of the amendment's final language capitalize the first letters of militia and arms. Rather than capitalize them, Cogan concludes that the versions with this orthography are printers' errors with the letters slightly out of alignment. For a good introduction to eighteenth-century theories of statutory construction, see William D. Popkin, Statutes in Court: The History and Theory of Statutory Interpretation (Durham, N.C., 1999). Sir William Blackstone, Commentaries on the Laws of England (1765; repr. Chicago, 1979), 1: 58–60; Giles Jacob, The Student's Companion: or, the Reason of the Laws of England (London, 1725), 191–92.

40. Coxe himself described his efforts as hasty and rushed: Tench Coxe to James Madison, June 18, 1789, CBR, 252–53. Coxe's "Remarks on the First Part of Amendments" was originally published in the Philadelphia Federal Gazette, June 18, 1789. Although some modern individual rights scholars have claimed that Madison endorsed Coxe's view of the Second Amendment, Madison only offered a general encouragement of Coxe's effort to win support for the proposed amendments. Moreover, Coxe's comments were made about an early draft of the amendment, not the final form in which Congress inserted the affirmation of a well-regulated militia in the preamble. For an analysis of the use and abuse of Coxe in modern Second Amendment scholarship, see Rakove, "Highest Stage of Originalism," 123, n. 48.

41. [Samuel Bryan], "Centinel Revived XXIX," Philadelphia Independent Gazetteer September 9, 1789; Thomas Tudor Tucker to St. George Tucker, October 2, 1789, CBR, 300; George Mason to Samuel Griffin, September 8, 1789, CBR, 292.

42. Samuel Nasson to George Thatcher, July 9, 1789, CBR, 261. For the social context of Maine Anti-Federalism and Nasson's connection to that world, see Alan

Taylor, *Liberty Men and Great Proprietors: The Revolutionary Settlement on the Maine Frontier, 1760–1820* (Chapel Hill, N.C., 1990).

43. William Petrikin to John Nicholson, March 23, 1789, *Documentary History of the First Federal Elections*, 1: 406; for a discussion of Pettit and other moderate Anti-Federalists and their reactions to popular radicalism, see Cornell, *Other Founders*, 136–43.

44. Charles Nisbet, quoted in Richard H. Kohn, *Eagle and Sword: The Federalists and the Creation of a Military Establishment in America, 1783–1802* (New York, 1975), 122; Gouverneur Morris to Moss Kent, in *The Founders' Constitution*, Philip B. Kurland and Ralph Lerner, eds. (Chicago, 1987), 3: 213.

45. The struggle over military policy in the new nation is discussed in the following works: Marcus Cunliffe, *Soldiers and Civilians: The Martial Spirit in America, 1775–1865* (Boston, 1968); Lawrence Delbert Cress, *Citizens in Arms: The Army and the Militia in American Society to the War of 1812* (Chapel Hill, N.C., 1982); Mark Pitcavage, "An Equitable Burden: The Decline of the State Militias, 1783–1858," Ph.D. dissertation, Ohio State University, 1995. The best account of the controversy generated by Knox's plan is Kohn, *Eagle and Sword*, 130–32. Linda Grant De Pauw et. al., eds., *The Documentary History of the First Federal Congress* (Baltimore, Md., 1986), 5: 1435, 1436–37, 1439, 1456 (hereafter, *DHFFC*).

46. De Witt Clinton, as quoted in Kohn, *Eagle and Sword*, 130.

47. "Speech of Elias Boudinot, December 25," in *DHFFC*, 14: 126.

48. "Speech of Mr. Burke, Dec. 22, 1790" and "Speech of Mr. Jackson, Dec. 22, 1790," ibid., 123.

49. *Annals of Congress*, 2nd Congress, 1st Session, March 6, 1792, 435.

50. *Gazette of the United States*, May 9, 1792; *National Gazette*, May 10, 1792.

51. "An Act More Effectually to Provide for the National Defense by Establishing an Uniform," 1 U.S. Statutes 271 (May 8, 1792); "An Act to Provide for the Calling Forth of the Militia," 1 U.S. Statutes 264 (May 2, 1792); "Speech of Mr. Steele," April 12, 1792, *Annals of Congress*, 2nd Congress, 1st Session, 553; "Speech of Mr. Benson," ibid.

52. Samuel Latham Mitchill, *An Oration, Pronounced before the Society of Black Friars* (New York, 1793), 26–27.

53. [Madison], "Federalist No 46," *DHRC* 15: 492.

Chapter Three

1. St. George Tucker Notebooks, Box 63, Vol. 4, Tucker-Coleman Papers, Swem Library, College of William and Mary, 127–28.

2. St. George Tucker, *Blackstone's Commentaries: With Notes of Reference, to the Constitution and Laws, of the Federal Government of the United States; and of the Commonwealth of Virginia . . .*, 5 vols. (1803).

3. St. George Tucker Notebooks, 4: 127–28. The Twelfth Amendment eventually became the Tenth once the first two provisions recommended by Congress were rejected by the states.

4. Alexander Addison, *Charges to the Grand Juries of the Counties of the Fifth Circuit in the State of Pennsylvania* (Philadelphia, 1800), 101, 104, 116.

5. William Pitt Smith, *Observations on Conventions, Made in a Tammanial Debate* (New York, 1793), 3, 12; on the Tammany Society, see Alfred Young, *The Democratic Republicans of New York: The Origins, 1763–1797* (Chapel Hill, N.C., 1967), 202–3, 316.

6. Marshall Smelser, "The Federalist Period as an Age of Political Passion," *American Quarterly* 10 (1958): 391–419; John R. Howe, "Republican Thought and the Political Violence of the 1790s," *American Quarterly* 19 (1967): 147–65; Simon P. Newman, *Parades and the Politics of the Street: Festive Culture in the Early American Republic* (Philadelphia, 1997); James Roger Sharp, *American Politics in the Early Republic: The New Nation in Crisis* (New Haven, Conn., 1993); Saul Cornell, *The Other Founders: Anti-Federalism and the Dissenting Tradition in America, 1788–1828* (Chapel Hill, N.C., 1999). On the Federalist vision of state, see Max M. Edling, *A Revolution in Favor of Government: Origins of the U.S. Constitution and the Making of the American State* (New York, 2003). For a general overview of the events leading up to the Whiskey Rebellion, see Thomas P. Slaughter, *The Whiskey Rebellion: Frontier Epilogue to the American Revolution* (New York, 1986).

7. Richard H. Kohn, *Eagle and Sword: The Federalists and the Creation of a Military Establishment in America, 1783–1802* (New York, 1975), 163. Governor Mifflin provided a more detailed explanation of his view that events in western Pennsylvania might be dealt with by the Pennsylvania courts: Mifflin to Washington, August 5, 1794, in *Pennsylvania Archives*, 2nd ser. (Harrisburg, Pa., 1896), 4: 105–9. The meeting included Secretary of State Edmund Randolph, Secretary of War Henry Knox, U.S. Attorney General William Bradford, Governor Thomas Mifflin of Pennsylvania, Chief Justice Thomas McKean of the Pennsylvania Supreme Court, State Attorney General Jared Ingersoll, and Pennsylvania's Secretary of State Alexander J. Dallas. A report of the meeting is available in Harold Syrett, ed., *The Papers of Alexander Hamilton* (New York, 1961–1987), 17: 9–14 (hereafter *Hamilton Papers*).

8. Kohn, *Eagle and Sword*, 161–70.

9. "Alexander Hamilton to George Washington," September 2, 1794, *Hamilton Papers*, 17: 187; "Extract from a Charge delivered by the Hon Judge Ruth to the Grand Jury of Berks County," *Gazette of the United States*, August 25, 1794.

10. William Findley, *A History of the Insurrection in the Four Western Counties . . .* (Philadelphia, 1796), 177, 285.

11. The documents are produced in Hugh Henry Brackenridge, *Incidents of the Insurrection in the Western Parts of Pennsylvania* (Philadelphia, 1795), 38–40, 58, 79. During the trials of the Whiskey Rebels, the prosecution focused on this usurpation of the forms of the militia as proof that the insurgents were not merely engaged in riotous behavior, but had engaged in treason against the government of the United States; see, for example, the charge of Judge Patterson in *United States v. Mitchell* in Francis Wharton, ed., *State Trials of the United States . . .* (Philadelphia, 1849), 182–83. Brackenridge, *Incidents*, 59, 77, 40, 58. See also Brackenridge to Tench Coxe, August 8, 1794, in *Pennsylvania Archives*, 4: 120.

12. Brackenridge, *Incidents*, 59, 77, 79, 40, 58.

13. "Deposition of Francis W. Gibson," October 11, 1794, Rawle Family Papers, Historical Society of Pennsylvania, 1: 49; Testimony of Mr. Pollack, Mr. Laird, and Samuel Irwine, Esq., ibid., 117; Testimony of Robert Whitehill, ibid., 119.

14. "Governor Mifflin to President Washington," August 5, 1794, *Pennsylvania Archives*, 2nd ser. (Harrisburg, Pa., 1896), 4: 91. A similar concern was expressed by Brackenridge in his letter to Coxe of August 8, 1794, ibid., 121.

15. Randolph to Washington, August 7, 1794, in Wharton, *State Trials*, 157. The notion that the militia of one state might not respond to a call from the president and might even be used to resist federal authority were possibilities that Randolph took seriously when he provided counsel to Washington; for evidence that Randolph's fears were not entirely unfounded, see Alexander Hamilton to Thomas Sim Lee, September 6, 1794, *Hamilton Papers*, 17: 201, and Thomas Sim Lee to Alexander Hamilton, September 13, 1794, ibid., 231–33. Modern critiques of the so-called states' rights view of the Second Amendment argue that the notion of the militia being used by the state to resist federal authority leads to absurd results; see Don Kates and Glenn Harlan Reynolds, "The Second Amendment and States' Rights: A Thought Experiment," *William and Mary Law Review* 36 (1995): 1737–68. Actually, as Randolph's letter to Washington demonstrates, such a possibility was not only possible, but in the view of many was also entirely plausible.

16. Thomas Mifflin to Joseph Hamar, September 8, 1794, *Gazette of the United States*, September 9, 1794; "Address of Governor Mifflin to the Militia of Lancaster, September 26, 1794," *Pennsylvania Archives*, 4: 312.

17. John Mellen, *The Great and Happy Doctrine of Liberty* (Boston, 1795), 10; Samuel Kendal, *A Sermon Delivered on the Day of National Thanksgiving, February 19, 1795* (Boston, 1795), 29, 28; Samuel Stanhope Smith, *The Divine Goodness of the United States of America* (Philadelphia, 1795), 27; Ebenzer Bradford, *The Nature of Humiliation* (Boston, 1795), 11; Thomas Thacher, *A Discourse, Delivered at the Third Parish in Dedham, 19th February, 1795* (Boston, 1795), 16; "The Late Insurrection in the Western Counties," *Washington Spy*, December 26, 1794.

18. Thomas P. Slaughter, "'The King of Crimes': Early American Treason Law, 1787–1860," in *Launching the Extended Republic: The Federalist Era*, Ronald Hoffman and Peter J. Albert, eds. (Charlottesville, Va., 1996); *United States v. Mitchell*, in Wharton, *State Trials*, 180, 183; *United States v. Mitchell*, 26 Fed. Cas. 1277, no. 15,788 (C.C.D.Pa. 1795), and *United States v. Vigol*, 28 Fed. Cas. 376, no. 16,621 (C.C.D.Pa. 1795).

19. Stanley Elkins and Eric McKitrick, *The Age of Federalism* (New York, 1993), 581–641.

20. Kohn, *Eagle and Sword*, 219–56.

21. Volunteer companies had existed since the Revolution and were usually composed of men of wealth, who could afford better equipment and uniforms than normal militia units. These companies were usually chartered by state law; see Kohn, *Eagle and Sword*, 224–30; Elkins and McKitrick, *Age of Federalism*, 594–99. "Speech of Mr. Nicholas," *Annals of Congress, 5th Congress, 2nd Session*, 1525; "Speech of Mr. Otis," ibid., 1526; "Speech of Mr. Sewall," ibid., 1528; "Speech of Mr. Harper," ibid., 1530. Representative Otis went so far as to claim that out of

seven thousand militia in North Carolina, only 500 were armed; ibid., 1643. Another representative drew attention to the lack of arms among city dwellers; see "Speech of Mr. Allen," ibid., 1755; "Speech of Mr. McDowell," ibid., 1536; "Speech of Mr. Williams," ibid., 1648; "Speech of Mr. Gallatin," ibid., 1728; "Speech of Mr. Sitgreaves," ibid., 1730–32; "Speech of Mr. Dayton," ibid., 1738; "Speech of M. Varnum," ibid., 1740; "Speech of Mr. Gallatin," ibid., 1726.

22.   "Speech of Mr. Gallatin," ibid., 1746. The language Gallatin quoted more closely paraphrased the language of Pennsylvania's 1790 constitutional provision on the right to bear arms than the syntax of the Second Amendment.

23.   Sharp, *American Politics in the Early Republic*, 175–76.

24.   "From *The Virginia Examiner*," June 21, 1799, *Philadelphia Aurora*; "Mentor," "To the Republican Citizens of Pennsylvania," May 21, 1799, *Philadelphia Aurora*. A cockade was a small ornament worn on a cap similar to a rosette. Thomas Jefferson to James Madison, May 10, 1798 in Paul Leicester Ford, ed., *The Writings of Thomas Jefferson* (New York, 1896), 7: 251. On the symbolic contest between Federalists and Republicans and the notion of a "black cockade fever," see Newman, *Parades and the Politics of the Street*, 160–65. The immediate context of the confrontation discussed by Jefferson is described by Merrill Peterson, *Thomas Jefferson and the New Nation* (New York, 1970), 598–99. Kohn, *Eagle and Sword*, 193–94. Adams's comment was made in a letter to Jefferson written more than a decade later; Adams to Jefferson, June 30, 1813, in Lester J. Cappon, ed., *The Adams-Jefferson Letters* (Chapel Hill, N.C., 1959), 2: 331. On the role of recent immigrants in the radicalization of Republicanism, see Michael Durey, "Thomas Paine's Apostles: Radical Emigres and the Triumph of Jeffersonian Republicanism," *William and Mary Quarterly* 44 (1987): 661–88.

25.   Congress passed the Naturalization Act (June 18, 1798), the Act Concerning Aliens (June 27, 1798), the Act Respecting Alien Enemies (July 6, 1798), and an Act for the Punishment of Certain Crimes (the Sedition Act) (July 14, 1798). For the historical background of the alien and sedition crises, see John C. Miller, *Crisis in Freedom: The Alien and Sedition Acts* (Boston, 1951), and James Morton Smith, *Freedom's Fetters: The Alien and Sedition Laws and American Civil Liberties*, rev. ed. (Ithaca, N.Y., 1966). The relationship between the Sedition Act and the development of a new libertarian theory of press freedom are discussed in Leonard Levy, *The Emergence of a Free Press* (New York, 1985), and Norman L. Rosenberg, *Protecting the Best Men: An Interpretive History of the Law of Libel* (Chapel Hill, N.C., 1986). Leonard Levy's original study of freedom of the press, *Legacy of Suppression*, was modified and presented in revised form in *Emergence of a Free Press*. Levy's original thesis was challenged by Walter Berns, "The Freedom of the Press and the Alien and Sedition Laws: A Reappraisal," *Supreme Court Review 1970* (1971): 109–59. The new First Amendment theorists included George Hay, *An Essay on the Liberty of the Press* (Philadelphia, 1799); Tunis Wortman, *A Treatise Concerning Political Inquiry and the Liberty of the Press* (New York, 1800); and St. George Tucker's appendix to *Blackstone's Commentaries*.

26.   Duane published all of the documents related to the trial as a pamphlet: *A Report of the Extraordinary Transactions which Took Place at Philadelphia, in February 1799*

(Philadelphia, 1799). The events were also picked up by the contemporary press; see *Albany (N.Y.) Centinel*, February 19, 1799; *Boston Columbian Centinel*, February 20, 1799; *New Haven (Conn.) Journal and Weekly Advertiser*, February 21, 1799.

27. *Report of the Extraordinary Transactions*, 30.

28. Ibid., 37.

29. On the duty to retreat, see Richard Brown, *No Duty to Retreat: Violence and Values in American History and Society* (New York, 1991).

30. *Report of the Extraordinary Transactions*, 33, 14.

31. The fact that neither side in this case cast the right of individual self-defense as a constitutional right is revealing. The orthodox view of the arms bearing provision of the Pennsylvania Constitution interpreted this right as civic in nature. An alternative individualistic view was starting to emerge among the most forward-looking legal thinkers of the day; see James Wilson, *The Works of the Honorable James Wilson* (Philadelphia, 1804), 3: 84.

32. On the Alien and Sedition Acts, see Miller, *Crisis in Freedom*, and James Morton Smith, *Freedom's Fetters*. On the Virginia and Kentucky resolutions, see Adrienne Koch and Harry Ammon, "The Virginia and Kentucky Resolutions: An Episode in Jefferson and Madison's Defense of Civil Liberties," *William and Mary Quarterly* 5 (1948): 147–76. On Kentucky's response, see James Morton Smith, "The Grass Roots Origins of the Kentucky Resolutions," *William and Mary Quarterly* 27 (1970): 221–45.

33. John Taylor to Thomas Jefferson, June 25, 1798, in William Dodd, ed., "John Taylor Correspondence," *The John P. Branch Historical Papers of Randolph-Macon College* 2 (1908): 271–76. On the importance of this letter to Jefferson's thought, see David N. Mayer, *The Constitutional Thought of Thomas Jefferson* (Charlottesville, Va., 1994), 199–208. For different readings of Jefferson's constitutional thought, see Garrett Ward Sheldon, *The Political Philosophy of Thomas Jefferson* (Baltimore, 1991), which stresses the democratic roots of this aspect of Jefferson's thought. Leonard Levy, *Jefferson and Civil Liberties: The Darker Side* (Cambridge, Mass., 1963), questions Jefferson's libertarian views. "The Kentucky Resolutions," in H. Jefferson Powell, *Languages of Power: A Sourcebook of Early American Constitutional History* (Durham, N.C., 1991), 130–33.

34. "Resolutions of a Company of Militia of Amelia County [Virginia]," *Alexandra Times*, September 12, 1798; *The Memorial of the Undersigned Freemen of the County of Rutland* [broadside] (Rutland, Vt., 1799); *There is a Snake in the Grass!!!* [broadside] (Lexington, Ky., 1798).

35. Nathaniel Pope, *A Speech Delivered by Nathaniel Pope . . .* (Richmond, Va., 1800), 34–35. Although there is fairly broad historical agreement that Federalists feared that Virginians were readying their militia, there is less agreement on the accuracy of their perceptions. James Roger Sharp, *American Politics in the Early Republic*, and Richard Kohn, *Eagle and Sword*, 251, each argue that leading Republicans were genuinely intent on using the militia against the federal government, while others, such as Richard Beeman, *The Old Dominion and the New Nation: 1788–1801* (Lexington, Ky., 1972), 202–4, discount the evidence for this as unreliable.

36. *The Address of the Minority of the Virginia Legislature* (Richmond, Va., 1798), 11; *The Communications of the Several States, on the Resolutions of the Legislature of Virginia* (Richmond, Va., 1799), 5.

37. John C. Miller, *The Federalist Era* (New York, 1960), 24; Robert H. Churchill, "Popular Nullification, Fries' Rebellion, and the Waning of Radical Republicanism, 1798–1801," *Pennsylvania History* 67 (2000): 105–40; Paul Douglas Newman, *Fries's Rebellion: The Enduring Struggle for the American Revolution* (Philadelphia, 2004).

38. "Testimony of Cephas Child," in Wharton, *State Trials*, 529; "Testimony of Colonel Nichols," ibid., 505–6; "Testimony of Colonel Nicholas," ibid., 503–4; "Testimony of James Chapman," ibid., 524. For discussions of the political culture of the predominantly German-speaking populations of southeastern Pennsylvania, see A. G. Roeber, "Citizens or Subjects? German Lutherans and the Federal Constitution in Pennsylvania, 1789–1800," *Amerikastudien/American Studies*, 34 (1989): 49–68. One of the lawyers for Fries tried to invoke the distinctiveness of his German heritage as a means for understanding his actions; see "Address of Ewing," in Wharton, *State Trials*, 555. "Testimony of Israel Roberts," in Wharton, *State Trials*, 552.

39. William Rawle, "Address," in Wharton, *State Trials*, 537. Rawle quoted from Judge Patterson's jury charge in the Whiskey Rebellion case of *U.S. v. Vigol*, which laid out a fairly expansive view of treason, consistent with this understanding.

40. Alexander Dallas, "Address," ibid., 544–47.

41. Judge Richard Peters, "Jury Charge," in Wharton, *State Trials*, 587.

42. For a somewhat anachronistic treatment of the relationship between the Second Amendment and the right of revolution in the early Republic, see David C. Williams, *The Mythic Landscape of the Second Amendment: Taming Political Violence in a Constitutional Republic* (New Haven, Conn., 2003). Williams devotes scant attention to the turbulent 1790s and mistakenly applies modern categories of scholarly analysis to these constitutional debates. The right of resistance was not, as Williams suggests, something that resided in the people collective as a unified organic whole. Jeffersonians clearly understood it as a right that could only be exercised by the states.

43. For a discussion of the role of the state militias in the Revolution of 1800, see Bruce Ackerman, *The Failure of the Founding Fathers: Jefferson, Marshall, and the Rise of Presidential Democracy* (Cambridge, Mass., 2005); Joanne B. Freeman, "The Election of 1800: A Study in the Logic of Political Change," *Yale Law Journal* 108 (1999): 1959–94; Sharp, *American Politics in the Early Republic*, 250–75; Daniel Sisson, *The American Revolution of 1800* (New York, 1974), 366–73, 420–26; Dumas Malone, *Jefferson and the Ordeal of Liberty* (New York, 1962), 503–5; John E. Ferling, *Adams vs. Jefferson: The Tumultuous Election of 1800* (New York, 2004).

44. *Washington Federalist*, February 12, 1801; Hugh Henry Brackenridge to Thomas Jefferson, January 19, 1801, Jefferson Papers, Library of Congress.

45. Albert Gallatin, "Plan at the Time of Balloting for Jefferson and Burr, Communicated to Nicholas and Jefferson," in Henry Adams, ed., *Writings of Gallatin* (Philadelphia, 1879), 1: 19–20.

46. Ibid.
47. John Beckly to Albert Gallatin, February 15, 1801, Gallatin Papers, New York Historical Society; James A. Bayard to Thomas Jefferson, February 17, 1801, Jefferson Papers, Library of Congress; Samuel Tyler to James Monroe, February 11, 1801, *William and Mary Quarterly* 1 (1892): 104. For additional confirmation of Pennsylvania's resolve to use its militia to thwart a possible Federalist coup, see Thomas McKean to Thomas Jefferson, March 21, 1801, Jefferson Papers, Library of Congress; Ezra Witter, *Two Sermons on the Party Spirit and Divided State of the Country, Civil and Religious* (Springfield, Mass., 1801), 11. *Washington Federalist*, February 12, 1801. The problem of arming the militia was a real one. Governor James Monroe's correspondence during Gabriel's Rebellion confirms that a significant portion of Virginia's militia lacked arms or powder; on this see Douglas R. Egerton, *Gabriel's Rebellion: The Virginia Slave Conspiracies of 1800 and 1802* (Chapel Hill, N.C., 1993). The details of Monroe's efforts are described by Sharp, *American Politics in the Early Republic*, 270–71.
48. Thomas Jefferson to James Monroe, February 15, 1801, Jefferson Papers, Library of Congress.
49. For a discussion of the concept of law and police and its connection to early American law, see Christopher L. Tomlins, "Law, Police, and Jeffersonian Political Theory," *Studies in American Political Development* 4 (1990): 3–45. Tucker, *Blackstone's Commentaries*.
50. St. George Tucker, *View of the Constitution of the United States with Selected Writings*, Clyde N. Wilson, ed. (Indianapolis, 1999), 227; 216, n. 67.
51. Ibid., 214.
52. Ibid., 293, 228–29. While Tucker's earliest discussion of the Second Amendment highlighted the connection of the right to bear arms to the defense of states' rights, Tucker shared with others of his generation a belief that the phrase "bear arms" was legally distinct from bearing or carrying a gun for personal use. Indeed, throughout his writings Tucker used this term in a manner consistent with this dominant military usage. The danger Tucker apprehended was that Congress might target military weapons—muskets and rifles—not sword canes, pistols, or other weapons with limited military value intended primarily for personal defense.
53. *Address of the Minority of the Virginia Legislature*, 11; Tucker, *View of the Constitution*, 227, 229.
54. John Danforth Dunbar, *An Oration Pronounced on the 4th of July 1805* (Boston, 1805), 13–15; Samuel Dana, *An Address on the Importance of a Well Regulated Militia* (Charlestown, Mass., 1801), 5, 10.

Chapter Four

1. John Adams to Benjamin Rush, September 19, 1806, in John Schutz and Douglas Adair, ed., *The Spur of Fame: Dialogues of John Adams and Benjamin Rush, 1805–1813* (San Marino, Calif., 1966), 66. On the role of dueling in early American politics, see Joanne B. Freeman, *Affairs of Honor* (New Haven,

Conn., 2001), chap. 4. Joanne B. Freeman, "Dueling as Politics: Reinterpreting the Burr-Hamilton Duel," *William and Mary Quarterly* 53 (1996): 289–318; William J. Rorabaugh, "The Political Duel in the Early Republic: Burr v. Hamilton" *Journal of the Early Republic* 15 (1995): 1–23.

2. *Trial of Thomas Selfridge, Attorney at Law, Before the Hon. Isaac Parker, Esq, For Killing Charles Austin* . . . (Boston, 1806); Thomas Selfridge, *A Correct Statement of the Whole Preliminary Controvesy between Tho. O. Selfridge and Benj. Austin* (Boston, 1807); *A Brief Account of the Catastrophe in State Street* . . . (Boston, 1807).

3. Thomas C. Amory, *Life of James Sullivan* (Boston, 1859), 2: 163.

4. *Boston Gazette*, August 4, 1806; *Boston Independent Gazetteer*, August 4, 1806. A detailed account of the dispute is available in Charles Warren, *Jacobin and Junto, or Early American Politics as Viewed in the Diary of Dr. Nathaniel Ames, 1758–1822* (1931; repr. New York, 1970), 183–214. For general discussions of politics in this period, see David Hackett Fischer, *The Revolution of American Conservatism: The Federalist Party in the Era of Jeffersonian Democracy* (New York, 1965), 186. See also Richard E. Ellis, *The Jeffersonian Crisis: Courts and Politics in the Young Republic* (New York, 1974), 218–19; Samuel Eliot Morison, *Harrison Gray Otis, 1765–1848: The Urbane Federalist* (Boston, 1969), 277–79, 536–37; Brook Thomas, *Cross-Examinations of Law and Literature: Cooper, Hawthorne, Stowe, and Melville* (Cambridge, U.K., 1987), 194–98.

5. Thomas Selfridge, *A Correct Statement*, 5. Nathaniel Ames, as quoted in Warren, *Jacobin and Junto*, 185. A copy of the circular announcement dated October 25, 1806, was reprinted in the *Boston Independent Chronicle*, November 6, 1806; see also Warren, *Jacobin and Junto*, 195–96.

6. Warren, *Jacobin and Junto*, 189, 191, 193; "Speech of Attorney Dexter," *Trial of Selfridge*, 117; Francis Wharton, *A Treatise on the Law of Homicide in the United States* (Philadelphia, 1855), 174–75, n. 1.

7. "Speech of the Attorney General," *Trial of Selfridge*, 77, 137; "Speech of Solicitor General," 20–21; "Speech of Attorney Gore," ibid., 41.

8. The common-law understanding of self-defense was elaborated in William Hawkins, *A Treatise of the Pleas of the Crown* . . . (London, 1716); Michael Foster, *A Report of Some Proceedings* . . . (Oxford, 1762); Sir Mathew Hale, *The History of the Pleas of the Crown* (London, 1800). "Speech of Attorney Gore," *Trial of Selfridge*, 41.

9. "Speech of Attorney Gore," *Trial of Selfridge*, 41.

10. "Jury Charge of Judge Parker," ibid., 164–65.

11. *Boston Independent Chronicle*, December 1, 1806; Dec 8, 1806; December 25, 1806; see also Warren, *Jacobin and Junto*, 197.

12. *Boston Independent Chronicle*, February 19, 1807; January 5, 1807; January 6, 1807; January 19, 1807; January 26, 1807; February 2, 1807.

13. "Mr. Selfridge," *Port Folio* 3 (1807), 259.

14. "Ames Diary," quoted in Warren, *Jacobin and Junto*, 205.

15. "Massachusetts Constitution," in Philip Kurland and Ralph Lerner, eds., *The Founders' Constitution* (Chicago, 1987), 1: 11–13; Benjamin Austin, *Memorial to the Legislature of Massachusetts* (Boston, 1808), 1–4. In the pamphlet, Austin noted that the judges had been divided in their rendering of this principle, a point

that he felt only underscored the need for the legislature to step in and settle
the matter.

16. Samuel Adams Drake, *Old Landmarks and Historic Personages of Boston* (Boston,
     1873), 114; "Case of Thomas Oliver Selfridge," *Boston Law Reporter* (July 1841):
     89–98; Wharton, *Treatise on the Law of Homicide in the United States*, 220,
     171–74, 222.

17. *Philadelphia Poulson's American Daily Advertiser*, March 29, 1809. For a brief nar-
     rative overview of the case, see George Lee Haskins and Hebert A. Johnson,
     *History of the Supreme Court of the United States: Foundations of Power: John
     Marshall, 1801–1815* (New York, 1981), 320–31, and Sanford W. Higginbotham,
     The Keystone in the Democratic Arch: Pennsylvania Politics, 1800–1816 (Harrisburg,
     Pa., 1952), 183–200. The best modern account of the legal issues involved
     in the Olmstead affair is Gary D. Rowe, "Constitutionalism in the Streets,"
     Southern California Law Review 78 (2005): 401–55.

18. *Philadelphia Aurora*, March 3, 1809. For a concise overview of the facts of the
     case, including the confrontation between the militia and the federal marshal,
     see "The Long and Litigated and Important Case of the Sloop *Active*," *The Gleaner,
     or Monthly Magazine* 1 (1809), 383–89.

19. *Statutes at Large, Pennsylvania*, April 3, 1803; *Acts of the General Assembly Com-
     monwealth of Pennsylvania* (Philadelphia, 1809), 200; Governor Simon Snyder to
     President James Madison, April 7, 1809, in *Pennsylvania Archives*, ser. 8, vol. 4
     (Harrisburg, Pa., 1931–1935), 2776. On the language of states' rights, see Saul
     Cornell, *The Other Founders: Anti-Federalism and the Dissenting Tradition in
     America, 1788–1828* (Chapel Hill, N.C., 1999); Forrest McDonald, *States' Rights
     and the Union: Imperium in Imperio, 1776–1876* (Lawrence, Kans., 2000). The
     politics of the embargo is discussed in Burton Spivak, *Jefferson's English Crisis:
     Commerce, Embargo, and the Republican Revolution* (Charlottesville, Va., 1979). On
     Madison's role in the embargo, see J. C. Stagg, *Mr. Madison's War: Politics,
     Diplomacy, and Warfare in the Early Republic, 1783–1830* (Princeton, N.J., 1983); the
     best short guide to Madison's presidency is Robert A. Rutland, *The Presidency
     of James Madison* (Lawrence, Kans., 1990).

20. *Philadelphia Poulson's American Daily Advertiser*, March 29, 1809. In the sub-
     sequent trial of the Pennsylvania militia officers the prosecution took every
     opportunity to stress the gravity of the constitutional crises precipitated by the
     Pennsylvania militia's actions; see *A Report of the Whole Trial of General Michael
     Bright and Others . . .* (Philadelphia, 1809).

21. *Carlisle (Pa.) Gazette*, March 10, 1809; *Journal of the Pennsylvania House of
     Representatives*, March 10, 1809 (Lancaster, Pa., 1810), 616; *Journal of the Senate of
     the Commonwealth of Pennsylvania* (Lancaster, Pa., 1810), 380.

22. "Mr. Scratch'em," *Philadelphia Tickler*, December 6, 1809, p. 3. General Michael
     Bright to Secretary of State Bolleau, March 25, 1809, in *Pennsylvania Archives*,
     ser. 9, vol. 4 (Harrisburg, 1931), 2773; *Philadelphia Aurora*, March 2, 1809.

23. *Philadelphia Aurora*, April 18, 1809.

24. *Report of the Whole Trial*, 19.

25. Ibid., 122.

26. Ibid., 89.

27. Ibid., 200–201; Thomas Leiper to James Madison, May 5, 1809, in *Papers of James Madison, Presidential Series*, Robert Rutland et al., eds. (Charlottesville, Va., 1984–92), 1: 172; Madison's pardon was issued on May 6, 1809; see ibid., 173. Thomas Jefferson to James Madison, May 21, 1809, in ibid., 198; *Carlisle (Pa.) Gazette*, June 2, 1809.

28. For an invocation of the "Pennsylvania Doctrine" during the nullification controversy, see Hampden, "Pennsylvania Doctrine of States Rights," *Washington, D.C., Banner of the Constitution*, July 6, 1831, p. 249, and "The Actual Crisis," ibid., December 5, 1832, pp. 414–17.

29. "Speech of Representative Randolph," *Annals of Congress*, 10th Congress, 1st Session (Washington, D.C., 1857–61), 1021.

30. "Return of Militia," *American State Papers: Military Affairs* (Washington, D.C., 1832–1861), 1: 230–34; "Speech of Representative Randolph," *Annals of Congress*, 10th Congress, 1st Session (Washington, D.C., 1857–61), 1021. "Representative Thomas" conceded that the militia lacked muskets but noted that the people were not entirely bereft of other armaments; ibid., 1027. "Speech of Representative Bacon," ibid., 1041.

31. McDonald, *States' Rights*, 64. On Federalist responses to the embargo, see James Banner, *To the Hartford Convention* (New York, 1969), 118–21, 300–301, 318; McDonald, *States' Rights*; Roger Brown, *The Republic in Peril: 1812* (New York, 1964); Steven Watts, *The Republic Reborn: War and the Making of Liberal America, 1790–1820* (Baltimore, 1987).

32. On the emergence of a new style of Federalist politician, see Fischer, *The Revolution of American Conservatism*.

33. Paul A. Gilje, "The Baltimore Riots of 1812 and the Breakdown of the Anglo-American Mob Tradition," *Journal of Social History* 13 (1980): 547–64; Donald R. Hickey, *The War of 1812: A Forgotten Conflict* (Urbana, Ill., 1989), chap. 3. The events of the siege of "Fort Hanson" can be pieced together from *The Report of the Committee of Grievances and Courts of Justice of the House of Delegates of Maryland on the Subject of the Recent Mobs and Riots in the City of Baltimore* (Annapolis, Md., 1813); see in particular, "Deposition of Henry C. Gaither," ibid., 192.

34. "Deposition of Henry C. Gaither," *Report of the Committee of Grievances*, 192.

35. Gilje, "Baltimore Riots of 1812"; Hickey, *War of 1812*.

36. "Dreadful Commotion," *Washington (D.C.) National Intelligencer*, August 1, 1812; "The Massacre at Baltimore," *Alexandria (Va.) Daily Gazette*, August 6, 1812.

37. *New York Commercial Advertiser*, August 4, 1812; "From the Spirit of 76," *Greenfield (Mass.) Franklin Herald*, August 11, 1812; *Greenfield (Mass.) Franklin Herald*, August 25, 1812; *New London (Conn.) Bee*, September 1, 1812; *Wilmington (Del.) American Watchmen*, August 5, 1812.

38. David Grimsted, *American Mobbing, 1828–1861: Toward Civil War* (New York, 1998).

39. One observer claimed that a single musket was carried into the premises in plain view and that the cache of arms had been disguised, but that the noise of the rattling betrayed the contents of the containers; "Deposition of John H. Payne," *Report of the Committee of Grievances*, 18–20.

40. Gilje, "Baltimore Riots of 1812."

41. Cruse recounted the events of the Baltimore Riot to Alexis de Tocqueville in 1831; see George Wilson Pierson, *Tocqueville in America* (New York, 1938), 505.

42. Banner, *To the Hartford Convention*; McDonald, *States' Rights*; Brown, *Republic in Peril*.

43. Daniel Webster, "Speech on the Conscription Bill, Dec. 9, 1814," *Papers of Daniel Webster* (Hanover, N.H., 1986), 1: 30.

44. "Governor Caleb Strong to Justices of the Supreme Court of the Commonwealth of Massachusetts, August 1, 1812" and the reply "To His Excellency the Governor," in Kurland and Lerner, *Founders' Constitution*, 3: 183.

45. "James Monroe to the Chairmen of the Senate Military Committee," February 1815, in ibid., 185–86.

46. *Houston v. Moore*, 18 U.S. 24, 26, 52–53 (1820). The connections between the case and the struggles to define federalism in the early republic are dealt with by G. Edward White, *The Marshall Court and Cultural Change, 1815–1835* (New York, 1991), 535–41. For a thoughtful discussion of the case and federalism, see Kurt T. Lash, "The Lost Jurisprudence of the Ninth Amendment," *Texas Law Review* 83 (2005): 597–716. For a somewhat anachronistic reading from the modern gun rights perspective, see Norman J. Heath, "Exposing the Second Amendment: Federal Preemption of State Militia Legislation," *Detroit Mercy Law Review* 79 (2001): 39–73.

47. Joseph Story, "Commentaries on the Constitution," in Kurland and Lerner, eds., *Founders' Constitution*, 3: 214.

48. R. Kent Newmyer, *Supreme Court Justice Joseph Story: Statesmen of the Old Republic* (Chapel Hill, N.C., 1985), chap. 5.

Chapter Five

1. Charles Dickens, *American Notes and the Uncommon Commercial Traveler* (Philadelphia, 1865), 277. The first edition of Dickens's work appeared in 1838, and it went through many subsequent printings. For other travel accounts noting the violent character of American life, see Frederick Law Olmstead, *A Journey through Texas; or a Saddle-Trip on the Southwestern Frontier* (New York, 1857), 20; John W. Forney, *Anecdotes of Public Men* (New York, 1873), 302–3. In addition to travelers' accounts, one can find additional evidence of the practice of individuals' arming themselves in newspapers. For a sample of such accounts, see *Middletown (Conn.) Middlesex Gazette*, November 7, 1827; *New Hampshire Sentinel*, May 4, 1837; *Newport (R.I.) Mercury*, May 12, 1838. Until mid-century handguns were generally seen as unreliable weapons for individuals interested in arming themselves for reasons of personal self-defense. In New York City guns accounted for only 30 percent of murders in the period before the Civil War; Eric Monkkonen, *Murder in New York City* (Berkeley, Calif., 2001), 26–55. For additional evidence that the practice of carrying concealed weapons was not exclusively a southern problem, see John Austin Stevens, *Progress of New York in a Century, 1776–1876* (New York, 1876), 84. Edwin G. Burrows and Mike Wallace, *Gotham: A History of New York City to 1898* (New York, 1999). Samuel

Colt was a key figure in the transformation of pistol technology and in popularizing pistols' role as effective tools for self-defense; see William Hosley, *Colt: The Making of an American Legend* (Amherst, Mass., 1996).

2. On the bowie knife, see Thomas A. Morris, *Miscellany: Consisting of Essays, Biographical Sketches and Notes of Travel* (Cincinnati, Ohio, 1854), 319.

3. Alexis de Tocqueville, trans. George Lawrence, *Democracy in America* (New York, 1966), 506–8; Sean Wilentz, *The Rise of American Democracy: Jefferson to Lincoln* (New York, 2005). For an argument that the War of 1812 marked a watershed in the evolution of the transition from republicanism to liberalism, see Steven Watts, *The Republic Reborn: War and the Making of Liberal America, 1790–1820* (Baltimore, Md., 1987).

4. Olmstead, *Journey through Texas*, 20; Richard Hildreth, *Despotism in America: An Inquiry into the Nature, Results, and Legal Basis of the Slave-Holding System* (Boston, 1854), 90–91. For comments on the different role of honor in northern and southern culture and its consequences for this issue, see Adam G. De Gurowski, *America and Europe* (New York, 1857), 219.

5. H. A. Boardmen, *The Low Value Set upon Human Life in the United States* (Philadelphia, 1853), 7; Hinton Rowan Helper, *The Land of Gold: Reality versus Fiction* (Baltimore, 1855), 68. For evidence that a similar perception existed in Boston, see "Going Armed," *The Boston Pearl, a Gazette of Polite Literature*, August 31, 1836. Establishing the connections between these perceptions and social reality is difficult. In his forthcoming study of violent death in America, historian Randolph Roth will provide a comprehensive account of this subject that will help determine the accuracy of these perceptions.

6. Joseph Gales, "Prevention of Crime," in *Early Indiana Trials: And Sketches*, Oliver Hampton Smith, ed. (Cincinnati, 1858), 465, 476.

7. Boardmen, *The Low Value Set upon Human Life in the United States*, 7; Helper, *Land of Gold*, 68; "D," "British Travelers in America No. 2," *Magnolia; or Southern Monthly* (1841–42), p. 363; Charles Augustus Murray, *Travels in North America*, 2 vols. (1839; repr. 1974).

8. For general discussions of rioting and mobbing, see Paul A. Gilje, *Rioting in America* (Indianapolis, 1996), and David Grimsted, *American Mobbing, 1828–1861: Toward Civil War* (New York, 1998).

9. Saul Cornell and Nathan Dedino, "A Well Regulated Right: The Early American Origins of Gun Control," *Fordham Law Review* 73 (2004): 487–529; Chap. 89, "An Act to Prevent persons in this Commonwealth from wearing concealed Arms, except in certain cases," *Acts Passed at the First Session of the Twenty-First General Assembly for the Commonwealth of Kentucky* (Frankfort, 1813), 100–101; "An Act against carrying concealed weapons, and going armed in public places in an unnecessary manner," *Acts Passed at the Second Session of the First Legislature of the State of Louisiana* (New Orleans, 1813), 172–75; *Acts of the General Assembly of the State of Georgia Passed in Milledgeville* (Milledgeville, 1838), 90–91. Interestingly, Clinton's speech was reported in the *Cleveland Register*, see *Annals of Cleveland, 1818–1935* (Cleveland, Ohio, 1938), 1037. "An Act to Prohibit the Carrying of Concealed Weapons," *The Revised Statutes of the State of Ohio* (Cincinnati, 1870), 1: 452; *Cleveland Morning Leader*, April 11, 1859,

and *Cincinnati Daily Times*, April 8, 1859. For an argument that concealed weapons were a southern problem, see Clayton Cramer, *Concealed Weapon Laws of the Early Republic: Dueling, Southern Violence, and Moral Reform* (Westport, Conn., 1999).

10.   For an overview of the scope of early American firearms regulations, see Cornell and Dedino, "A Well Regulated Right." For a general discussion of the police powers, see William J. Novak, *The People's Welfare: Law and Regulation in Nineteenth-Century America* (Chapel Hill, N.C., 1996). For examples of the types of laws legislatures enacted, see "An Act to Prevent the Wearing of Dangerous and Unlawful Weapons" (passed October 19, 1821), *Tennessee State Sessions Laws* [microform], chap. 13, pp. 15–16 (fiche 29–30); "An Act to Prevent the Carrying of Concealed Weapons" (passed February 2, 1838), *Virginia State Sessions Laws* [microform], chap. 101, pp. 76–77 (fiche 87); "An Act to Suppress the Sale and Use of Bowie Knives and Arkansas Tooth Picks in This State" (passed January 27, 1838), *Tennessee State Sessions Laws* [microform], chap. 137, pp. 200–201 (fiche 79).

11.   *The Debates and Journals of the Constitutional Convention of the State of Maine, 1819–1820* (Augusta, 1894). The important change in the language of state con-stitutions on bearing arms is elided by modern individual rights scholars who conflate the language of eighteenth-century constitutions with that of the early nineteenth century; for an illustration of the misreading of this history, see Eugene Volokh, "The Commonplace Second Amendment," *New York University Law Review* 73 (1998): 793–821. For a critique of Volokh's misread-ing, see Saul Cornell, "Don't Know Much about History: The Current Crisis in Second Amendment Scholarship," *Northern Kentucky Law Review* 29 (2002): 657–81. The literature on the debates over the relative importance of repub-lican and liberal ideas in American life is enormous. For a useful overview of the historiography, see Daniel T. Rodgers, "Republicanism: The Career of a Concept," *Journal of American History* 76 (1992): 11–38. Republicanism, it is worth stressing, had managed to creatively synthesize many elements of an emerging liberal ethos by the end of the eighteenth century; see James T. Kloppenberg, "Republicanism in American History and Historiography," *Tocqueville Review* 13 (1992): 119–36. On change in Jacksonian America, see Charles G. Sellers, *The Market Revolution: Jacksonian America, 1815–1846* (New York, 1991). For a different view, see Daniel Feller, *The Jacksonian Promise: America, 1815–1840* (Baltimore, Md., 1995). On the radical changes wrought by the Revolution and its impact on republicanism, see Gordon S. Wood, *The Radicalism of the American Revolution* (New York, 1992). For a wonderfully evocative study of the changes in American society in the early republic, see Jack Larkin, *The Reshaping of Everyday Life, 1790–1840* (New York, 1988). On the character of Jacksonian constitutionalism, see Laura J. Scalia, *America's Jeffersonian Experiment: Remaking State Constitutions, 1820–1850* (DeKalb, Ill., 1999). For a discussion of the original conception of the right to assemble, see Richard A. Primus, *The American Language of Rights* (Cambridge, U.K., 1999).

12.   Harold M. Dorr, ed., *The Michigan Constitutional Conventions of 1835–36: Debates and Proceedings* (Ann Arbor, Mich., 1940), 283.

13. *Bliss v. Commonwealth*, 12 KY (2 Litt.) 90, 13 Am. Dec. 251 (1822), 92.
14. *Journal of the Kentucky House of Representatives* (Frankfort, 1837), 73–75.
15. Ibid.
16. Ibid.; see also Robert Ireland, "The Problem of Concealed Weapons in 19th Century Kentucky," *Register of the Kentucky Historical Society* 91 (1993): 370–85.
17. *Aymette v. State*, 21 Tenn (2 Hump) 154 (1840).
18. *State v. Buzzard*, 4 Ark (2 Pike) 18 (1842) at 21–22.
19. *A Full and Authentic Report of the Testimony on the Trial of Matt. F. Ward* (New York, 1854).
20. "Speech of Thomas Marshall," *A Full and Authentic Report*, 71.
21. Ibid.; "Speech of Governor Helm," ibid., 82; "Speech of Mr. Wolfe," ibid., 111.
22. "Speech of Mr. Wolfe," ibid., 105; "Speech of Mr. Crittenden," ibid., 130.
23. The Ward trial was widely covered in the national press; for a good sampling of this coverage, see "The Ward Trial," *Amherst (N.H.) Farmers Cabinet*, May 11, 1854; ibid., June 11, 1854; ibid., November 17, 1853; *Pittsfield (Mass.) Sun*, May 18, 1854.
24. "The Ward Trial," *Monthly Law Reporter* 7(1854): 129, 134, 137, 149, 151, 154. The distinction between the right to keep or carry firearms and the right to keep and bear arms in the militia was discussed as an aside in the most infamous case of the nineteenth century, the Dred Scott case. In that case the U.S. Supreme Court considered questions of black citizenship and the constitutionality of slavery in the territories. Chief Justice Roger Taney used the examples as a way of demonstrating the limits of congressional power in the territories and the limited scope of African-American rights under the Constitution. To accept the proposition that African-Americans were entitled to the privileges and immunities of federal citizenship would have included the right to "keep and carry arms wherever they went." Taney's choice of terms is important. He did not use the right to bear arms as his example, but he spoke about a right to keep and carry arms. The subject of bearing arms came up in an entirely different context in the opinion when Taney noted that Congress could no more abrogate the right to bear arms in the territories than it could restrict any other aspect of the Bill of Rights; *Dred Scott v. Sanford*, 19 Howard 393 (1857), 417. All of these discussions were not part of the holding in the case but were *obiter dicta*. The classic study of the case is Don E. Fehrenbacher, *The Dred Scott Case: Its Significance in American Law and Politics* (New York, 1978). The ambiguous status of free African-Americans, particularly in the South, offered another opportunity for judges to think hard about the meaning of the right to bear arms. As a matter of law free blacks occupied an intermediate status, enjoying some basic individual liberties, but not all those associated with full citizenship. In *State v. Newsome* (1844), the supreme court of North Carolina upheld a state law limiting the access of "free persons of color" to firearms. Newsome had been indicted for carrying a gun without a license as required by law. The court acknowledged that the law treated blacks and whites differently. Where the right to bear arms was concerned, however, blacks' inferior status was not at issue. The court further noted that had the law impinged on the state's ability to maintain its well-regulated militia, it would be subject to stricter scrutiny

and might be subject to constitutional challenge. "The defendant is not indicted for carrying arms in defense of the state, nor does the act of 1840 prohibit him from doing it"; *State v. Newsome*, 27 N.C. (5 Ired.) 250 (1844) at 253–54. In 1848, the supreme court of Georgia further elaborated the distinction between the rights of citizens and free people of color in *Cooper and Worsham v. Savannah*: "Free persons of color have never been recognized here as citizens; they are not entitled to bear arms, vote for members of the legislature, or to hold any civil office." Moreover, the court ruled, "They have no *political* rights, but they have *personal* rights, one of which is personal liberty"; *Cooper and Worsham v. Savannah*, 4 Ga 68 (1848). Taney's discussion of the right to keep and carry firearms was linked to the right to travel, another common-law right not expressly mentioned in the Bill of Rights. Taney approached both of these common-law rights as though they had been included in the privileges and immunities clause of the Constitution. For a different reading of Taney's dicta that interprets his decision as articulating an individual rights view of the Second Amendment, see David B. Kopel, "The Second Amendment in the Nineteenth Century," *Brigham Young University Law Review* 4 (1998): 1359–1545.

25.   Furman Sheppard, *The Constitutional Text-Book: A Practical and Familiar Exposition of the Constitution of the United States* (Philadelphia, 1855), 3–4; Edward Deering Mansfield, *The Political Grammar of the United States . . .* (New York, 1834); Francis Fellowes, *Youth's Manual of the Constitution of the United States* (Hartford, Conn., 1835); B.E. Hale, *Familiar Conversations upon the Constitution of the United States; Designed for the Use of Commons Schools* (West Bradford, Mass., 1835). For a somewhat dated but still useful overview of early constitutional commentaries, see Elizabeth Bauer, *Commentaries on the Constitution, 1790–1860* (New York, 1952). On American legal education in the antebellum era, see William P. Lapiana, *Logic and Experience: The Origin of Modern American Legal Education* (New York, 1994). William Rawle, *A View of the Constitution of the United States of America* (Philadelphia, 1825), 121–23. For biographical sketches of Rawle, see Evert A. Duyckinck and George L. Duyckinck, *Cyclopedia of American Literature*, 2 vols. (Philadelphia, 1881), 697–98, and Henry Vethake, *Encyclopedia Americana* (Boston, 1851), 14: 512–14. For Rawle the meaning of the Second Amendment was clearly controlled by its preamble, which placed the subject of the right to bear arms within the context of the militia. Indeed, Rawle treated the second clause of the amendment as a corollary of the preamble, which asserted the necessity of a well-regulated militia. The purpose of the militia was to repel invasion, to suppress insurrection, and preserve the good order and peace of government. The right of the people to keep and bear arms was therefore indispensably necessary to the goal of maintaining this valuable public institution. Regulation was not antithetical to the exercise of this right in Rawle's view, but was essential for its free exercise. "The duty of the state government is to adopt such regulations as will tend to make good soldiers with the least interruptions of the ordinary and useful occupations of civil life." For Rawle, bearing arms was, as it had been for virtually all previous writers, a military obligation of citizens. In arguing that the Second Amendment was

binding on the states, Rawle articulated a view of the Bill of Rights that the Supreme Court would explicitly reject within a decade in the case of *Barron v. Baltimore*, a decision which held that the provisions of the federal Bill of Rights were not binding on the states; Rawle, *A View of the Constitution*, 142, 122; *Barron v. Baltimore*, 7 Peters 243 (1833).

26. Joseph Story, *A Familiar Exposition of the Constitution of the United States* (New York, 1840), 264–65.

27. Joseph Story, *Commentaries on the Constitution*, 3 vols. (Boston, 1833), 3: 746–47. On the jeremiad as an important American literary form, see Sacvan Bercovitch, *The American Jeremiad* (Madison, Wis., 1978). On the decline of the militia as an institution in the early republic, see Mark Pitcavage, "An Equitable Burden: The Decline of the State Militias, 1783–1858," Ph.D. dissertation, Ohio State University, 1995.

28. Furman Sheppard, author of a popular guide to the Constitution published a decade after Story's influential treatise, also viewed the Second Amendment through the framework provided by the preamble's affirmation of the need for a well-regulated militia. "If citizens are allowed to keep and bear arms, it will be likely to operate as a check upon their rulers, and restrain them from acts of tyranny and usurpation. The necessity of maintaining a large standing army is also diminished by arming and disciplining the citizens generally, so that they may be ready and qualified at any time, to defend the country in a sudden emergency." Sheppard's main point was underscored by the study question he posed in the back of his book: "What diminishes the necessity of maintaining a large standing army?" His answer: the Second Amendment. His popular summary presented the Second Amendment as a civic right inextricably linked to participation in the militia; Sheppard, *The Constitutional Text-Book*, 247.

29. Benjamin L. Oliver, *The Rights of an American Citizen with Commentary on State Rights, and on the Constitution and Policy of the United States* (1832; repr. New York, 1970), 176–77. At the time that Oliver was writing, the only case in point was the Kentucky case of *Bliss v. Commonwealth*, which declared a ban on concealed weapons unconstitutional. A year after Oliver's book appeared, an Indiana court took the opposite view in *State v. Mitchell*.

30. Lewis Perry, *Radical Abolitionism: Anarchy and the Government of God in Anti-Slavery Thought* (Ithaca, N.Y., 1973); John Demos, "The Anti-Slavery Movement and the Problem of Violent Means," *American Quarterly* 37 (1964): 501–26; David S. Reynolds, *John Brown, Abolitionist: The Man Who Killed Slavery, Sparked the Civil War, and Seeded Civil Rights* (New York, 2005).

31. For a general history of abolitionism, see James Brewer Stewart, *Holy Warriors: The Abolitionists and American Slavery* (New York, 1996).

32. Joel Tiffany, *A Treatise on the Unconstitutionality of Slavery* (Cleveland, Ohio, 1849), 117–18; Lysander Spooner, *The Unconstitutionality of Slavery* (Boston, 1845), 66, 98; Lysander Spooner, *An Essay on the Trial by Jury* (Boston, 1852), 17–18.

33. *The Liberator*, October 4, 1850, p. 3, quoted in Perry, *Radical Abolitionism*, 237–38.

34. *New York Tribune*, February 8, 1856. In a travel account written six years later, one writer noted that western Indian tribes not only had old muskets, but also

Sharps breachloaders, which he described as Beechers Bibles; Richard F. Burton, *The City of the Saints and Across the Rocky Mountains to California* (New York, 1862), 119. On the role of Sharps rifles in the Kansas conflict, see W. H. Isley, "The Sharps Rifle Episode in Kansas History," *American Historical Review* 12 (1907): 546–66.

35. *New York Tribune*, May 23, 1856; "Speech of Sumner," *Congressional Globe*, appendix, 34th Congress, 1st Session (May 20, 1856), 539. Butler explained his intention in a response to Charles Sumner, delivered after Sumner's "Crime against Kansas Speech"; "Speech of A.P. Butler," *Congressional Globe*, appendix, 34th Congress, 1st Session, 1093 (June 13, 1856).

36. [Robert Turnbull], "Brutus," *The Crisis* (Charleston, 1827), 15, 152. Compare Calhoun's less aggressive notion of constitutional resistance: Charles J. McDonald to John C. Calhoun, May 30, 1831, *The Papers of John C. Calhoun*, Robert L. Meriwether et al., eds. (Columbia, S.C., 1959), 11: 396; Calhoun to James Hamilton, Jr., August 28, 1832, in *Calhoun Papers*, 627–28; The best account of the development of nullification theory in South Carolina is William Freehling, *Prelude to Civil War: The Nullification Controversy in South Carolina, 1816–1836* (New York, 1965). On the theory of states' rights, see Richard E. Ellis, *The Union at Risk: Jacksonian Democracy, States' Rights, and the Nullification Crisis* (New York, 1987). For a fascinating modern discussion of Calhoun's theory, see Hannah Arendt, *Crises of the Republic: Thoughts on Politics and Revolution* (New York, 1972).

37. The arsenal incident is discussed in Patrick T. Conley, *Democracy in Decline: Rhode Island's Constitutional Development, 1776–1841* (Providence, R.I., 1977), 339–42, and George Marshall Dennison, *The Dorr War: Republicanism on Trial, 1831–1861* (Lexington, Ky., 1976).

38. *Luther v. Borden*, 48 U.S. (7 How.) 1 (1849).

39. Story, *Commentaries*, 3: 746–47; Joseph Story, "Charge to Grand Jury Treason," 30 *Federal Cases* 1046 (1842).

40. Philip B. Kurland and Gerhard Casper, eds., *Landmark Briefs and Arguments of the Supreme Court of the United States: Constitutional Law* (Washington, D.C., 1978), 2: 721, 723, 768, 778, 793–94.

41. All of the materials in *State v. Dorr*, including a full transcript of the trial, are available in Edmund Burke's report, a detailed investigation by Congress into unrest in Rhode Island, *Rhode Island—Interference of the Executive in Affairs of*, 28th Congress, 1st Session, Rep. No. 546 (Washington, 1844–45), 865–1052.

42. For explicit references to the problem of concealed weapons, see *Report of the Debates in the Convention of California, on the Formation of the State Constitution: 1849* (Washington, 1849), 47, and *Report of the Debates and Proceedings of the Convention for the Revision of the Constitution of the State of Indiana: 1850* (Indianapolis, Ind., 1850–51). "Speech of Mr. Ochilttree," "Speech of Mr. Baylor," "Speech of Mr. Hemphill," *Debates of the Texas Convention* (Houston, 1846), 311–12.

43. *Report of the Debate and Proceedings of the Convention for the Revision of the Constitution of the State of Indiana* (Indianapolis, 1850), 1391.

44. On the Philadelphia riot, see Maxwell Bloomfield, *American Lawyers in a Changing Society, 1776–1876* (Cambridge, Mass., 1976), and J. Thomas Scharf and Thompson Westcott, *History of Philadelphia, 1609–1884*, 3 vols. (Philadelphia, 1884), 1: 664–67.

45. Nicholas B. Wainwright, ed., *A Philadelphian Perspective: The Diary of Sidney George Fisher Covering the Years 1834–1871* (Philadelphia, 1967), 166, 168.

46. "Philadelphia Riot Cases 1844," in Francis Wharton, *A Treatise on the Law of Homicide* (Philadelphia, 1855), 352, 465, 480.

47. William Hosley, *Colt: The Making of an American Legend* (Amherst, Mass., 1996), 71; Eric Monkkonen, *Police in Urban America, 1860–1920* (Cambridge, U.K., 1981); Sidney L. Haring, *Policing a Class Society: The Experience of American Cities, 1865–1915* (New Brunswick, N.J., 1983).

48. James N. McElligott, *The American Debater: Being a Plain Exposition of the Principles and Practices of Public Debate* (New York, 1855), 227.

49. Ibid., 219, 216.

Chapter Six

1. For a narrative overview of Civil War politics, see James McPherson, *Battle Cry of Freedom: The Civil War Era* (New York, 1988). The standard narrative account of Reconstruction is Eric Foner, *Reconstruction: America's Unfinished Revolution, 1863–1877* (New York, 1988).

2. The black codes were collected and republished along with congressional civil rights legislation by the clerk of the House of Representatives; Edward McPherson, *The Political History of the United States during the Period of Reconstruction* (Washington, D.C., 1875), 32, 35.

3. "The Labor Question at the South," *Harper's Weekly*, January 13, 1866; "Order of General Sickles, Disregarding the Code, January 17, 1866," in McPherson, *Political History*, 36–37. For a contemporary discussion of the significance of Sickles's actions and those of other military figures in the South who attempted to dismantle the black codes, see William H. Barnes, *History of the Thirty-Ninth Congress of the United States* (New York, 1868), 214.

4. The text of the Civil Rights Act and the extension of the Freedmen's Bureau were included in a collection appropriately titled *Key-Notes of Liberty* (New York, 1866), 239–61.

5. *Key-Notes of Liberty*, 239–61.

6. Henry J. Raymond, *Congressional Globe*, 39th Congress, 1st Session, 1266 (March 8, 1866); Lyman Trumbull, *Congressional Globe*, 39th Congress, 1st Session, 474 (January 24, 1866); William Lawrence, *Congressional Globe*, 39th Congress, 1st Session, 1832 (April 7, 1866).

7. Sidney Clarke, *Congressional Globe*, 39th Congress, 1st Session, 1838 (April 7, 1866).

8. Modern debates over the Fourteenth Amendment have focused on the question of incorporation, the idea that the Fourteenth Amendment intended to make the provisions of the Bill of Rights applicable to the states. Opponents of the idea of incorporation have argued that such a view would have violated the strong commitment to federalism and run afoul of the deeply rooted racist

views of the majority of northerners. The literature on incorporation is immense. For a useful guide to this literature and to the tendency toward overstatement by both sides of the modern incorporation debate, see Bret Boyce, "Originalism and the Fourteenth Amendment," *Wake Forest Law Review* 33 (1998): 909–1034. For a sensible effort to chart the middle ground, see William Nelson, *The Fourteenth Amendment* (Cambridge, Mass., 1988). Opponents of incorporation include Charles Fairman, "Does the Fourteenth Amendment Incorporate the Bill of Rights? The Original Understanding," *Stanford Law Review* 2 (1949): 5–139, and Raoul Berger, *Government by Judiciary: The Transformation of the Fourteenth Amendment* (Cambridge, Mass., 1977). More recent scholarship has generally endorsed the incorporation thesis; see, in particular, Michael Kent Curtis, *No State Shall Abridge: The Fourteenth Amendment and the Bill of Rights* (Durham, N.C., 1986), and Akhil Amar, *The Bill of Rights: Creation and Reconstruction* (New Haven, Conn., 1998). For an interesting discussion of the modern uses of incorporation rhetoric by the courts, see Pamela Brandwein, *Reconstructing Reconstruction: The Supreme Court and the Production of Historical Truth* (Durham, N.C., 1999).

9.   Jacob Howard, *Congressional Globe*, 39th Congress, 1st Session, 2765 (March 23, 1866); Samuel Pomeroy, ibid., 1182 (March 5, 1866); Luke Poland, ibid., 2961 (June 5, 1866).

10. Richard L. Aynes, "The Antislavery and Abolitionist Background of John A. Bingham," *Catholic University Law Review* 37 (1988): 881–933; Aynes, "On Misreading John Bingham and the Fourteenth Amendment," *Yale Law Journal* 103 (1993): 57–104; Aynes, "The Continuing Importance of Congressman John A. Bingham and the Fourteenth Amendment," *Akron Law Review* 36 (2003): 589–615. Although Aynes's reading of Bingham makes sense, his suggestion that Bingham's views were widely shared seems less persuasive. Aynes argues that Luke Poland could not have intended Section 1 to protect the same privileges and immunities associated with Article IV, Section 2 of the Constitution since that would have made the Fourteenth Amendment redundant. Yet, Poland quite explicitly noted that rise of states' rights had made enforcement practically impossible and that Section 1 of the Fourteenth Amendment would give Congress explicit authority to enforce Article IV, Section 2 claims against the states. There was absolutely nothing superfluous or redundant about Poland's more narrow interpretation of the Fourteenth Amendment. Compare Aynes's claims about Poland, "On Misreading John Bingham," 81–82, with Poland's speech, *Congressional Globe*, 39th Congress, 1st Session, 1269 (June 5, 1866). For Bingham, see *Congressional Globe*, 39th Congress, 1st Session, 1088, 1094, 1034, 1292 (February 26–28, 1866).

11. There is quite a bit of evidence to suggest that the views of the congressional framers of the amendment were not echoed in the state legislatures or the public campaign to sell the amendment; see James E. Bond, "Ratification of the Fourteenth Amendment in North Carolina," *Wake Forest Law Review* 20 (1984): 89–119, and "The Original Understanding of the Fourteenth Amendment in Illinois, Ohio, and Pennsylvania," *Akron Law Review* 18 (1985): 435–67; and Lambert Gingras, "Congressional Misunderstandings and the Ratifiers' Understanding:

The Case of the Fourteenth Amendment," *American Journal of Legal History* 40 (1996): 41–71. The latter concludes there was not even a consensus among the framers of the amendment within Congress. A number of legal scholars have read the absence of explicit discussions of incorporation during public debate as a sign that this idea enjoyed widespread support; see in particular, Curtis, *No State Shall Abridge*; Stephen Halbrook, *Freedmen and the Fourteenth Amendment* (Westport, Conn., 1998); and Amar, *Bill of Rights*. For a critique of arguments from silence, see Boyce, "Originalism and the Fourteenth Amendment." The main focus of contemporary debate was not on Section 1, but on other provisions of the amendment that addressed issues relevant to establishing governments in the South and preventing confederate sympathizers from regaining power.

12. Bingham, "Politics in Ohio," *Cincinnati Commercial*, August 10, 1866; Bingham, "The Constitutional Amendment," *Cincinnati Commercial*, August 27, 1866. A survey of the stump speeches made during the congressional campaign of 1866 in Ohio, Indiana, and Kentucky provides scant evidence that Section 1 was widely understood to have incorporated the first eight amendments of the Bill of Rights; *Speeches of the Campaign of 1866, in the States of Ohio, Indiana, and Kentucky . . .* (Cincinnati, Ohio, 1866).

13. Wilson, *Congressional Globe*, 39th Congress, 1st Session, 914 (February 19, 1866); Saulsbury, ibid.; For the middle ground, see Wartman T. Willey, *Congressional Globe*, 39th Congress, 2nd Session, 1848–49 (February 26, 1867); President Andrew Johnson echoed these concerns when he argued that this policy was "contrary to the express declaration of the Constitution" on the right to bear arms; "President Johnson's Last Annual Message, December 7, 1868," in McPherson, *Political History*, 385. The debate over the disarmament of the militias has not figured prominently in modern Second Amendment scholarship. Indeed, a number of scholars have mistakenly claimed that the states' rights view was a modern invention. Thus, David Kopel erroneously declares that Saulsbury's statement was the only example of the states' rights view in the nineteenth century; see David B. Kopel, "The Second Amendment in the Nineteenth Century," *Brigham Young University Law Review* (1998): 1453, n. 357. The controversy over what to do about the southern militias is briefly mentioned by Carl T. Bogus, "What Does the Second Amendment Restrict? A Collective Rights Analysis," *Constitutional Commentary* 18 (2002): 485–516.

14. Charles Buckalew, *Congressional Globe*, 40th Congress, 3rd Session, 84 (December 15, 1868).

15. Otis Singletary, *Negro Militia and Reconstruction* (Austin, Tex., 1957); Herbert Shapiro, "The Ku Klux Klan during Reconstruction: The South Carolina Episode," *Journal of Negro History* 49 (1964): 34–55; Joel Williamson, *After Slavery: The Negro in South Carolina during Reconstruction, 1861–1877* (Chapel Hill, N.C., 1965); Richard Zuczek, *State of Rebellion: Reconstruction in South Carolina* (Columbia, S.C., 1996); Stephen Kantrowitz, "One Man's Mob is Another Man's Militia: Violence, Manhood, and Authority in Reconstruction South Carolina," in *Jumpin' Jim Crow: Southern Politics from Civil War to Civil Rights*, Jane Dailey, Glenda E. Gilmore, and Bryant Simon, eds. (Princeton, N.J.,

2000), 67–87. A number of modern accounts of Reconstruction sympathetic to the individual rights reading of the Second Amendment have ignored the rise of the black militia, arguing that Republicans during Reconstruction showed little interest in the militia; see Amar, *Bill of Rights*; Kopel, "Second Amendment in the Nineteenth Century," 1453; Halbrook, *Freedmen and the Fourteenth Amendment*.

16. *Report of the Joint Select Committee to Inquire into the Condition of Affairs in the Late Insurrectionary States*, 42nd Congress, 2nd Session, Report No. 22 (Washington, D.C., 1872).

17. Ibid.

18. Henry T. Thompson, *Ousting the Carpetbagger from South Carolina* (1926; repr., New York, 1969), 47.

19. *Report of the Joint Select Committee to Inquire into the Condition of Affairs in the Late Insurrectionary States*, 540–45.

20. *Report of the Joint Select Committee to Inquire into the Condition of Affairs in the Late Insurrectionary States*, 2. For more sympathetic accounts, see the testimony of the state attorney general, D. H. Chamberlin, ibid., 48–59, and Judge Williard of the South Carolina Supreme Court, ibid., 59–62.

21. *Testimony Taken by Joint Select Committee to Inquire into the Condition of Affairs in the Late Insurrectionary States, Vol. l, South Carolina* (Washington, D.C., 1872), 77.

22. Kermit L. Hall, "Political Power and Constitutional Legitimacy: The South Carolina Ku Klux Klan Trials, 1871–1872," *Emory Law Journal* 33 (1984): 921–51; Lou Falkner Williams, *The Great South Carolina Ku Klux Klan Trials, 1871–1872* (Athens, Ga., 1996); Robert J. Kaczorowski, *The Nationalization of Civil Rights: Constitutional Theory and Practice in a Racist Society, 1866–1883* (New York, 1987); Kaczorowski, *The Politics of Judicial Interpretation: The Federal Courts, Department of Justice and Civil Rights, 1866–1876* (Dobbs Ferry, N.Y., 1985).

23. Daniel Corbin to Amos Akerman, November 13, 1871, Letters Received by the Department of Justice, from South Carolina, 1871–1884, RG 60, M947, Microfilm Reel 1, National Archives, Washington, D.C.

24. Ibid.; Amos Akerman to Daniel Corbin, November 16, 1871, Letters Sent by Department of Justice, Instruction to U.S. Attorney's Book, RG 60, Microfilm Reel M701, National Archives, Washington, D.C.

25. As a result of the Judiciary Act of 1869 federal prosecutions were handled by teams of judges, a district court judge, and a circuit court judge. The new system was designed to both relieve Supreme Court justices of the burdens of riding on circuit and project a more nationalist conception of law into the states by creating a new cohort of circuit court judges. Hall explores the legal and jurisprudential context of the trial in "Ku Klux Klan Trials."

26. The first Second Amendment case, *U.S. v. Avery*, became bogged down on the complex question of federal jurisdiction over crimes such as murder. The case was eventually heard by the Supreme Court, *U.S. v. Avery*, 80 U.S. 253 (13 Wall) 251 (1871), which ducked the federalism issue by arguing that the Supreme Court lacked jurisdiction in such a case. For a useful discussion of the legal issues in the Avery case, see Hall, "Ku Klux Klan Trials."

27. Daniel Corbin, "Opening Statement," *"The Case of Robert Hays Mitchell" et al. in Proceedings in the Ku Klux Klan Trials at Columbia, S.C.* (1872; repr. New York, 1969), 147–48.

28. Stanbery, ibid., 146–47; Johnson, ibid., 150–51; *U. S. v. Avery*, 80 U.S. 253 (13 Wall.) (1871).

29. Johnson, ibid., 150–51.

30. For evidence of the states' rights view in Democratic constitutional thinking before Reconstruction, see C. Chauncey Burr, *Notes on the Constitution of the United States* (New York, 1864), 34, 80–81; Samuel Cox, *Congressional Globe*, 37th Congress, 3rd Session, 1269 (February 24, 1863).

31. "Speech of Mr. Stanbery," *Proceedings in the KKK Trials*, 296.

32. Corbin, ibid., 151–52.

33. Ibid., 296, 151.

34. Ibid., 164; "Testimony of Andy Tims," ibid., 221; Louis Post Papers, Library of Congress, Container 9, KKK Trial Scrapbook; Corbin, *Proceedings in the KKK Trials*, 164; "Testimony of Andy Tims," ibid., 223.

35. Louis F. Post, "A 'Carpetbagger' in South Carolina," *Journal of Negro History* 10 (1925): 61.

36. "Examination of John A. Moroso," *Proceedings in the KKK Trials*, 293; "Speech of Mr. Stanbery," ibid., 296; "Cross examination of Mr. Hart," ibid., 228; "Re-cross examination of Mr. Hart," ibid., 230; "Cross examination of Elias Ramsay," ibid., 269. Stanbery turned the tables on the prosecution on the issue of voter intimidation. "The only interference with the exercise of that right," he asserted, "was by the Negro militias who mustered around Election Day and verbally and physically harassed opponents of the Republican Party. Although Stanbery's argument was exaggerated, the Negro militia had been used by Republicans to organize and protect voters; "Speech of Mr. Stanbery," ibid., 296.

37. Williams, *The Great South Carolina Ku Klux Klan Trials*, chap. 6.

38. The opening arguments of the prosecution and defense are available in *Proceedings in the KKK Trials*, 147–52. The divisions among the judges and lawyers in this case about the meaning of the Second Amendment effectively refute claims that a strong consensus existed on the connections between the right to bear arms and the Fourteenth Amendment. For problematic efforts to make such a claim, see Amar, *Bill of Rights*; Halbrook, *Freedmen and the Fourteenth Amendment*; and Kopel, *Second Amendment in the Nineteenth Century*.

39. Williams, *The Great South Carolina Ku Klux Klan Trials*, chap. 7.

40. John Norton Pomeroy, *An Introduction to the Constitutional Law of the United States* (New York, 1868), 152–53.

41. Ibid., 150–51.

42. Joel Prentiss Bishop, *Commentaries on the Law of Statutory Crimes* (Boston, 1873), 494, 497, 498. The Arkansas doctrine was articulated in *State v. Buzzard*, 4 Ark. 18; other cases following this line of thought included *Aymette v. the State*, 2 Humph. 154; *State v. Reid*, 1 Ala. 612; and *State v. Mitchell*, 3 Blackf. 229. A highly regarded text from this era was Calvin Townsend's *Analysis of Civil Government* (1869). Townsend described the meaning of the Second Amendment as a

militia right: "The right of the people to keep and bear arms, with which the General Government is herein prohibited from interfering, refers to the organization of the militia of the States"; Calvin Townsend, *Analysis of Civil Government* (New York, 1869), 224. For a sample of a glowing review of the book, see *Michigan University Magazine* 3 (1869): 199; "Book Notices," *Massachusetts Teacher and Journal of Home and School Education* 22 (1869): 74; and *Lippincott's Magazine of Literature, Science, and Education* 3 (1869): 463. One of the most expansive articulations of the civic conception of bearing arms was elaborated by the distinguished jurist Thomas M. Cooley. His vision of a universal militia encompassing all citizens capable of bearing arms was stated in forceful terms in his writings. Still, although Cooley viewed the militia in expansive terms, his vision was still quintessentially civic in nature, and he conceded that the state might regulate the use of firearms, even in this military context; Thomas Cooley, *A Treatise on Constitutional Limitations* (Boston, 1868); Cooley, *General Principles of Constitutional Law* (Boston, 1880), 271. The strongest statement of his civic conception of the Second Amendment occurs in Cooley, "The Abnegation of Self Government," *Princeton Review* 12 (1883): 226.

43. John Forrest Dillon and S. D. Thompson, "The Right to Keep and Bear Arms for Private and Public Defense," *Central Law Journal* 1(1874): 260. For a brief biography of Dillon, see George S. Clay, "John Forrest Dillon," *The Green Bag* 23 (1911): 447–55. Timothy R. Mahoney, "Dillon, John Forrest," http://www.anb.org/articles/11/11-00243.html. The Eighth Circuit spanned an enormous geographical region including, sections of the Southeast and Midwest: Iowa, Minnesota, Missouri, Kansas, Arkansas, Nebraska, and eventually Colorado. Dillon later was president of the American Bar Association and left Columbia for a professorship at Yale.

44. Dillon and Thompson, "The Right to Keep and Bear Arms for Private and Public Defense," 260, 273.

45. Ibid., 286.

46. Ibid., 287.

47. Ibid., 296.

48. *U.S. v. Cruikshank*, 92 U.S. 568 (1875).

49. The historical context of the Colfax Massacre and the subsequent legal battles that culminated in the *Cruikshank* case are dealt with in Robert M. Goldman, *Reconstruction and Black Suffrage: Losing the Vote*, in Reese and Cruikshank (Lawrence, Kans., 2001), and Kaczorowski, *The Politics of Judicial Interpretation.* Congress investigated violence in Louisiana, including the Colfax Massacre, and its report and the documents collected by the committee were published as *The Report of the Select Committee on the Portion of the President's Message Relating to the Condition of the South* (Washington, D.C, 1875).

50. The Democrats were technically a coalition that included some conservative Republicans and were known locally as the "Fusion Party" or "Fusionists"; see Goldman, *Reconstruction and Black Suffrage,* 43–46, and Joe Gray Taylor, *Louisiana Reconstructed, 1863–1877* (Baton Rouge, La., 1974).

51. *Report of the Select Committee on the Portion of the President's Message,* 14–15; *New York Times,* September 23, 1874; Goldman, *Reconstruction and Black Suffrage,* 42–60.

52. Goldman, *Reconstruction and Black Suffrage*, 50–52; Taylor, *Louisiana Reconstructed*, 267–71.

53. "An Act to Enforce the Right of Citizens," in McPherson, *Political History*, 547.

54. Goldman, *Reconstruction and Black Suffrage*, 54–59. Modern scholarship is divided over how to interpret *Cruikshank* and its connection to the history of incorporation. One of the most interesting issues deals with *Cruikshank*'s connection to the Slaughter House Cases, 16 Wall. 36 (1873). Traditionally, legal scholarship has treated Slaughter House as marking the end of the Republican goal of incorporation. Recent revisionist scholarship has questioned this interpretation, suggesting that *Cruikshank*, not Slaughter House, may have been the case that undermined incorporation; see Kevin Christopher Newsom, "Setting Incorporationism Straight: A Reinterpretation of the Slaughter-House Cases [83 U.S. (16 Wall.) 36 (1873)]," *The Yale Law Journal* 109 (2000): 643–744, and Robert C. Palmer, "The Parameters of Constitutional Reconstruction: Slaughter-House [Slaughter-House Cases, 83 U.S. (16 Wall.) 36], Cruikshank [United States v. Cruikshank, 92 U.S. 542], and the Fourteenth Amendment," *University of Illinois Law Review* 1984 (1984): 739–70. For a thoughtful overview of these issues, see Bryan H. Wildenthal, "The Lost Compromise: Reassessing the Early Understanding in Court and Congress on Incorporation of the Bill of Rights in the Fourteenth Amendment," *Ohio State Law Journal* 61 (2000): 1051–1173. While generally quite helpful, Wildenthal does accept somewhat uncritically Amar's and Halbrook's problematic interpretations of the connection between the Second Amendment and the Fourteenth Amendment.

55. Judge Woods's elaboration of the scope of the right to bear arms is available in "Charge of Hon. W. B. Woods, *The United States v. William J. Cruikshank et al.*," *Report of the Select Committee on the Portion of the President's Message*, 861; P. Phillips and David S. Bryon, "Brief for the Defendants, *United States v. C. C. Nash, et al.*," in Philip B. Kurland and Gerhard Casper, eds., *Landmark Briefs and Arguments of the Supreme Court of the United States*, (Washington, D.C., 1975–), 7: 325–26. R. H. Mar, "Brief for the Defendants, *The United States vs. Cruikshank, Irwin, and Hadnot*," ibid., 373.

56. David Dudley Field, "Brief for the Defendants, *United States vs. William I. Cruikshank and Two Others*," ibid., 416–17.

57. *U.S. v. Cruikshank*, 92 U.S. 542 (1876) at 553.

58. The situation at the state level was far more complex and unsettled. In a survey of state jurisprudence published in the early part of the twentieth century, Daniel J. McKenna noted a variegated patchwork quilt of laws and decisions at the state level that left "many elements of confusion and uncertainty." This chaos stemmed from state constitutions, which used a bewildering array of formulations to describe the right to bear arms. Twenty-four constitutions used a more collective formulation while thirteen used more individualistic language. While there was broad agreement that citizens could not be deprived of weapons suitable for use in the militia, the meaning of this principle was that "the Constitution expects the citizens to carry such weapons only as actual or potential members of the local militia." Other states adopted a more individualistic reading of the right to bear arms unconnected to participation in the

militia; see Daniel J. McKenna, "The Right to Keep and Bear Arms," *Marquette Law Review* 12 (1927–28): 138–49.

59. S. T. Ansell, "Legal and Historical Aspects of the Militia," *Yale Law Journal* 26 (1916–17): 471–80; H. Richard Uviller and William G. Merkel, *The Militia and the Right to Arms: Or, How the Second Amendment Fell Silent* (Durham, N.C., 2002); "Dr. Cadman on Military Training in the Schools," in Lamar T. Beman, ed., *Military Training Compulsory in Schools and College* (New York, 1926) 132.

60. *New York Times*, August 10, 1910; *New York Times*, August 31, 1911. For a general discussion of this event and its connection to the adoption of the Sullivan law, see Alexander DeConde, *Gun Violence in America: The Struggle for Control* (Boston, 2001). Larmar T. Beman, ed., *Outlawing the Pistol* (New York, 1926).

61. Lucillus A. Emery, "The Constitutional Right to Keep and Bear Arms," *Harvard Law Review* 28 (1914–15): 473–77. Emery asserted that states might even regulate the way militia weapons were carried in the open and not merely nonmilitary weapons carried outside of the context of militia service. To support this claim he cited *Presser v. Illinois*, 116 U.S. 264, a case that built on the legacy of *Cruikshank* and upheld an Illinois statute that prohibited citizens from parading with arms. Emery's formulation of the right to bear arms was picked up by a number of subsequent commentators; see McKenna, "The Right to Keep and Bear Arms"; John Brabner-Smith, "Firearm Regulation," *Law and Contemporary Problems* 1 (1933–34): 400–414; cited for authority in a commentary on the constitutionality of the National Firearms Act, "Notes and Comments," *Cornell Law Quarterly* 21 (1935–36): 106–7; and cited by the government in the most important twentieth-century Second Amendment case, *U.S. v. Miller*, see Brief of the United States, *U.S. v. Miller*, 307 U.S. 174 (1939) (No. 696) at 4–5; *U.S. v. Miller*, 307 U.S. 174 (1939) (No. 696).

62. Emery, "Constitutional Right to Keep and Bear Arms," 473, 476–77; although Emery did not cite *Salina v. Blaksley*, 72 Kan. 230 (1905), the Kansas Supreme Court had used a similar formulation of the right to bear arms a decade earlier, describing this right as one that "refers to the people as a collective body." One measure of Emery's influence may be found in an essay written by the eminent Harvard Law professor Zechariah Chafee, Jr. Following Emery's lead, Chafee concluded that "unlike the neighboring amendments, this clause safeguards individual rights very little and relates mainly to our federal scheme of government." Chafee went on to note that "the Second Amendment is thus concerned with the militia and army clauses in the original constitution"; Chafee, "Right to Bear Arms," *Encyclopedia of the Social Sciences* (New York, 1930), 2: 209–10. For another good illustration of Emery's influence, see Brabner-Smith, "Firearm Regulation," 411.

63. McKenna, "The Right to Keep and Bear Arms."

64. DeConde, *Gun Violence in America*; Osha Grey Davidson, *The NRA and the Battle for Gun Control* (New York, 1993); Robert J. Spitzer, *The Politics of Gun Control*, 3rd ed. (Washington, D.C., 2004).

65. For a brief overview of the case, see DeConde, *Gun Violence in America*. A number of modern individual rights scholars have attempted to reinterpret *Miller* as being either agnostic on the individual rights question or even supportive

of an individual right; see Brannon P. Denning, "Can the Simple Cite Be Trusted? Lower Court Interpretations of *United States v. Miller* [59 S. Ct. 816 (1939)] and the Second Amendment," *Cumberland Law Review* 26 (1995/96): 961–1004. Brannon P. Denning and Glenn H Reynolds, "Telling *Miller*'s Tale: A Reply to David Yassky," *Law and Contemporary Problems* 65 (2002): 113–23; Eugene Volokh et al., "The Second Amendment as Teaching Tool in Constitutional Law Classes," *Journal of Legal Education* 48 (1998): 591–614. For a critique of these revisionist arguments about *Miller*, see Mathew S. Nosanchuk, "The Embarrassing Interpretation of the Second Amendment," *Northern Kentucky Law Review* 29 (2002): 705–803. While *Miller* did not use this language, no contemporary commentator read the interpretation as asserting an individual rights view of the amendment.

66. Brief of the United States, *U.S. v. Miller*, 307 U.S. 174 (1939) (No. 696) at 4–5, 21, 16. *U.S. v. Miller*, 307 U.S. 174 (1939) (No. 696); *U.S. v. Miller*, 26 F. Supp 1002 (W.D. Ark 1939), *rev'd*, 307 U.S. 174.

67. "Supreme Court Bars Sawed-Off Shotgun: Denies Constitution Gives Right to Carry This Weapon," *New York Times*, May 16, 1939. It is impossible to say why the Court accepted the conclusion of the government's brief without adopting its language. Some modern gun rights scholars have read the failure to employ this nomenclature as evidence that the Court either embraced or was agnostic on the individual rights character of the amendment. Such a view rests on a false dichotomy which assumes that the Second Amendment protects an individual right or a collective right. Actually, the Court's argument was entirely consistent with the dominant civic paradigm of the Second Amendment that defined mainstream constitutional commentary for most of the nineteenth century. The Court's language placed it closer to antebellum jurisprudence than it did to *Cruikshank* and the line of cases descended from it. For a critique of the fallacy of false dichotomous questions in the Second Amendment debate, see Saul Cornell, "A New Paradigm for the Second Amendment," *Law and History Review* 22 (2004): 161–67.

68. *United States v. Miller*, 307 U.S. 174.

69. The modern revisionist view that Miller supported an individual rights view was explicitly rejected when the First Circuit Court of Appeals took up the Second Amendment three years later in *Cases v. U.S.*, 131 F.2d 916, 1st Cir (1942), *cert denied*, 319 U.S. 770 (1943). Two larger historical contexts are important in thinking about the Court's state of mind when deciding this case. First, the Court was mindful of the rise of organized crime, a social ill that had prompted passage of the first federal gun control laws. Second, growing concerns about Hitler's aggression in Europe sensitized the Court to the need for providing future flexibility regarding the militia's composition and range of armaments. To gain some sense of the way the Nazi threat loomed in contemporary thought, one need only look at the May 16, 1939, issue of the *New York Times*, which reported the *Miller* decision. For some sense of the level of anxiety see in particular the following two articles: "Nazi Inquiry in Quebec: Fascist Bodies in Province Are Also Investigated" and "German Fort Line Held Impregnable: Hitler Continues His Tour of 'West Wall.'"

70. "Case Notes," *California Law Review* 13 (1939–40): 130; "Recent Cases," *George Washington Law Review* 8 (1939–40): 231; "Recent Decisions," *St. John's Law Review* 14 (1939–40): 168; "Recent Decisions," *Michigan Law Review* 38 (1939–40): 404; Robert E. Cushman, "Constitutional Law in 1938–1939: The Constitutional Decisions of the Supreme Court of the United States in the October Term, 1938," *American Political Science Review* 34 (1940): 266.

71. "U.S. High Court Bars Sawed Off Shotgun Sales," *Chicago Tribune*, May 16, 1939.

72. James Jacobs, *Can Gun Control Work?* (New York, 2002), chap. 3; Abigail A. Kohn, *Shooters: Myths and Realities of America's Gun Cultures* (New York, 2004), chap. 7.

73. Robert J. Spitzer, "Lost and Found: Researching the Second Amendment," *Chicago Kent Law Review* 76 (2000): 349–401.

74. Erwin Chemerinsky, "Putting the Gun Control Debate in Social Perspective: Keynote Address," *Fordham Law Review* 73 (2004): 477–85.

75. For other cases offering a states' rights reading of *Miller*, see *U.S. v. Tot*, 131 F.2d 261 (3rd Cir. 1942), *re'd (on other grounds)*, 319 U.S. 463 (1943); for militia based readings, see *Cases v. U.S.*, 131 F. 2d 916 (1st Cir. 1942), *cert. denied*, 319 U.S. 770 (1943). The first case to adopt the collective rights language explicitly was *U.S. v. Johnson, Jr.*, 441 F. 2d. 1134 (5th Cir. 1971). Most federal courts continue to accept the orthodox reading of *Miller*. Two notable exceptions are *United States v. Emerson*, 270 F.3d 203 (5th Cir.), *reh'g and reh'g en banc denied*, 281 F.3d 1281 (5th Cir. 2001), *cert. denied*, 122 S. Ct. 2362 (2002); and the dissent by Judge Alex Kozinski for petition for en banc review in *Silveira v. Lockyer*, 328 F.3d 567, 568 (9th Cir. 2003) (Kozinski, J. dissenting) (dissenting from denial of a petition for rehearing en banc).

Conclusion

1. The question of how to remain faithful to the text of the Constitution and not fall victim to the static and overly simplistic notions of history that plague so much constitutional originalism has perplexed many constitutional theorists; for some thoughtful comments on this problem, see the essays collected in "Fidelity in Constitutional Theory: Symposium," *Fordham Law Review* 65 (1997): 1247–1818.

2. Even if one accepts Justice William Brennan's notion of majestic generalities, it is hard to justify simply erasing part of a provision of the Bill of Rights because it seems not to fit with a particular ideological stance, either pro-gun or pro-control. On Justice Brennan's notion of majestic generalities, and a living Constitution, see William Brennan, "The Constitution of the United States: Contemporary Ratification," in *Interpreting the Constitution: The Debate over Original Intent*, Jack N. Rakove, ed. (Boston, 1990).

3. For an interesting, but not entirely persuasive, argument that accepting the individual rights view would facilitate progress in this debate, see Abigail A. Kohn, *Shooters: Myths and Realities of America's Gun Cultures* (New York, 2004). For a thoughtful defense of the individual rights view from a living Constitution perspective, see Jonathan Simon, "Gun Rights and the Constitutional Significance of Violent Crime," *William and Mary Bill of Rights Journal* 12 (2004): 335–56.

For a libertarian defense of gun rights that seeks to overturn the New Deal reconfiguration of American law, see Randy Barnett, *Restoring the Lost Constitution: The Presumption of Liberty* (Princeton, 2004). For calls to repeal the Second Amendment, see Lewis S. Dabney, "The Second Amendment Should Be Repealed," *Boston Globe*, July 3, 2000; William Safire, "An Appeal for Repeal," *New York Times*, June 10, 1999. On the irony of judicial activism on behalf of a powerful lobby, see Michael C. Dorf, "Identity Politics and the Second Amendment," *Fordham Law Review* 73 (2004): 549–72.

4. J. G. A. Pocock, *The Machiavellian Moment: Florentine Political Thought and the Atlantic Republican Tradition* (Princeton, N.J., 1975).

5. For a not particularly persuasive argument that the original Second Amendment was premised on an ideal of a unified America that no longer exists, see David Williams, *The Mythic Meanings of the Second Amendment* (New Haven, Conn., 2003). For trenchant critique of the dubious historical foundations for Williams's account, see Stuart Banner, "The Second Amendment, So Far," *Harvard Law Review* 117 (2004): 898–917.

6. Stephen P. Halbrook, "Nazi Firearms Law and the Disarming of the German Jews," *Arizona Journal of International and Comparative Law* 17 (2000): 483–532; Daniel P. Polsby and Don B. Kates, "Of Holocausts and Gun Control," *Washington University Law Quarterly* 75 (1997): 1237–75. For a critique of this interpretation, see Bernard E. Harcourt, "On Gun Registration, the NRA, Adolf Hitler, and Nazi Gun Laws: Exploding the Gun Culture Wars," *Fordham Law Review* 73 (2004): 653–80.

7. Conservative legal scholar and gun rights advocate Nelson Lund has advocated using insurance markets to achieve reasonable gun regulation; see Nelson Lund, "The Second Amendment, Political Liberty, and the Right to Self Preservation," *Alabama Law Review* 103 (1987–88): 39–67. The idea of gun insurance has also been suggested by proponents of gun regulation; see David Hemenway, *Private Guns, Public Health* (Ann Arbor, Mich., 2004), 216.

INDEX

CPSIA information can be obtained
at www.ICGtesting.com
Printed in the USA
LVHW011559020920
664875LV00003B/289

9 780195 341034